Atlas of the
Universe

SIMON & SCHUSTER BOOKS FOR YOUNG READERS
An imprint of Simon & Schuster Children's Publishing Division
1230 Avenue of the Americas, New York, New York 10020

Conceived and produced by Weldon Owen Pty Ltd
61 Victoria Street, McMahons Point
Sydney, NSW 2060, Australia

Group Chief Executive Officer John Owen
President and Chief Executive Officer Terry Newell
Publisher Sheena Coupe
Creative Director Sue Burk
Editorial Coordinator Mike Crowton
Vice President, International Sales Stuart Laurence
Vice President, Sales and New Business Development Amy Kaneko
Vice President, Sales Asia and Latin America Dawn Low
Administrator, International Sales Kristine Ravn

Author Dr. Mark A. Garlick
Consultant Editor Dr. John O'Byrne
Project Editor Paul McNally
Designer Alex Frampton

A WELDON OWEN PRODUCTION

SIMON & SCHUSTER BOOKS FOR YOUNG READERS is a trademark of Simon & Schuster, Inc.
The text of this book is set in Adobe Garamond and Frutiger.

Color reproduction by Chroma Graphics (Overseas) Pte Ltd
Printed by Tien Wah Press Pte Ltd
Manufactured in Singapore

10 9 8 7 6 5 4 3 2 1

Cataloging-in-publication data for this book is available from the Library of Congress.

ISBN-13: 978-1-4169-5558-0
ISBN-10: 1-4169-5558-5

Atlas of the Universe

Dr. Mark A. Garlick

SIMON & SCHUSTER BOOKS FOR YOUNG READERS
New York London Toronto Sydney

Contents

Stargazing 74

Into Space 104

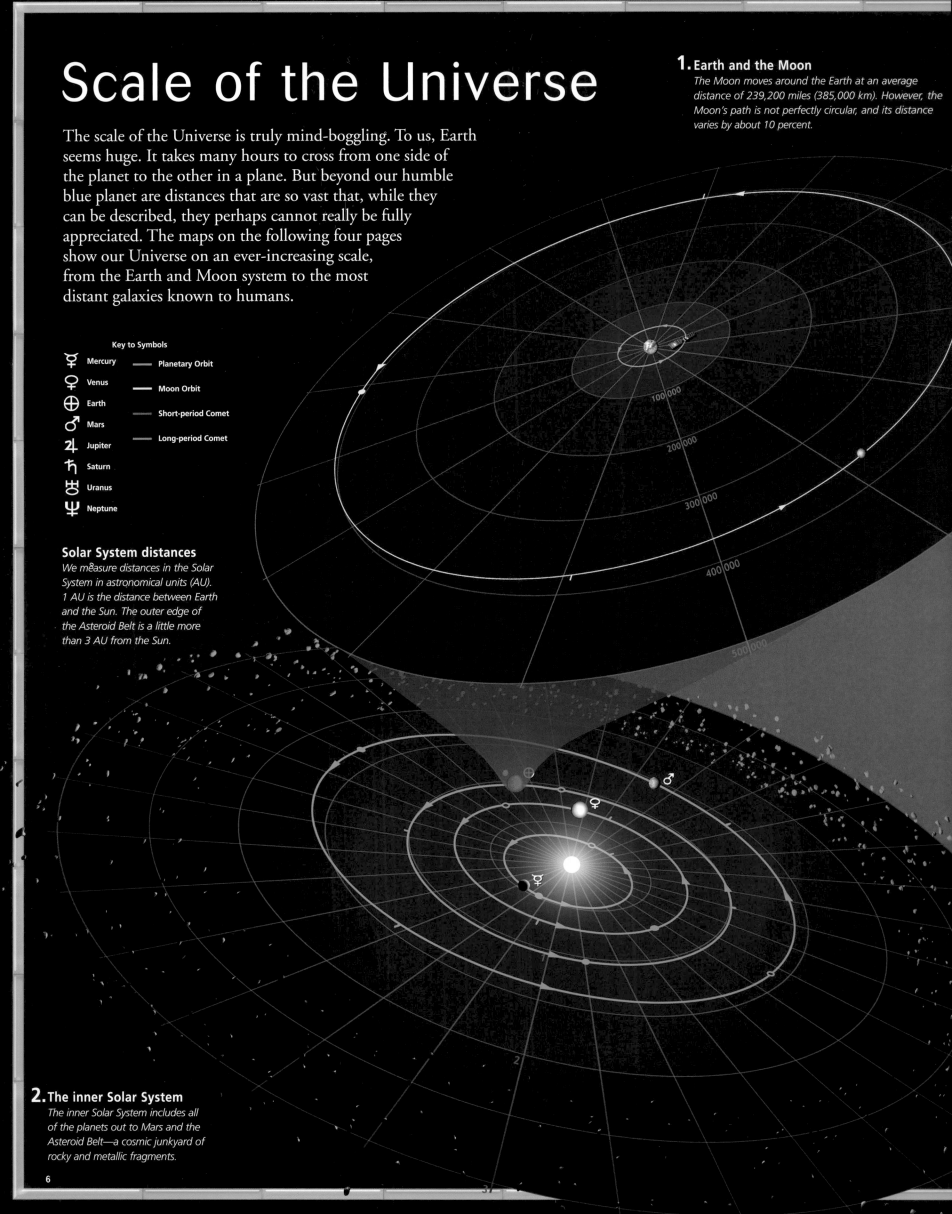

Scale of the Universe

The scale of the Universe is truly mind-boggling. To us, Earth seems huge. It takes many hours to cross from one side of the planet to the other in a plane. But beyond our humble blue planet are distances that are so vast that, while they can be described, they perhaps cannot really be fully appreciated. The maps on the following four pages show our Universe on an ever-increasing scale, from the Earth and Moon system to the most distant galaxies known to humans.

Key to Symbols

☿	Mercury	——	Planetary Orbit
♀	Venus	——	Moon Orbit
⊕	Earth	——	Short-period Comet
♂	Mars	——	Long-period Comet
♃	Jupiter		
♄	Saturn		
♅	Uranus		
♆	Neptune		

Solar System distances
We measure distances in the Solar System in astronomical units (AU). 1 AU is the distance between Earth and the Sun. The outer edge of the Asteroid Belt is a little more than 3 AU from the Sun.

1. Earth and the Moon
The Moon moves around the Earth at an average distance of 239,200 miles (385,000 km). However, the Moon's path is not perfectly circular, and its distance varies by about 10 percent.

2. The inner Solar System
The inner Solar System includes all of the planets out to Mars and the Asteroid Belt—a cosmic junkyard of rocky and metallic fragments.

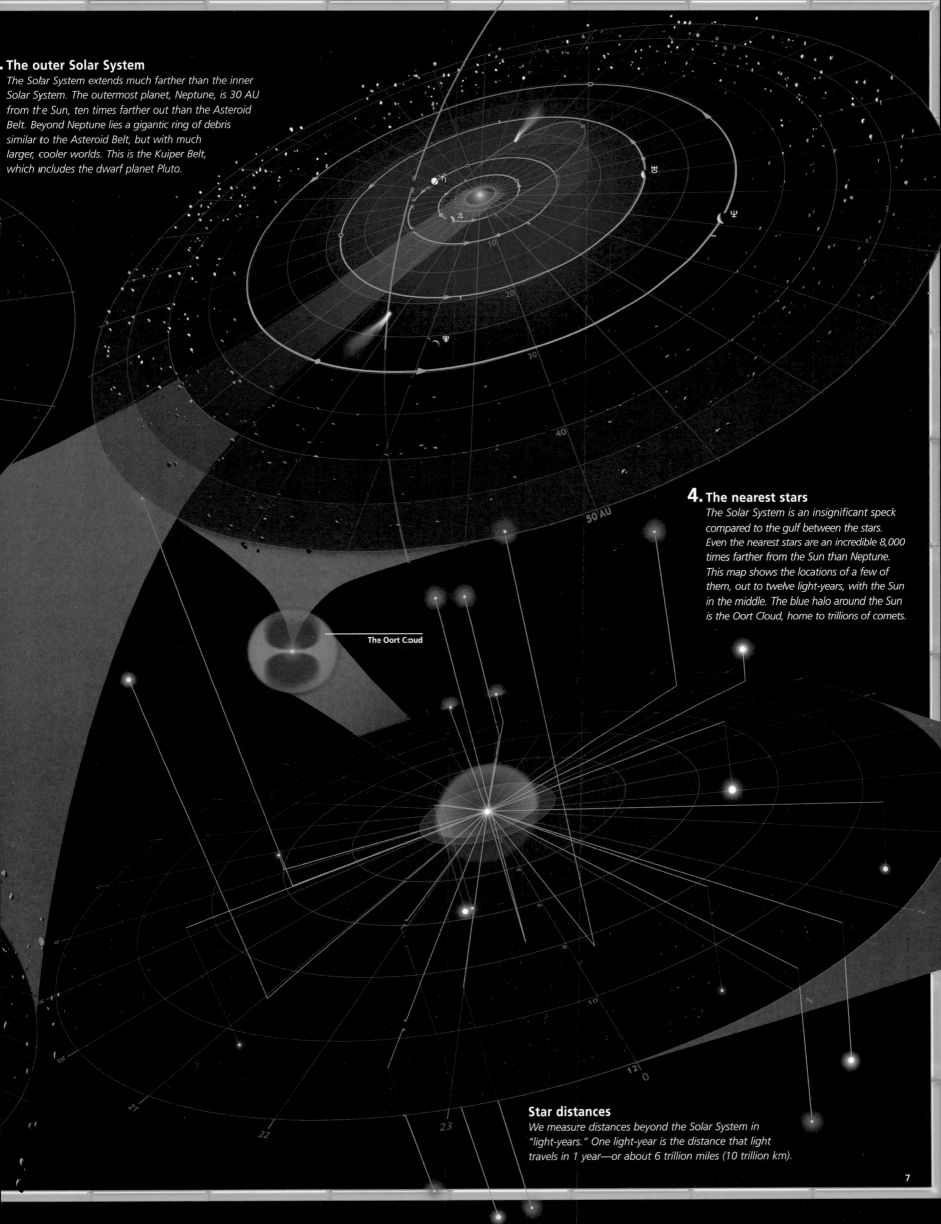

The outer Solar System

*The Solar System extends much farther than the inner
Solar System. The outermost planet, Neptune, is 30 AU
from the Sun, ten times farther out than the Asteroid
Belt. Beyond Neptune lies a gigantic ring of debris
similar to the Asteroid Belt, but with much
larger, cooler worlds. This is the Kuiper Belt,
which includes the dwarf planet Pluto.*

The Oort Cloud

4. The nearest stars

*The Solar System is an insignificant speck
compared to the gulf between the stars.
Even the nearest stars are an incredible 8,000
times farther from the Sun than Neptune.
This map shows the locations of a few of
them, out to twelve light-years, with the Sun
in the middle. The blue halo around the Sun
is the Oort Cloud, home to trillions of comets.*

Star distances

*We measure distances beyond the Solar System in
"light-years." One light-year is the distance that light
travels in 1 year—or about 6 trillion miles (10 trillion km).*

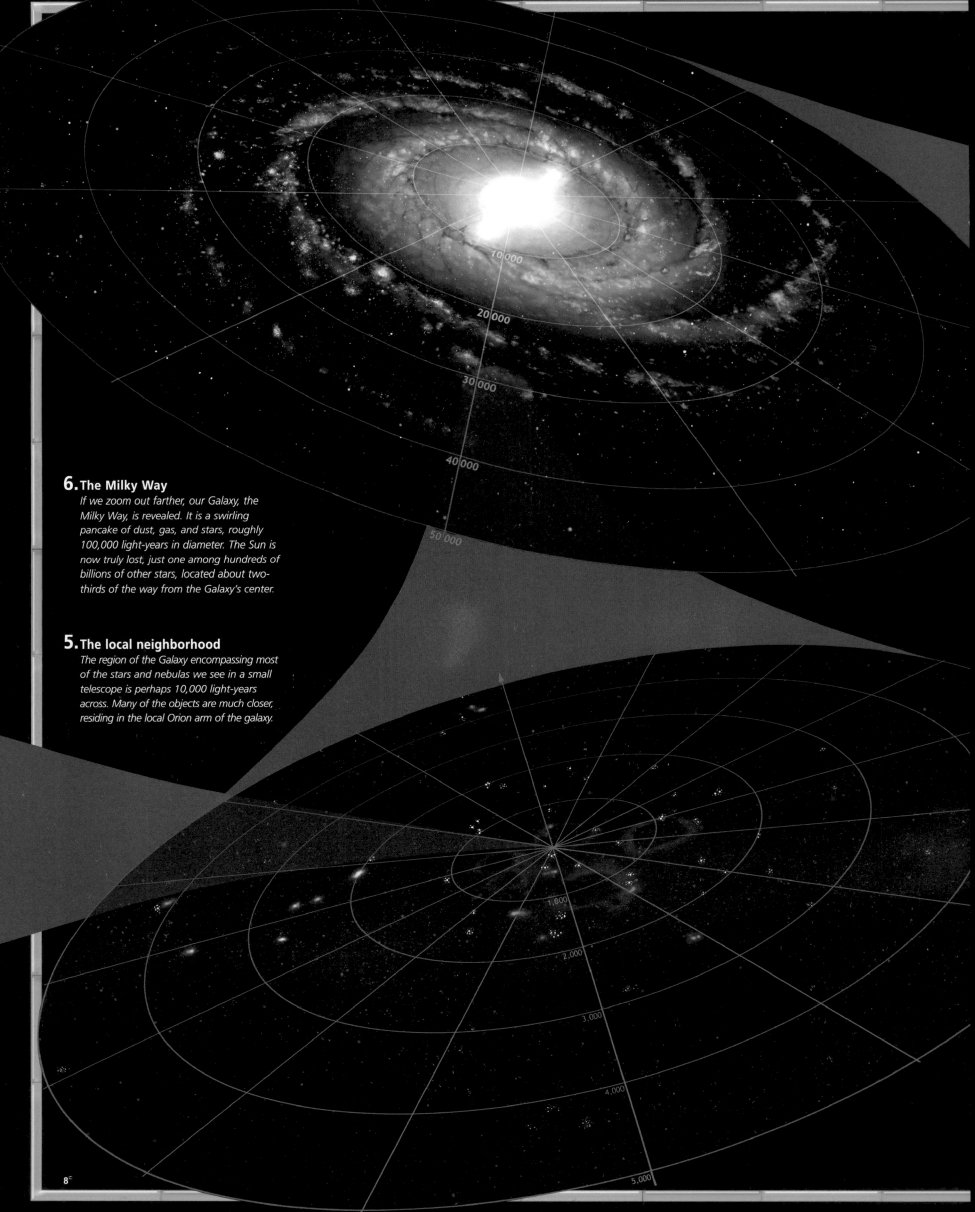

6. **The Milky Way**
If we zoom out farther, our Galaxy, the Milky Way, is revealed. It is a swirling pancake of dust, gas, and stars, roughly 100,000 light-years in diameter. The Sun is now truly lost, just one among hundreds of billions of other stars, located about two-thirds of the way from the Galaxy's center.

5. **The local neighborhood**
The region of the Galaxy encompassing most of the stars and nebulas we see in a small telescope is perhaps 10,000 light-years across. Many of the objects are much closer, residing in the local Orion arm of the galaxy.

10,000

20,000

30,000

40,000

50,000

1,000

2,000

3,000

4,000

5,000

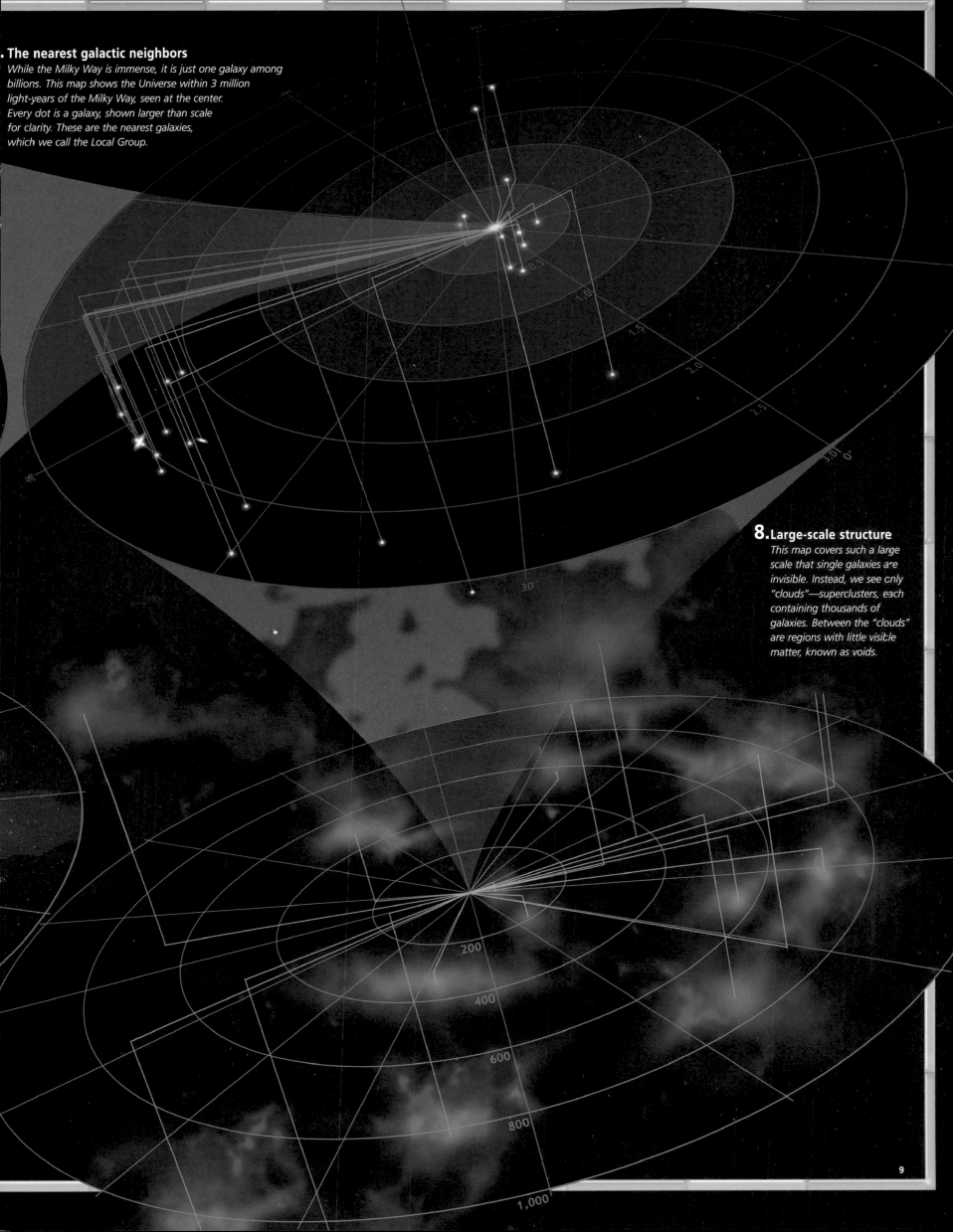

The nearest galactic neighbors

While the Milky Way is immense, it is just one galaxy among billions. This map shows the Universe within 3 million light-years of the Milky Way, seen at the center. Every dot is a galaxy, shown larger than scale for clarity. These are the nearest galaxies, which we call the Local Group.

8.Large-scale structure

This map covers such a large scale that single galaxies are invisible. Instead, we see only "clouds"—superclusters, each containing thousands of galaxies. Between the "clouds" are regions with little visible matter, known as voids.

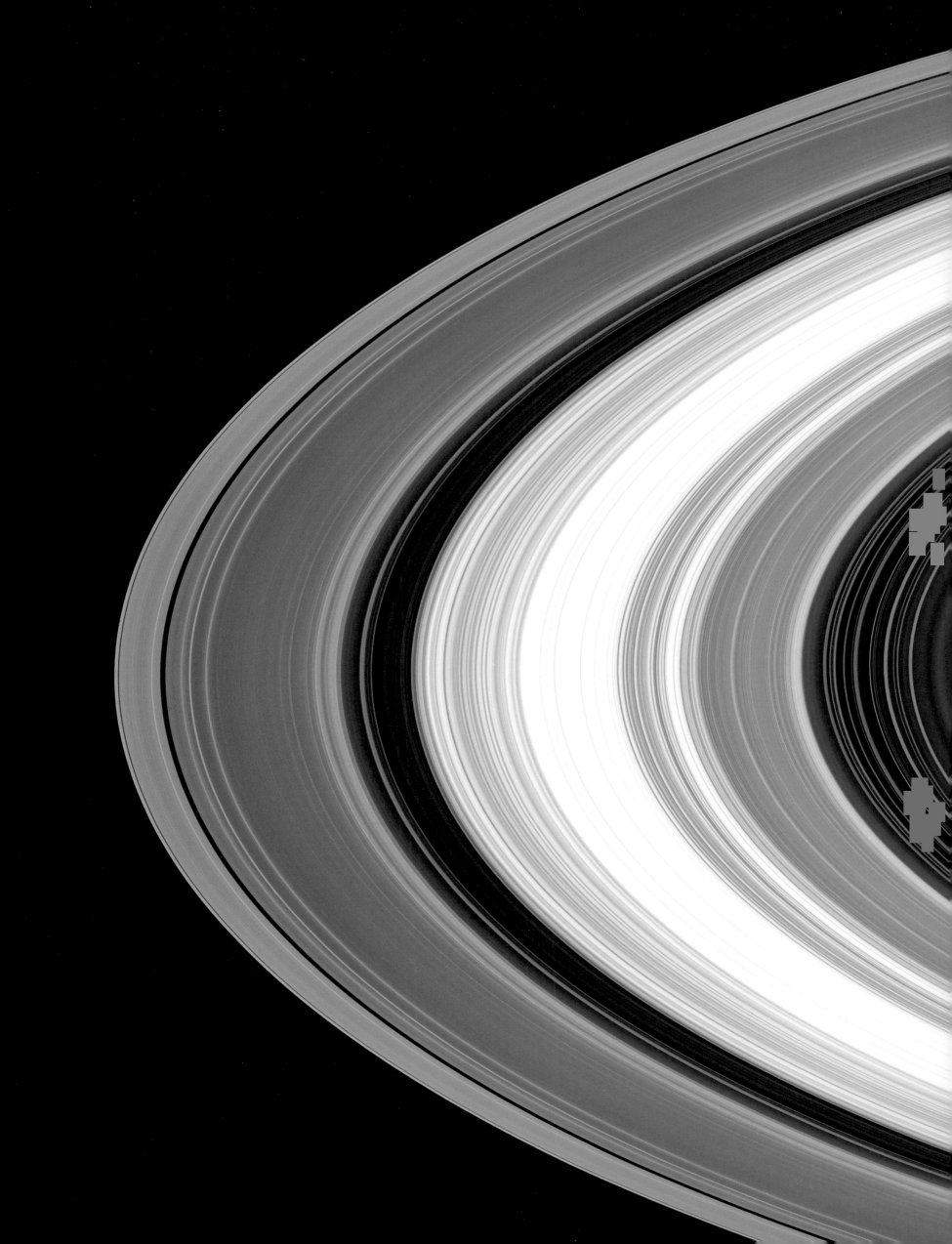

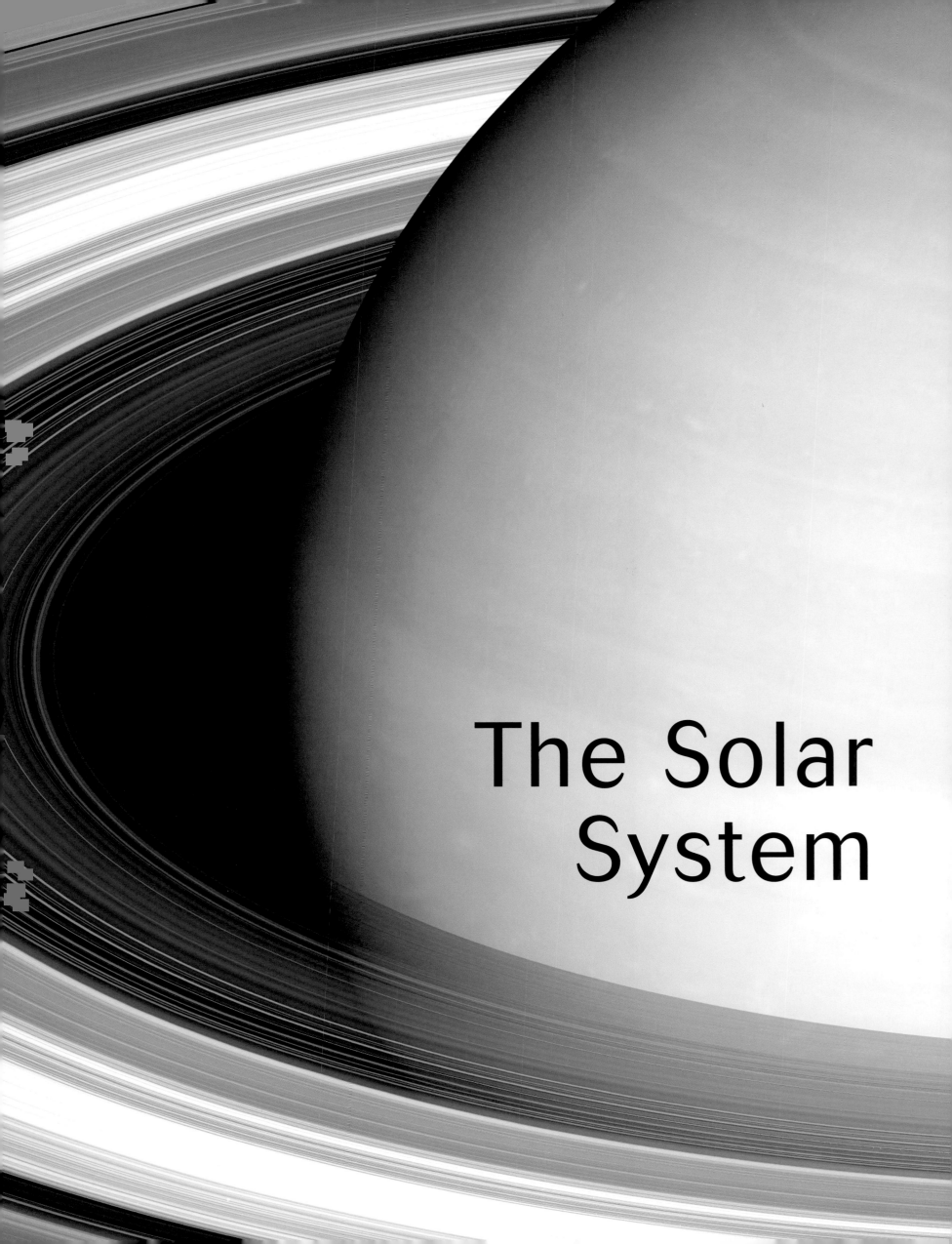

The Solar System

The Solar System

Mercury

Mercury is the smallest planet, whose iron and nickel core is almost as big as the planet itself. Its surface is totally covered in impact craters. Orbiting close to the Sun, Mercury is the hottest planet after Venus.

Venus

Despite being farther from the Sun than Mercury, Venus is the hottest planet, because its thick atmosphere traps the Sun's heat like a giant greenhouse. Venus is so hot that a bar of solid lead would melt there like butter.

Jupiter

Jupiter is bigger and more massive than all the other planets put together. It has no solid surface, being composed instead of a deep atmosphere overlying a fluid interior. Astronomers call it a gas giant. Jupiter has a faint ring system and dozens of small moons.

Mars

Mars is the smallest planet after Mercury. Its surface has a characteristic red color and there is evidence that water once flowed on the planet. Mars is heavily cratered and dotted with vast volcanoes, now probably extinct.

Asteroid Belt

Beyond Mars is the domain of the asteroids—small, irregularly shaped worlds made of rock, iron, or materials rich in carbon. Some are several hundred miles across, but these are rare. Most are hundreds of times smaller.

Earth

Earth is our home planet, third from the Sun, and the only planet that we know has life. More than two-thirds of its surface is covered in liquid water, many miles deep in places.

Neptune

The farthest planet from the Sun is Neptune. It is almost the same size as Uranus, but has a much more colorful atmosphere, blue with faint bands of clouds. It has many moons and a series of dark rings.

Uranus

Uranus is a smaller gas giant, about four times the diameter of Earth. It has an almost featureless atmosphere, its clouds hidden by layers of methane haze.

Saturn

Saturn, another gas giant, is a little like a pale version of Jupiter, but slightly smaller. Its main claim to fame is its ring system, made of countless icy boulders that encircle the planet like tiny moons.

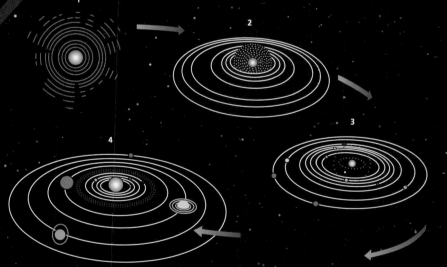

How the Solar System formed

The Solar System is about 4.6 billion years old. It was created when a cloud of gas and dust called a nebula started to shrink under its own gravity (1). As it shrank, the cloud got hotter, flatter, and started to spin, until it transformed into a gigantic disk (2). Particles inside this disk immediately started to stick together. They grew and grew until they reached the size of small moons (3). These then attracted each other, colliding to form ever-larger worlds. The Sun formed at the center, where it was hottest. The gas planets probably formed first. Then the smaller, rocky planets formed out of the remaining debris (4).

Apollo,
Greek Sun god

Jupiter

The Sun

The Sun

ORIGIN OF NAME
SOL, THE LATIN WORD FOR "SUN"

DISCOVERED
KNOWN SINCE ANTIQUITY

DIAMETER AT THE EQUATOR
865,000 MILES (1,392,000 KM)

MASS
333,000 X EARTH'S MASS

SURFACE TEMPERATURE
9,900°F (5,500°C)

CORE TEMPERATURE
28,000,000°F (15,500,000°C)

SOHO observatory

The Solar and Heliospheric Observatory (SOHO) was launched in December 1995 to study the Sun. Its twelve instruments continually monitor the solar surface, winds, and corona.

The Sun's face

In close-up, the surface of the Sun has a grainy appearance, known as solar granulation. Individual grains are typically about 600 miles (1,000 km) across. Solar granulation is the result of hot gas rising from the Sun's interior, which spreads out and disperses once it reaches the surface.

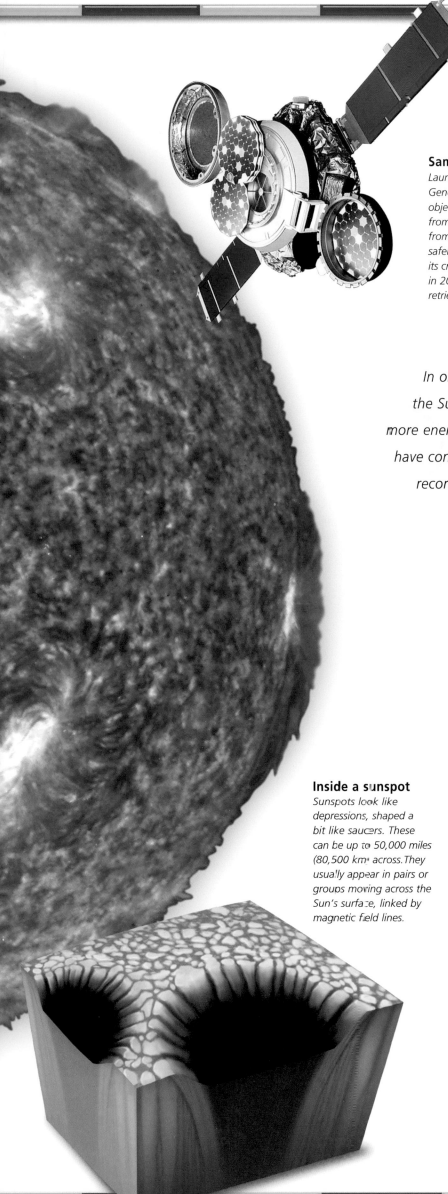

Sampling the Sun
Launched in 2001, NASA's Genesis mission had a bold objective—to capture particles from the solar wind blustering out from the Sun, and to return them safely to Earth for study. Despite its crash landing in the Utah desert in 2004, scientists were able to retrieve some of its precious cargo.

*In one second,
the Sun sends out
more energy than humans
have consumed in all of
recorded history.*

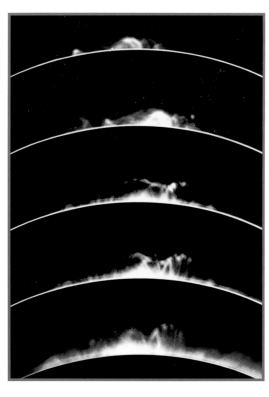

Flaring up!
This image is an eight-hour photographic sequence showing a solar flare eruption. Some solar flares can eject material out through the solar corona.

Corona

The corona is the Sun's atmosphere, extending out several million miles from the Sun's visible face, the photosphere. Despite its extent, it is exceedingly faint, shining with only one-millionth as much light as the photosphere. For this reason the corona is most easily photographed during a solar eclipse, when the photosphere is blocked by the Moon. A cupful of gas from the photosphere contains a trillion times more gas particles than a cupful from the corona.

Inside a sunspot
Sunspots look like depressions, shaped a bit like saucers. These can be up to 50,000 miles (80,500 km) across. They usually appear in pairs or groups moving across the Sun's surface, linked by magnetic field lines.

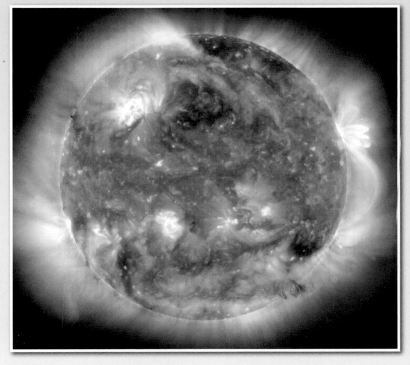

This photograph of the Sun reveals its turbulent atmosphere. The white regions are where the magnetic field is most highly concentrated.

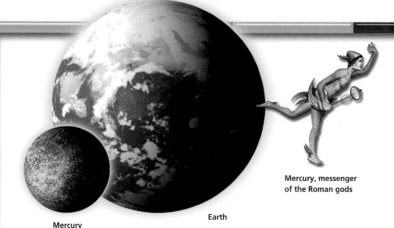

Mercury

Earth

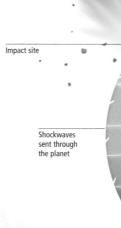

Mercury, messenger
of the Roman gods

Mercury

ORIGIN OF NAME
MERCURIUS, MESSENGER OF THE ROMAN GODS

DISCOVERED
KNOWN SINCE ANTIQUITY

DISTANCE FROM THE SUN
36 MILLION MILES (57.9 MILLION KM)

DIAMETER AT THE EQUATOR
3,032 MILES (4,879 KM)

MASS
5% OF EARTH'S MASS

MOONS
0

LENGTH OF YEAR
88 EARTH DAYS

Huge crash!
Mercury's largest known feature, Caloris, is a huge impact basin (larger than the state of Texas) formed by an object slamming into Mercury about 3.9 billion years ago.

Impact site

Shockwaves
sent through
the planet

Mercury's dense core of iron and nickel is larger than our Moon.

Suisei Planitia

Turg

• Strin

• Shakespeare

De

Sobkou
Planitia

• Couperin

Odin
Planitia

Budh
Planitia

Hee

Tir Planitia

• Harunobu

• Phidias

• Lysi

• Goya

• Tolstoj

• Milton

Beethov

• Valmiki

• Takayoshi

Pour Quoi Pas Rupes

Delacro

• Vincente

On the surface

Mercury's surface resembles the Moon—most of the planet is covered in giant cratered regions called highlands. But, as on the Moon, there are also smoother, slightly younger areas known as lowland plains, which were formed when molten rock from the planet's interior—or from the impact of giant meteorites—spilled onto the surface and froze. Surface temperatures on Mercury range from about -293°F to 806°F (-180°C to 430°C). This makes it the hottest planet after Venus.

The surface of Mercury, as revealed by the Mariner 10 spacecraft. Part of the circular rim of the Caloris basin can be seen on the left of this photo.

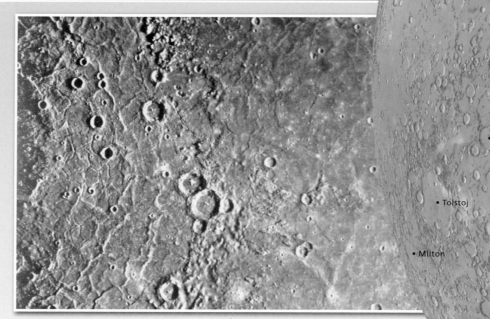

Future missions
A new mission to Mercury, the BepiColombo, is due for launch between 2009 and 2012. The mission will consist of two identical orbiters (right) and, for the first time, possibly a lander.

Messenger
This artist's impression shows Messenger, a NASA mission launched toward Mercury in 2004. After brief encounters with Mercury in 2008 and 2009, the spacecraft will enter into orbit around the planet in 2011.

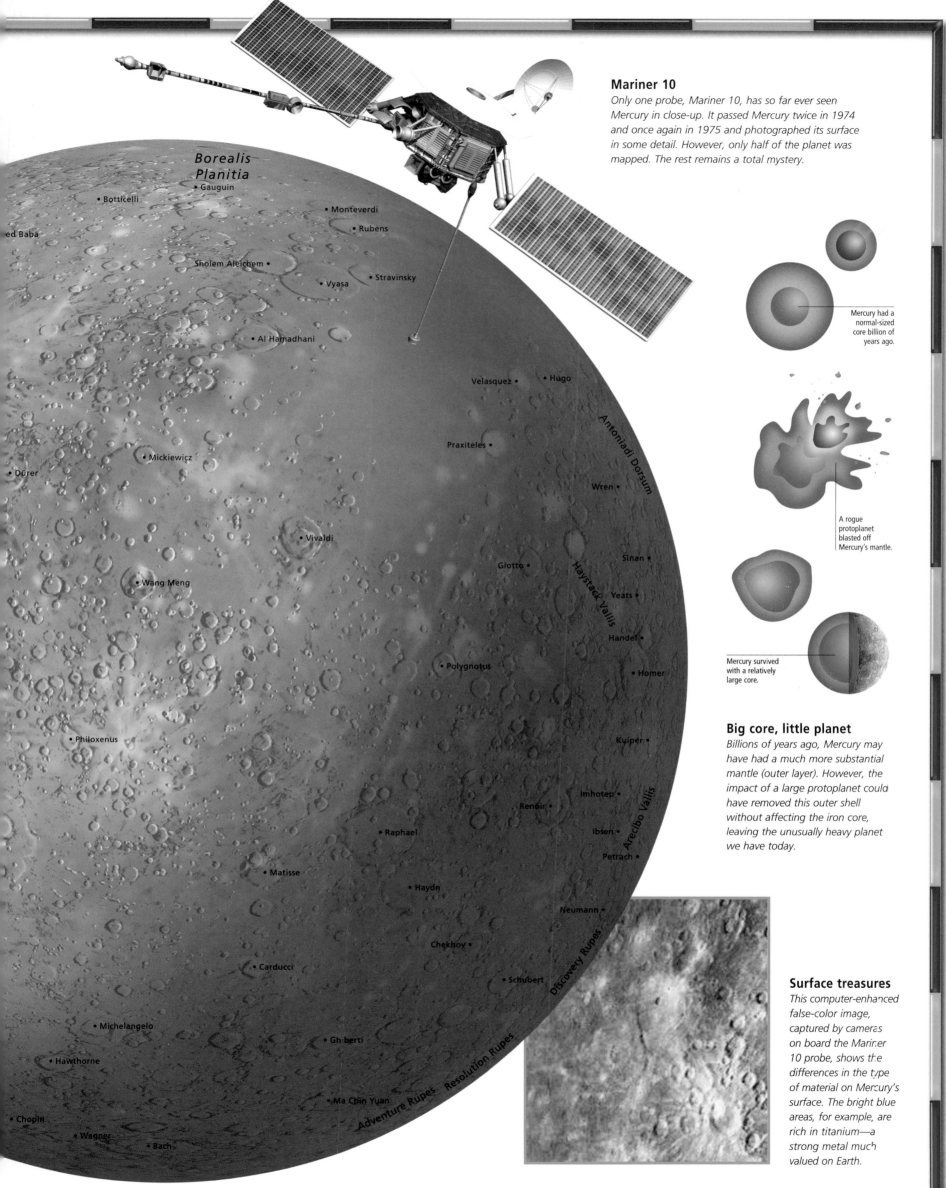

Borealis
Planitia

- Gauguin
- Botticelli
ed Baba
Sholem Aleichem •
- Vyasa   • Stravinsky
- Monteverdi
- Rubens
- Al Hamadhani

- Mickiewicz
- Dürer

- Vivaldi
- Wang Meng

- Philoxenus

Velasquez •   • Hugo

Praxiteles •

Giotto •

Polygnotus •

- Matisse

- Raphael

- Haydn

Chekhov •

- Carducci

- Michelangelo

- Ghiberti

- Hawthorne

- Chopin
- Wagner
- Bach
- Ma Chin Yuan

Antoniadi Dorsum

Wren •

Sinan •

Yeats •

Handel •

- Homer

Kuiper •

Imhotep •

Renoir •

Ibsen •

Petrach •

Neumann •

Schubert •

Haystack Vallis
Arecibo Vallis
Discovery Rupes
Adventure Rupes Resolution Rupes

Mariner 10

Only one probe, Mariner 10, has so far ever seen Mercury in close-up. It passed Mercury twice in 1974 and once again in 1975 and photographed its surface in some detail. However, only half of the planet was mapped. The rest remains a total mystery.

Mercury had a normal-sized core billion of years ago.

A rogue protoplanet blasted off Mercury's mantle.

Mercury survived with a relatively large core.

Big core, little planet

Billions of years ago, Mercury may have had a much more substantial mantle (outer layer). However, the impact of a large protoplanet could have removed this outer shell without affecting the iron core, leaving the unusually heavy planet we have today.

Surface treasures

This computer-enhanced false-color image, captured by cameras on board the Mariner 10 probe, shows the differences in the type of material on Mercury's surface. The bright blue areas, for example, are rich in titanium—a strong metal much valued on Earth.

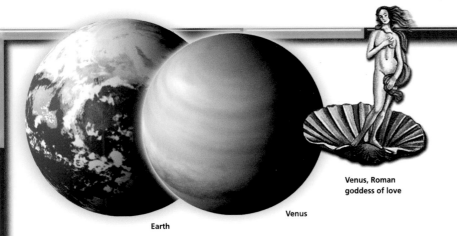

Earth

Venus

Venus, Roman goddess of love

Venus

ORIGIN OF NAME
VENUS, THE ROMAN GODDESS OF LOVE

DISCOVERED
KNOWN SINCE ANTIQUITY

DISTANCE FROM THE SUN
67 MILLION MILES (108 MILLION KM)

DIAMETER AT THE EQUATOR
7,521 MILES (12,104 KM)

MASS
81.5% OF EARTH'S MASS

MOONS
0

LENGTH OF YEAR
225 EARTH DAYS

Only one feature on Venus is named after a man: Maxwell Montes are named after James Clerke Maxwell. The rest are named for famous women.

Transit of Venus

Occasionally, observers on Earth can watch Venus pass across the face of the Sun. These rare events are called transits of Venus. In the past, astronomers used these events to measure the distance between Earth and Venus. James Cook's first voyage of exploration in the Pacific included observing a transit of Venus before he went on to discover new lands.

The portable observatory used by James Cook in Tahiti

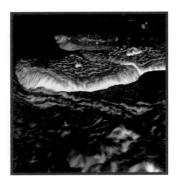

Pancakes on Venus
This image, created from data provided by the Magellan probe in 1989, shows three "pancake domes" on the Alpha Regio highland plateau. These volcanic features are about 2,400 feet (750 m) high.

Thermal control pipes

Antenna
Aerobrake

Photometer

Camera

Venera lander
The Soviet Venera program launched sixteen probes to study Venus from 1967 to 1983. This illustration shows the odd shape of landers 9 to 14. They were designed to absorb the shock of landing, as well as the high temperature and pressure of Venus.

Landing platform   Lightning detector

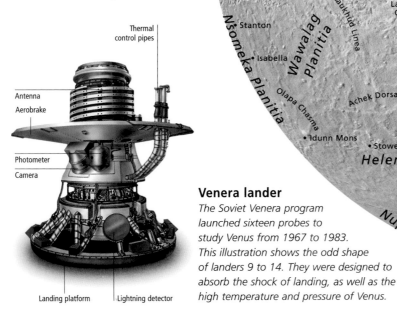

Snegurochka Planitia
Vinmara Planitia
Ganiki Planitia
Bachue Corona
Iris Dorsa
Mist Chasma
Feronia Corona
Rananeida Corona
Duncan
Lampedo Linea
Ishtar Terra
Sapph-
Patera
Eist
Reg
Libuse Planitia
Deken Dorsa
Sedna Planitia
Sekmet Mons
Yuki-Onne Tessera
Rauni Corona
Shishimora Dorsa
Ki Corona
Kawelu Planitia
Asteria Regio
Beta Regio
Emegen Corona
Breksta Linea
Guinevere Planitia
Vener
Abe-Mango Dorsa
Bellona Dorsa
Mentha Tholus
Venera 9
Renenti Corona
Atla Regio
Ulfrun Regio
Ixtab Mons
Hecate Chasma
Latona Chasma
Devana Chasma
Hyndla Regio
Purandhi Corona
O'Keefe
Taranga Corona
Sinlaku Corona
Zverine Chasma
Venera 10
Undine Planitia
Seymour
Pani Corona
Wheatley
Nang-byon Chasma
Uottakh-silus Vallis
Cashan-Ki Corona
Nedolya Tesserae
Somagali
Montes
Tkashi-mapa Chasma
Zewana Chasma
Aruru Corona
Tuulikki Mons
Rhpisunt Mohs
Pioneer Venus 2 Large Probe
Sapas Mons
Ozza Mons
Langdin Corona
Hinemoa Planitia
Venera 12
Venera 13
Venera 8
Vene
Maat Mons
Ongwuti Mons
Kicheda Chasma
Dhorani Corona
Phoebe Regio
Dzerassa Planitia
Venera 11
Venera 14
Hithyia Mons
Bhumidevi Corona
Zewana Chasma
Parga Chasmata
Thaukhud Linea
Mbokomu Mons
Lal Atete Corona
Uretsete Mons
Pinga Chasma
Atai Mons
Iweridd Corona
Nsomeka Planitia
Stanton
Isabella
Wawalag Planitia
Parga Chasma
Lalohonua Corona
Pioneer Venus 2 Day Probe
Dione Regio
Cipactli Mons
Olapa Chasma
Achek Dorsa
Gertjon Corona
Oakley
Furachoga Corona
Semi-ramus Corona
Themis Regio
Kata Linea
Hathor Mons
Kankey Pl
Idunn Mons
Stowe
Helen Planitia
Abeona Mons
Shiwanokia Corona
Bibi-Patma Corona
Magu Tessera
Lavinia Planitia
Nuptadi Planitia
Sui-ur Linea
Sinann Vallis
Natami Dorsa
Vesuna Corona
Ponselie
Morgan Linea

✛ = Spacecraft landing sites

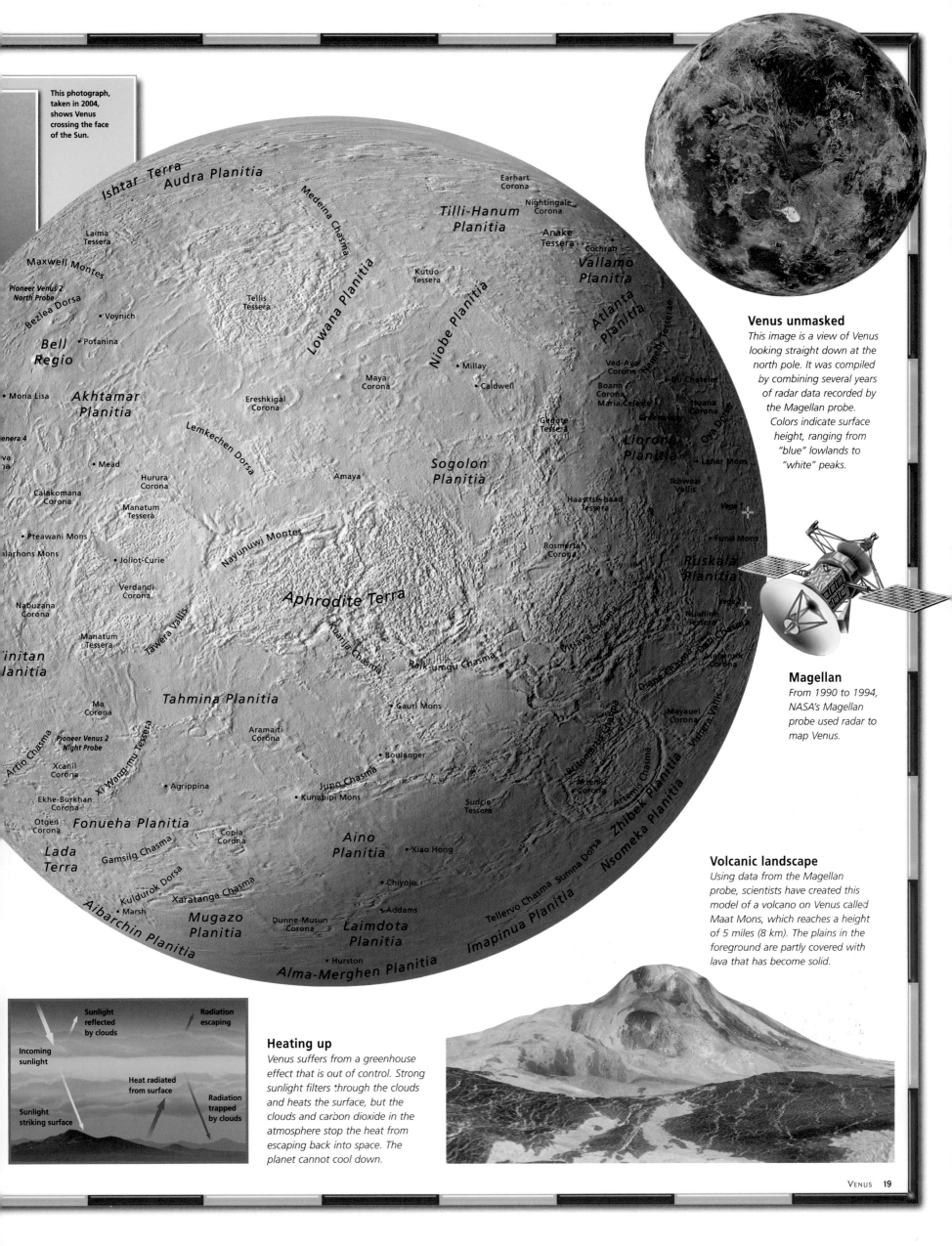

This photograph, taken in 2004, shows Venus crossing the face of the Sun.

Venus unmasked
This image is a view of Venus looking straight down at the north pole. It was compiled by combining several years of radar data recorded by the Magellan probe. Colors indicate surface height, ranging from "blue" lowlands to "white" peaks.

Magellan
From 1990 to 1994, NASA's Magellan probe used radar to map Venus.

Volcanic landscape
Using data from the Magellan probe, scientists have created this model of a volcano on Venus called Maat Mons, which reaches a height of 5 miles (8 km). The plains in the foreground are partly covered with lava that has become solid.

Heating up
Venus suffers from a greenhouse effect that is out of control. Strong sunlight filters through the clouds and heats the surface, but the clouds and carbon dioxide in the atmosphere stop the heat from escaping back into space. The planet cannot cool down.

Sunlight reflected by clouds
Radiation escaping
Incoming sunlight
Heat radiated from surface
Radiation trapped by clouds
Sunlight striking surface

Ishtar Terra
Audra Planitia
Medeina Chasma
Earhart Corona
Nightingale Corona
Tilli-Hanum Planitia
Anake Tessera
Cochran
Vallamo Planitia
Laima Tessera
Maxwell Montes
Kutuo Tessera
Lowana Planitia
Atlanta Planitia
Pioneer Venus 2 North Probe
Tellis Tessera
Niobe Planitia
Bezlea Dorsa
Voynich
Bell Regio
Potanina
Ved-Aya Corona
Gu Chatelet
Boann Corona
Maria Celeste
Nemesis Tesserae
Ituana Corona
Mona Lisa
Akhtamar Planitia
Ereshkigal Corona
Maya Corona
Caldwell
Millay
Lemkechen Dorsa
Greenaway
Oya Dorsa
Llorona Planitia
Lahar Mons
Venera 4
Mead
Hurura Corona
Amaya
Sogolon Planitia
Gegute Tessera
Ikhwezi Vallis
Calakomana Corona
Manatum Tessera
Haasttse-baad Tessera
Vega 1
Pteawani Mons
Joliot-Curie
Nayunuwi Montes
Rosmerta Corona
Funu Mons
Alarhons Mons
Verdandi Corona
Ruskala Planitia
Nabuzana Corona
Tawera Vallis
Aphrodite Terra
Vega 2
Nuahine Tessera
Manatum Tessera
Kuanja Chasma
Rarahmahtr Corona
Inatitan Planitia
Ma Corona
Tahmina Planitia
Gauri Mons
Relk-umgu Chasma
Musa Chasma
Diana Chasma
Dali Chasma
Parn Chasma
Pioneer Venus 2 Night Probe
Aramaiti Corona
Boulanger
Mayauel Corona
Artio Chasma
Xcanil Corona
Xi Wang-mu Tessera
Agrippina
Juno Chasma
Kunapipi Mons
Britomartis Chasma
Artemis Chasma
Zhibek Planitia
Vahmera Vallis
Ekhe-Burkhan Corona
Artemis Corona
Otgen Corona
Fonueha Planitia
Copia Corona
Aino Planitia
Sudice Tessera
Nsomeka Planitia
Lada Terra
Gamsilg Chasma
Xiao Hong
Kuldurok Dorsa
Xaratanga Chasma
Chiyojo
Tellervo Chasma
Sumna Dorsa
Marsh
Mugazo Planitia
Dunne-Musun Corona
Addams
Laimdota Planitia
Imapinua Planitia
Aibarchin Planitia
Hurston
Alma-Merghen Planitia

Earth
Sumerian Earth goddess
The Moon
Earth

Earth

ORIGIN OF NAME
EARTHE, THE ANGLO-SAXON WORD FOR "LAND"

DISTANCE FROM THE SUN
92.9 MILLION MILES (149.6 MILLION KM)

DIAMETER AT THE EQUATOR
7,926 MILES (12,756 KM)

MASS
6×10^{24} TONS (5.5×10^{24} TONNES)

MOONS
1

LENGTH OF YEAR
365.24 DAYS

Curtain of light
The auroras—the Northern and Southern lights—are caused by charged particles streaming from the Sun. Upon reaching our planet, they get caught up in Earth's magnetic field and collide with molecules in the atmosphere, making them glow.

200 million years ago

90 million years ago

Today

On the move
The continents are in continuous motion. Some 200 million years ago Earth had a single supercontinent. But it broke up and the fragments separated to make the pattern of continents so familiar today.

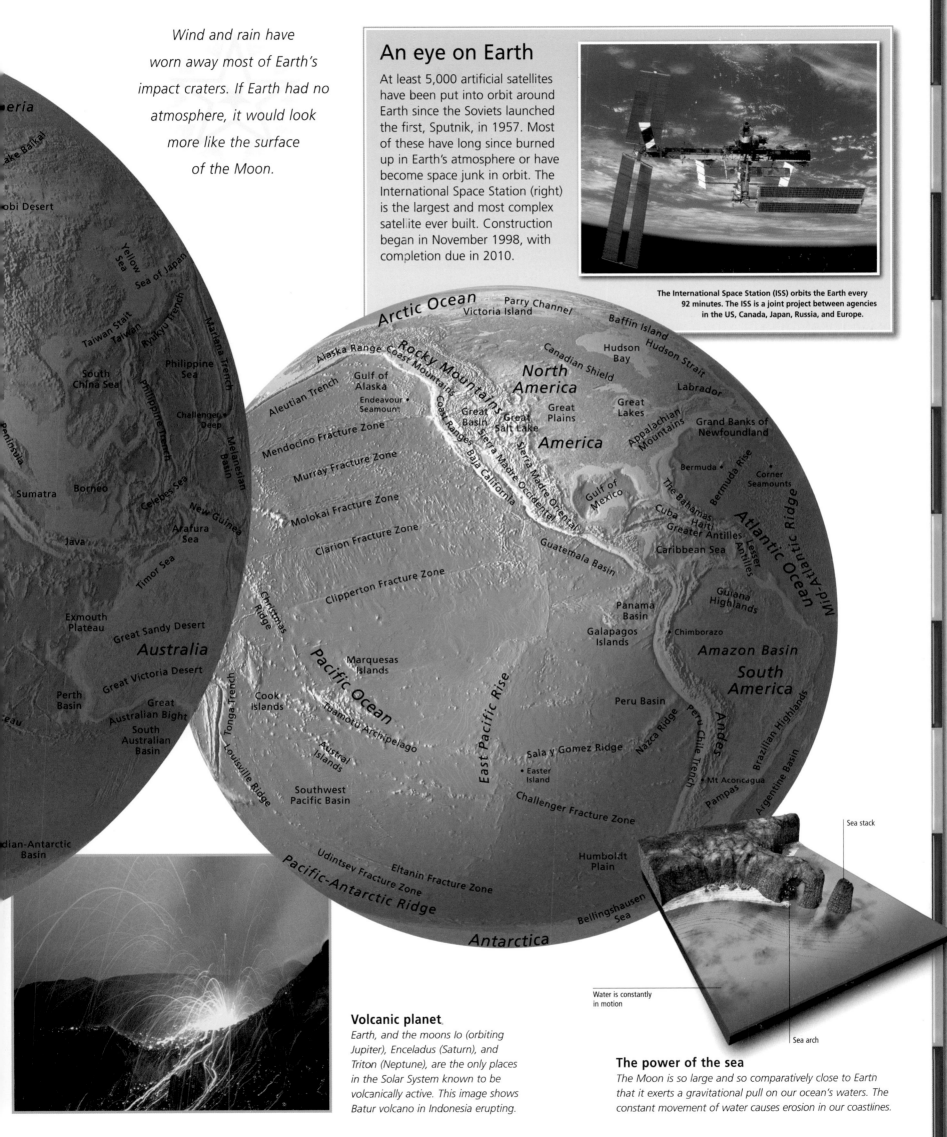

Wind and rain have worn away most of Earth's impact craters. If Earth had no atmosphere, it would look more like the surface of the Moon.

An eye on Earth

At least 5,000 artificial satellites have been put into orbit around Earth since the Soviets launched the first, Sputnik, in 1957. Most of these have long since burned up in Earth's atmosphere or have become space junk in orbit. The International Space Station (right) is the largest and most complex satellite ever built. Construction began in November 1998, with completion due in 2010.

The International Space Station (ISS) orbits the Earth every 92 minutes. The ISS is a joint project between agencies in the US, Canada, Japan, Russia, and Europe.

Volcanic planet
Earth, and the moons Io (orbiting Jupiter), Enceladus (Saturn), and Triton (Neptune), are the only places in the Solar System known to be volcanically active. This image shows Batur volcano in Indonesia erupting.

The power of the sea
The Moon is so large and so comparatively close to Earth that it exerts a gravitational pull on our ocean's waters. The constant movement of water causes erosion in our coastlines.

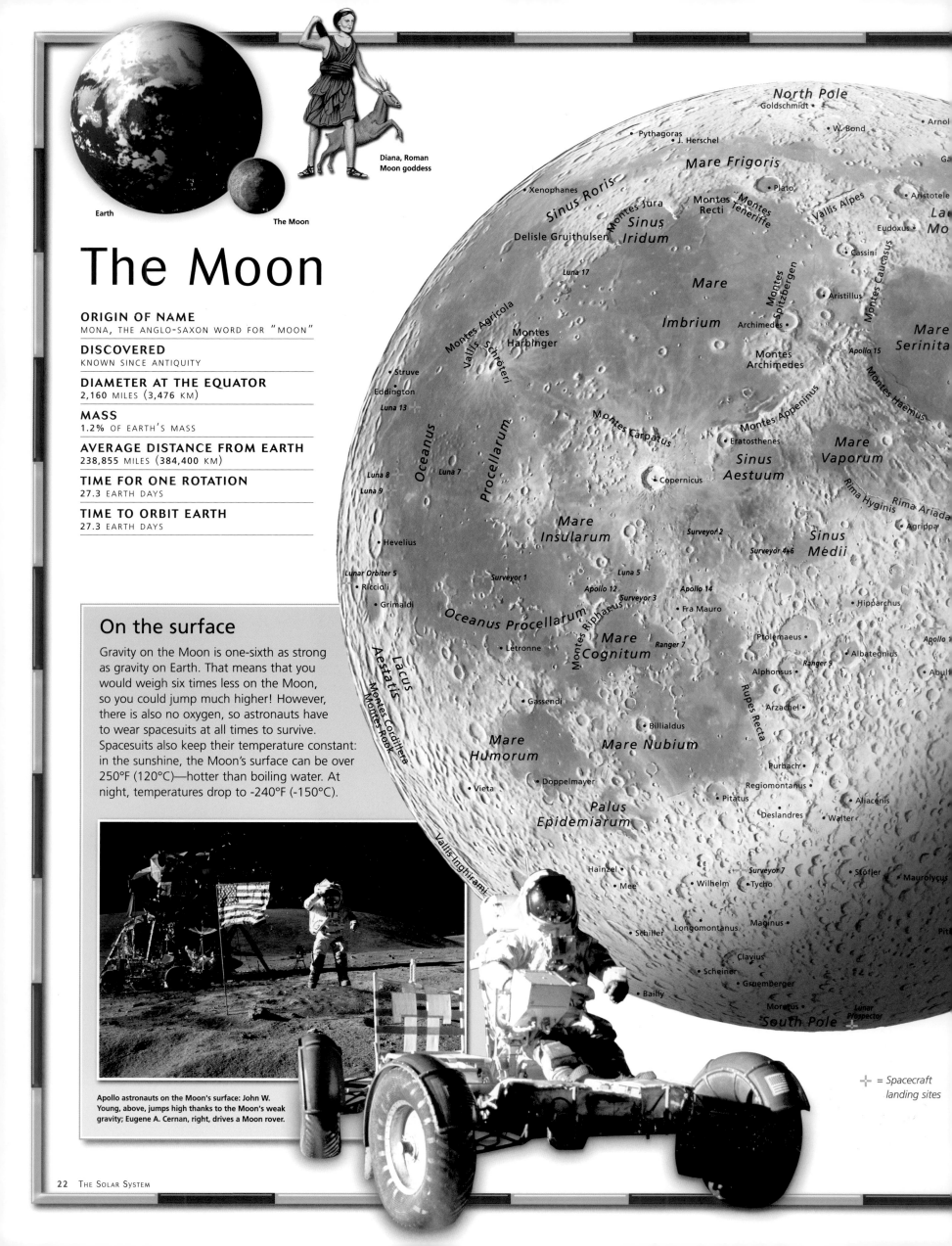

Earth   The Moon

Diana, Roman
Moon goddess

The Moon

ORIGIN OF NAME
MONA, THE ANGLO-SAXON WORD FOR "MOON"

DISCOVERED
KNOWN SINCE ANTIQUITY

DIAMETER AT THE EQUATOR
2,160 MILES (3,476 KM)

MASS
1.2% OF EARTH'S MASS

AVERAGE DISTANCE FROM EARTH
238,855 MILES (384,400 KM)

TIME FOR ONE ROTATION
27.3 EARTH DAYS

TIME TO ORBIT EARTH
27.3 EARTH DAYS

On the surface

Gravity on the Moon is one-sixth as strong as gravity on Earth. That means that you would weigh six times less on the Moon, so you could jump much higher! However, there is also no oxygen, so astronauts have to wear spacesuits at all times to survive. Spacesuits also keep their temperature constant: in the sunshine, the Moon's surface can be over 250°F (120°C)—hotter than boiling water. At night, temperatures drop to -240°F (-150°C).

Apollo astronauts on the Moon's surface: John W. Young, above, jumps high thanks to the Moon's weak gravity; Eugene A. Cernan, right, drives a Moon rover.

North Pole
Goldschmidt •
• Pythagoras   • W. Bond   • Arnol
• J. Herschel
• Xenophanes   Sinus Roris   Mare Frigoris   • Aristotele
• Plato   Vallis Alpes   La
Montes Jura   Montes   Montes   Eudoxus •   Mo
Delisle Gruithulsen   Sinus   Recti Teneriffe   • Cassini
Iridum   Montes Caucasus
Luna 17   Mare   • Aristillus
Montes Agricola   Montes   Imbrium   Montes   Mare
Harbinger   Spitzbergen   Serinita
Montes   Archimedes •   Apollo 15
Vallis Schröteri   Archimedes   Mare
• Struve   Montes   Montes Haemus
Eddington   Montes Carpatus   Appeninus
Luna 13   • Eratosthenes   Mare
Oceanus   Sinus   Vaporum
• Copernicus   Aestuum   Rima Hyginis
Procellarum   Rima Ariada
Luna 8   Luna 7   • Agrippa
Luna 9   Sinus
Mare   Surveyor 2   Medii
Hevelius   Insularum   Surveyor 4+6
Lunar Orbiter 5   Luna 5   • Hipparchus
• Riccioli   Surveyor 1   Apollo 12   Apollo 14
• Grimaldi   Surveyor 3   • Fra Mauro   Ptolemaeus
Oceanus Procellarum   Ranger 7   • Albategnius   Apollo
Montes Riphaeus   Mare   Ranger 9   Alphonsus   Abul
• Letronne   Cognitum   Rupes Recta
Lacus   Arzachel
Aestatis   • Gassendi   • Billialdus
Montes Cordillera   Mare Nubium   Purbach
Montes Rook   Mare   Regiomontanus   • Aliacensis
• Doppelmayer   Humorum   Pitatus   Deslandres   • Walter
• Vieta
Palus   Surveyor 7   • Stöfler
Vallis Inghirami   Epidemiarum   • Maurolycus
Hainzel •   • Wilhelm   Longomontanus   Maginus   Pit
• Mee   • Tycho
• Schiller   Clavius
• Scheiner   Gruemberger
• Bailly   Moretus   Lunar
Prospector
South Pole

✛ = Spacecraft
landing sites

22 THE SOLAR SYSTEM

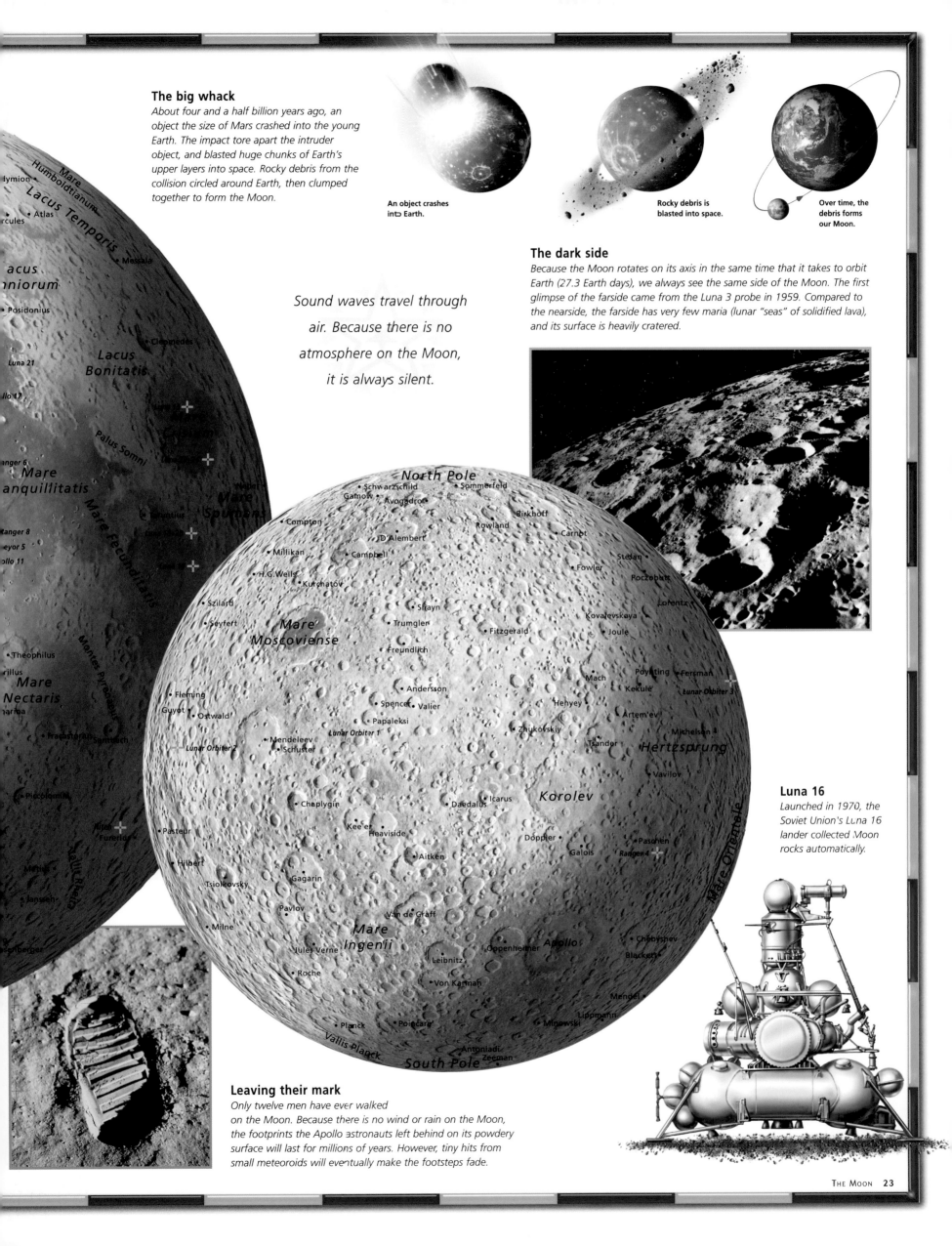

The big whack

About four and a half billion years ago, an object the size of Mars crashed into the young Earth. The impact tore apart the intruder object, and blasted huge chunks of Earth's upper layers into space. Rocky debris from the collision circled around Earth, then clumped together to form the Moon.

An object crashes into Earth.

Rocky debris is blasted into space.

Over time, the debris forms our Moon.

The dark side

Because the Moon rotates on its axis in the same time that it takes to orbit Earth (27.3 Earth days), we always see the same side of the Moon. The first glimpse of the farside came from the Luna 3 probe in 1959. Compared to the nearside, the farside has very few maria (lunar "seas" of solidified lava), and its surface is heavily cratered.

Sound waves travel through air. Because there is no atmosphere on the Moon, it is always silent.

Luna 16

Launched in 1970, the Soviet Union's Luna 16 lander collected Moon rocks automatically.

Leaving their mark

Only twelve men have ever walked on the Moon. Because there is no wind or rain on the Moon, the footprints the Apollo astronauts left behind on its powdery surface will last for millions of years. However, tiny hits from small meteoroids will eventually make the footsteps fade.

Meteors and Meteorites

The Solar System is a messy place. The tails of gas and dust that make comets so spectacular litter their passage with trails of cometary dust. Asteroids lack the tails of comets but scatter fragments of rock and iron across the Solar System when they collide. Some of these small meteoroids and the cometary dust strike Earth's atmosphere. The smaller particles burn up in the atmosphere and form a glowing streak across the sky, which we call a meteor. Larger particles that survive the fiery encounter and reach the ground are classified as meteorites.

Space debris
Children were once able to climb on the Willamette Meteorite, which now resides at the American Museum of Natual History. This 15-ton chunk of nickel-iron fell to Earth thousands of years ago after spending billions of years in space.

Iron meteorite

Stony meteorite

Stony-iron meteorite

Barringer Crater
Located in Arizona, USA, this impact crater was formed about 50,000 years ago. It measures 0.76 mile (1.2 km) in diameter—and yet, the object that caused it was only around 160 feet (50 m) across. The great size of the crater is due to the tremendous speed of the impact, at several miles per second.

Kinds of meteorites
Meteorites come in different varieties, depending on their origins in the Solar System. These illustrations show (left to right) examples made from iron, stone, and a mixture of both.

Inside a meteorite

This magnified cross section of a meteorite from Chile shows its makeup. The golden bits are chunks of rock, while the blue material that surrounds them is metal, mainly iron and nickel.

Shooting stars

Meteors are often called "shooting stars," although they have nothing to do with stars. They are fragments of dust that enter our planet's atmosphere. As they pass through the air, their rapid motions heat the atmospheric gases in their wake and create beautiful, glowing streaks. Most meteors are caused by flecks no larger than a grain of sand. But occasionally, larger, pea-sized fragments burn up, producing unusually bright streaks called fireballs.

In this photo, several meteors are seen streaking across the starry sky on the night of a meteor shower. On rare occasions, when the number of meteors is very high, we call it a meteor storm.

Impact!

This illustration shows something we should all hope never to experience—our planet being hit by a large object from space. When comets or asteroids collide with Earth, they do so at incredible speed. This generates so much heat that the object is vaporized and leaves a melted hole called a crater in the ground, dozens of times its original size. Some 65 million years ago, the impact of a comet or asteroid 6 miles (10 km) across may have hit Earth and killed off the dinosaurs and other species.

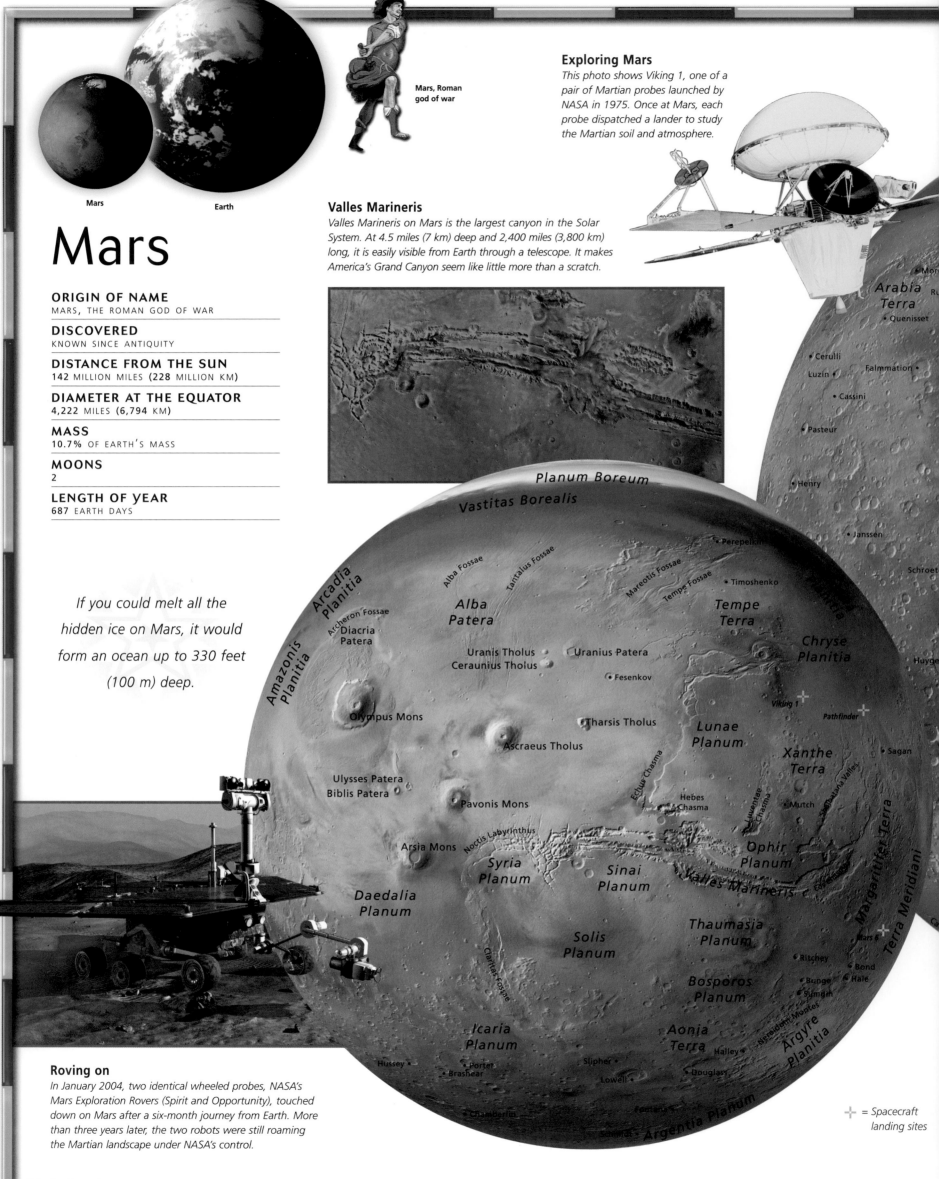

Mars

Mars, Roman god of war

Exploring Mars
This photo shows Viking 1, one of a pair of Martian probes launched by NASA in 1975. Once at Mars, each probe dispatched a lander to study the Martian soil and atmosphere.

Valles Marineris
Valles Marineris on Mars is the largest canyon in the Solar System. At 4.5 miles (7 km) deep and 2,400 miles (3,800 km) long, it is easily visible from Earth through a telescope. It makes America's Grand Canyon seem like little more than a scratch.

Mars **Earth**

ORIGIN OF NAME
MARS, THE ROMAN GOD OF WAR

DISCOVERED
KNOWN SINCE ANTIQUITY

DISTANCE FROM THE SUN
142 MILLION MILES (228 MILLION KM)

DIAMETER AT THE EQUATOR
4,222 MILES (6,794 KM)

MASS
10.7% OF EARTH'S MASS

MOONS
2

LENGTH OF YEAR
687 EARTH DAYS

If you could melt all the hidden ice on Mars, it would form an ocean up to 330 feet (100 m) deep.

Roving on
In January 2004, two identical wheeled probes, NASA's Mars Exploration Rovers (Spirit and Opportunity), touched down on Mars after a six-month journey from Earth. More than three years later, the two robots were still roaming the Martian landscape under NASA's control.

Planum Boreum
Vastitas Borealis
Arcadia Planitia
Alba Fossae
Tantalus Fossae
Mareotis Fossae
Tempe Fossae
Perepelkin
Timoshenko
Tempe Terra
Chryse Planitia
Arabia Terra
Quenisset
Cerulli
Falmmation
Luzin
Cassini
Pasteur
Henry
Janssen
Schroet
Amazonis Planitia
Archeron Fossae
Diacria Patera
Alba Patera
Uranis Tholus
Ceraunius Tholus
Uranius Patera
Fesenkov
Olympus Mons
Ascraeus Tholus
Tharsis Tholus
Lunae Planum
Viking 1
Pathfinder
Xanthe Terra
Sagan
Ulysses Patera
Biblis Patera
Pavonis Mons
Echus Chasma
Hebes Chasma
Mutch
Ophir Planum
Huyge
Arsia Mons
Noctis Labyrinthus
Syria Planum
Sinai Planum
Valles Marineris
Margaritifer Terra
Daedalia Planum
Solis Planum
Thaumasia Planum
Terra Meridiani
Claritas Fossae
Bosporos Planum
Mars 6
Ritchey
Bond
Bunge
Hale
Sumgin
Icaria Planum
Aonia Terra
Argyre Planitia
Hussey
Porter
Brashear
Slipher
Halley
Douglass
Lowell
Chamberlin
Argentia Planum

+ = *Spacecraft landing sites*

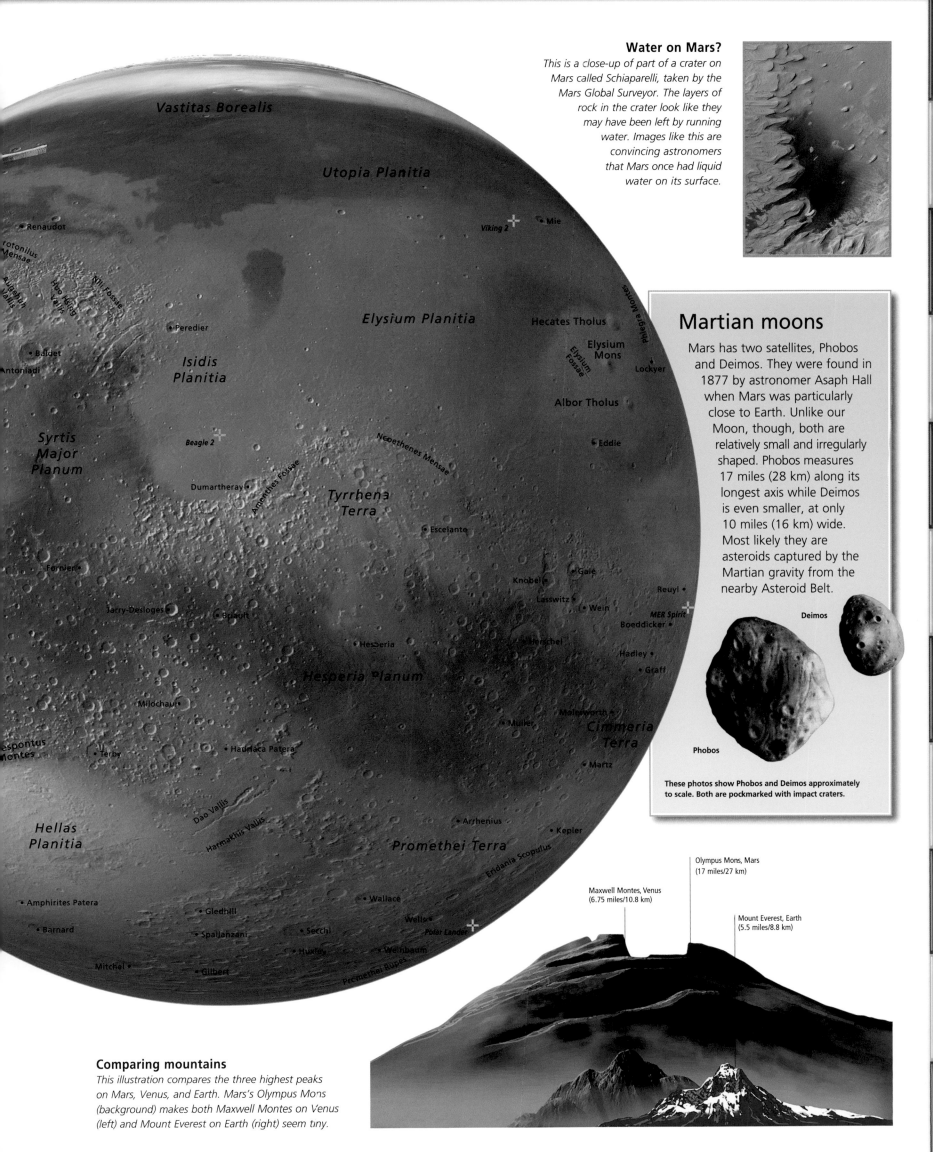

Vastitas Borealis

Utopia Planitia

• Renaudot

rotonilus
Mensae

• Peredier

• Baldet

Antoniadi

**Isidis
Planitia**

Elysium Planitia

Hecates Tholus

Phlegra Montes

Elysium
Mons

Elysium
Fossae

Lockyer

Albor Tholus

Viking 2 ✛   • Mie

**Syrtis
Major
Planum**

Beagle 2 ✛

Neoethenes Mensae

Amenthes Fossae

Dumartheray

**Tyrrhena
Terra**

• Escelante

Eddie

• Gale

Fornier

Knobel •

Reuyl •

Jarry-Desloges •

• Briault

Lasswitz •

• Wein

MER Spirit

Boeddicker •

Milochau •

• Hesseria

• Herschel

Hadley •

• Graff

Hesperia Planum

• Muller

Molesworth •

**Cimmeria
Terra**

• Martz

espontus
Montes

• Terby

• Hadriaca Patera

Dao Vallis

Harmakhis Vallis

• Arrhenius

• Kepler

Promethei Terra

Eridania Scopulus

**Hellas
Planitia**

• Amphirites Patera

• Gledhill

• Wallace

• Barnard

• Spallanzani

• Secchi

Wells •

Polar Lander ✛

• Huxley

• Weinbaum

Mitchel •

• Gilbert

Promethei Rupes

Water on Mars?
This is a close-up of part of a crater on Mars called Schiaparelli, taken by the Mars Global Surveyor. The layers of rock in the crater look like they may have been left by running water. Images like this are convincing astronomers that Mars once had liquid water on its surface.

Martian moons

Mars has two satellites, Phobos and Deimos. They were found in 1877 by astronomer Asaph Hall when Mars was particularly close to Earth. Unlike our Moon, though, both are relatively small and irregularly shaped. Phobos measures 17 miles (28 km) along its longest axis while Deimos is even smaller, at only 10 miles (16 km) wide. Most likely they are asteroids captured by the Martian gravity from the nearby Asteroid Belt.

Deimos

Phobos

These photos show Phobos and Deimos approximately to scale. Both are pockmarked with impact craters.

Olympus Mons, Mars
(17 miles/27 km)

Maxwell Montes, Venus
(6.75 miles/10.8 km)

Mount Everest, Earth
(5.5 miles/8.8 km)

Comparing mountains
This illustration compares the three highest peaks on Mars, Venus, and Earth. Mars's Olympus Mons (background) makes both Maxwell Montes on Venus (left) and Mount Everest on Earth (right) seem tiny.

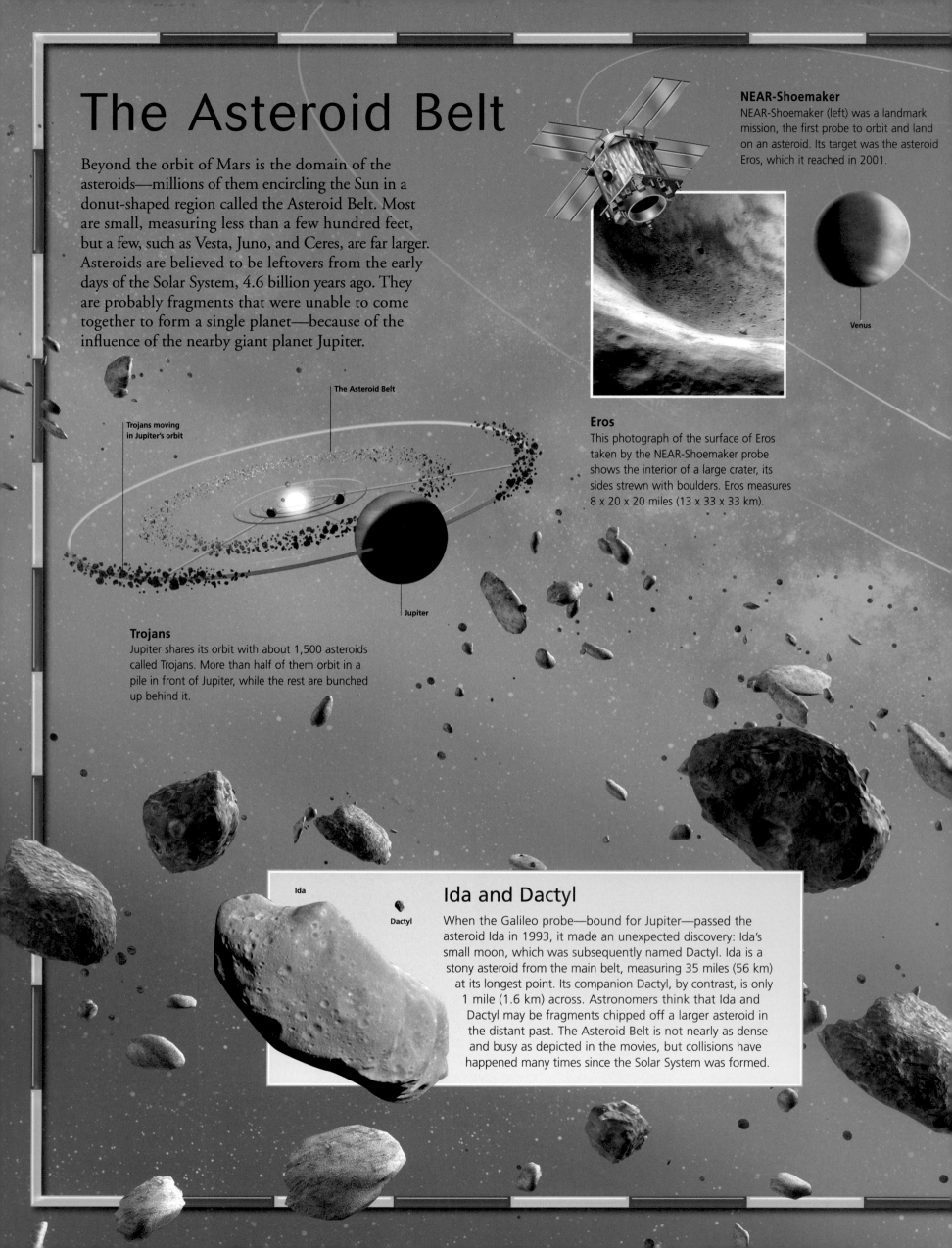

The Asteroid Belt

Beyond the orbit of Mars is the domain of the asteroids—millions of them encircling the Sun in a donut-shaped region called the Asteroid Belt. Most are small, measuring less than a few hundred feet, but a few, such as Vesta, Juno, and Ceres, are far larger. Asteroids are believed to be leftovers from the early days of the Solar System, 4.6 billion years ago. They are probably fragments that were unable to come together to form a single planet—because of the influence of the nearby giant planet Jupiter.

NEAR-Shoemaker
NEAR-Shoemaker (left) was a landmark mission, the first probe to orbit and land on an asteroid. Its target was the asteroid Eros, which it reached in 2001.

Venus

Eros
This photograph of the surface of Eros taken by the NEAR-Shoemaker probe shows the interior of a large crater, its sides strewn with boulders. Eros measures 8 x 20 x 20 miles (13 x 33 x 33 km).

The Asteroid Belt

Trojans moving in Jupiter's orbit

Jupiter

Trojans
Jupiter shares its orbit with about 1,500 asteroids called Trojans. More than half of them orbit in a pile in front of Jupiter, while the rest are bunched up behind it.

Ida

Dactyl

Ida and Dactyl

When the Galileo probe—bound for Jupiter—passed the asteroid Ida in 1993, it made an unexpected discovery: Ida's small moon, which was subsequently named Dactyl. Ida is a stony asteroid from the main belt, measuring 35 miles (56 km) at its longest point. Its companion Dactyl, by contrast, is only 1 mile (1.6 km) across. Astronomers think that Ida and Dactyl may be fragments chipped off a larger asteroid in the distant past. The Asteroid Belt is not nearly as dense and busy as depicted in the movies, but collisions have happened many times since the Solar System was formed.

Mercury

Earth

Moon

Hayabusa

In 2003, the Japanese probe Hayabusa was launched toward the asteroid Itokowa with an ambitious mission: to land on the asteroid, collect samples, and return them to Earth. Upon arrival in 2005, the probe failed to make its historic touchdown.

Ceres

Ceres, the largest known asteroid, was the first one to be discovered, in 1801. Measuring 605 miles (675 km) across, it is the only spherical asteroid, and the only one belonging to the new class of astronomical objects called dwarf planets, which includes Pluto.

Mars

The Inner Solar System

Mars takes 687 Earth days to orbit the Sun.

Earth takes 365 days to orbit the Sun.

Venus takes 225 Earth days to orbit the Sun.

Mercury takes 88 Earth days to orbit the Sun.

The Asteroid Belt

WHAT'S OUT THERE?

Terrestrial planets
The four planets closest to the Sun are Mercury, Venus, Earth, and Mars. They are called terrestrial planets after the Latin word for "Earthlike."

Asteroids
Just beyond Mars, millions of fragments of rock, metal, and other minerals called asteroids are in orbit. Most are tiny; some are small worlds in their own right.

Meteors and meteorites
Meteors are fragments of comet dust that burn up in our atmosphere. Larger fragments of space debris that land on Earth are called meteorites.

PLANET AND MOON SIZES

Mercury 3,032 miles (4,879 km) in diameter

Venus 7,521 miles (12,104 km) in diameter

Earth 7,926 miles (12,756 km) in diameter

The Moon 2,160 miles (3,476 km) in diameter

Mars 4,222 miles (6,794 km) in diameter

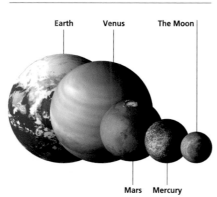

Earth　Venus　The Moon

Mars　Mercury

SIZE COMPARED WITH EARTH

Mercury 38%

Venus 91%

The Moon 27%

Mars 53%

NUMBER OF MOONS

Mercury 0

Venus 0

Earth 1

Mars 2

INSIDE AND OUTSIDE

Mercury THE IRON PLANET
Mercury, the smallest major planet, has a gigantic core of iron that takes up most of its interior. Its surface is cratered and barren.

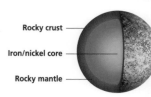

Rocky crust

Iron/nickel core

Rocky mantle

Venus THE HELL PLANET
Venus is almost the same size as Earth but otherwise utterly different. Its thick, choking atmosphere traps the Sun's heat and rains sulfuric acid.

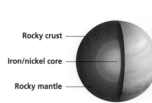

Rocky crust

Iron/nickel core

Rocky mantle

Earth THE WATERWORLD
Earth is the only place in the Solar System where surface liquid water is known to exist. Its distance from the Sun makes it ideal for life.

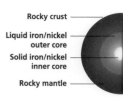

Rocky crust

Liquid iron/nickel outer core

Solid iron/nickel inner core

Rocky mantle

The Moon
The Moon is Earth's only natural satellite. Its surface is a mixture of ancient craters and slightly younger "seas"— made of solid lava, not water.

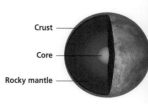

Crust

Core

Rocky mantle

Mars THE RED PLANET
Mars is a small, dusty world with a thin atmosphere. It has craters, vast volcanoes, and caps of water ice and frozen carbon dioxide.

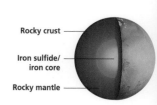

Rocky crust

Iron sulfide/ iron core

Rocky mantle

Distance from the Sun

Mercury	Venus	Earth	Mars	The Asteroid Belt
36.0 million miles (57.9 million km)	67 million miles (108 million km)	92.2 million miles (149.6 million km)	142 million miles (228 million km)	190–300 million miles (310–490 million km)

NOTABLE NUMBERS

1801 *Year Giuseppe Piazzi discovered the first asteroid, Ceres. Today it is classified as a dwarf planet.*

12 *Number of astronauts who have walked on the Moon.*

3 *Time in minutes it would take to travel from Earth to Mars at the speed of light when Mars is close to Earth.*

107 *Time in years it would take to travel from Earth to Mars at 60 mph (96 kph) when Mars is close to Earth.*

22,000 *Number of meteorite discoveries on Earth.*

88 *Earth days in a Mercurial year.*

1970 *Year the probe Venera 7 became the first man-made object to land on another planet—Venus.*

4,600,000,000 *Time in years our Solar System has been around—give or take a few hundred million years.*

83 *Number of days Mars Pathfinder sent back signals from the Red Planet.*

2880 *Year the asteroid 1950 DA will pass close to Earth— the greatest known impact hazard we face.*

1 *Number of planets in the Solar System with liquid water on the surface. It's our planet, Earth.*

Astronaut Edward "Buzz" Aldrin on the Moon.

If you weigh 80 pounds (36 kg) on Earth, you would weigh 73 pounds (33 kg) on Venus, 30 pounds (14 kg) on Mercury and Mars, and only 14 pounds (6 kg) on the Moon.

Mars attacks!

Could Martians conquer Earth? In 1897, H. G. Wells wrote the science-fiction novel *The War of the Worlds*, about a Martian invasion of Earth. A 1938 radio broadcast of the story scared thousands of people into thinking that Martians were really invading. We now know that Mars is unable to support advanced life—Martians do not exist.

Touchdown!

On July 4, 1997, the Mars Pathfinder mission touched down on the Red Planet and deployed the first Martian rover. Known as Sojourner, the probe was remotely steered by NASA mission scientists on Earth and used to analyze the structure and material of several Martian boulders. Since Pathfinder's trail-blazing mission, two more rovers have been deployed on Mars—Spirit and Opportunity. More are planned.

INNER SOLAR SYSTEM RECORDS

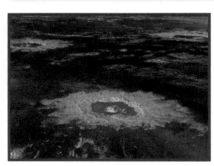

Three impact craters are seen at Lavinia Planitia, Venus.

Hottest planet in the Solar System

Because of its heat-trapping atmosphere, the surface of Venus can reach 867°F (464°C), making it the hottest in the Solar System. However, Mercury is not far behind; it can reach 800°F (430°C).

Highest mountain in the Solar System

Olympus Mons on Mars rises 17 miles (27 km) above the local surface, its base 340 miles (550 km) across. By comparison, Earth's biggest peak, Mount Everest, stands 5.5 miles (8.8 km) above sea level.

Smallest planet in the Solar System

Mercury is the innermost and smallest planet in the Solar System. It is only 38 percent the size of Earth, but 1.4 times the size of our Moon.

Mercury   Earth

Largest canyon in the Solar System

Valles Marineris on Mars is roughly 2,400 miles (3,800 km) long, with a depth of 4.5 miles (7 km). If it were in the United States, this canyon would extend from San Francisco on the west coast to the Appalachian Mountains near the east coast. In Europe, it would stretch from Paris to Russia's Ural Mountains.

Largest object in the Asteroid Belt

The dwarf planet Ceres—originally classified as an asteroid—is by far the largest known object in the Asteroid Belt. It measures 605 miles (975 km) in diameter. Ceres was also the first object identified in the Asteroid Belt, when it was discovered on January 1, 1801.

Ceres

Greatest meteor shower

The Leonids on November 13, 1833, showered down up to 200,000 meteors per hour. Onlookers said that the meteors "fell like snowflakes," while many thought the world would come to an end. The remarkable display helped astronomers realize that meteors were entering Earth's atmosphere from outer space, and were not an Earth-based event, like rain.

EXPLORATION AT A GLANCE

DISCOVERING THE INNER SOLAR SYSTEM

1610
Galileo Galilei becomes the first person to use a telescope for astronomy. He discovers, among other things, the craters on the Moon.

1877
The two moons of Mars, Phobos and Deimos, are discovered.

1959
The Soviets launch Luna 1, the first successful space probe, which sails past the Moon and sends back data.

1962
The American Mariner 2 becomes the first probe to reach another planet—Venus.

1965
Mariner 4 becomes the first probe to fly past Mars. It reveals an unexpectedly cratered surface.

1969
Apollo 11 lands the first men on the Moon— Neil Armstrong and Buzz Aldrin.

Neil Armstrong on the Moon

1970
Venera 7, launched by the US, becomes the first craft to land on another planet—Venus.

1976
NASA lands the first two craft on Mars—Vikings 1 and 2. They provide the first photographs of the Red Planet's landscape and test its soil for evidence of chemistry that might indicate life. None is found.

Viking 1's view of Mars

1990
NASA's Magellan probe reaches Venus and radar-maps its entire surface.

1991
NASA's Galileo, on its way to Jupiter, becomes the first probe to pass an asteroid (Gaspra) and photographs it in close-up.

1997
Mars Pathfinder touches down on the Red Planet and deploys the first Martian rover, known as Sojourner.

2000
The probe NEAR-Shoemaker becomes the first to orbit and map an asteroid, called Eros. Afterward the craft went on to land on the asteroid—a bonus, as it was not a scheduled part of the mission.

NEAR-Shoemaker

Earth · Jupiter

Jupiter, ruler of the Roman gods

Jupiter

ORIGIN OF NAME
JOVE, ROMAN GOD OF HEAVEN AND EARTH

DISCOVERED
KNOWN SINCE ANTIQUITY

DISTANCE FROM THE SUN
483.8 MILLION MILES (778.6 MILLION KM)

DIAMETER AT THE EQUATOR
88,846 MILES (142,984 KM)

MASS
318 x EARTH'S MASS

MOONS
AT LEAST 63

LENGTH OF YEAR
11.9 EARTH YEARS

Jupiter's moons

Jupiter hosts an entire family of at least 63 moons, more than any other planet. Most are merely captured asteroids, so they tend to be small and irregularly shaped. But there are also four of the largest satellites in the Solar System, each of them unique. Io's surface is covered in sulfurous volcanoes. Ganymede is the largest known moon (larger even than Mercury). Along with that of Europa, its surface is covered in a shell of solid water ice with, possibly, an ocean of liquid water beneath. And Callisto's battered face is the most cratered in the Solar System.

Europa · Ganymede · Io · Callisto

Far Northern Temperate Belt

Northern Temperate Belt

Northern Equatorial Belt

Circling Jupiter

This diagram plots the orbits of most of Jupiter's 63 known satellites. The innermost orbit shown is Callisto's. To give an idea of the scale of Jupiter's family, the outermost moons here are about 60 times farther from Jupiter than the Moon is from Earth.

Southern Equatorial Belt

Southern Temperate Belt

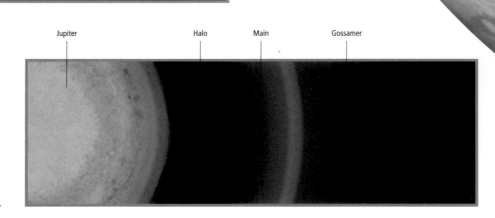

Jupiter · Halo · Main · Gossamer

Sooty rings

Jupiter's rings are nothing like the famous rings of its planetary neighbor Saturn, for they are dark—reflecting only 5 percent of sunlight reaching them—and made of tiny particles resembling grains of soot. This diagram shows the view from above, illustrating how the rings are divided into three broad regions: the halo nearest the planet, the slightly denser main ring farther out, and the pale gossamer ring on the outskirts.

Far Southern Temperate Belt

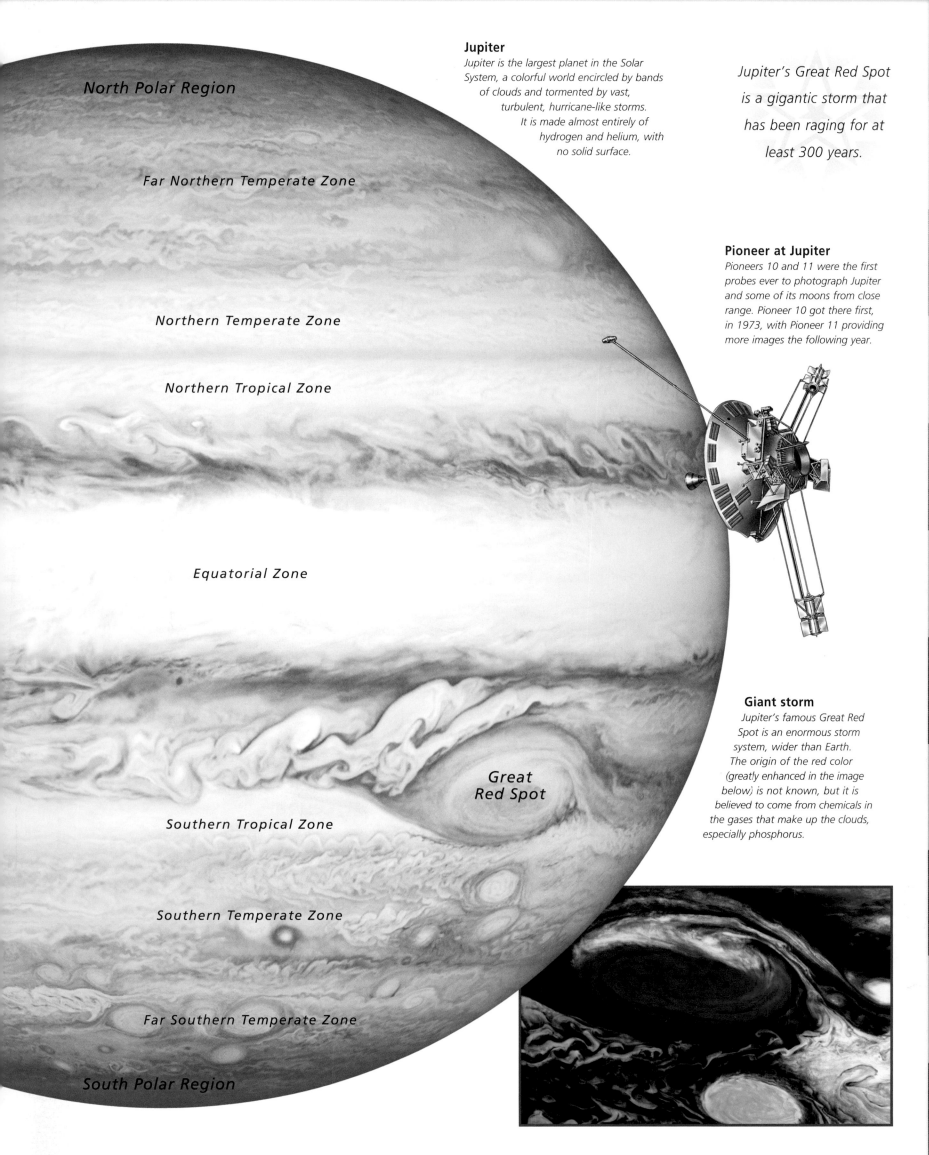

North Polar Region

Far Northern Temperate Zone

Northern Temperate Zone

Northern Tropical Zone

Equatorial Zone

**Great
Red Spot**

Southern Tropical Zone

Southern Temperate Zone

Far Southern Temperate Zone

South Polar Region

Jupiter

Jupiter is the largest planet in the Solar System, a colorful world encircled by bands of clouds and tormented by vast, turbulent, hurricane-like storms. It is made almost entirely of hydrogen and helium, with no solid surface.

Jupiter's Great Red Spot is a gigantic storm that has been raging for at least 300 years.

Pioneer at Jupiter

Pioneers 10 and 11 were the first probes ever to photograph Jupiter and some of its moons from close range. Pioneer 10 got there first, in 1973, with Pioneer 11 providing more images the following year.

Giant storm

Jupiter's famous Great Red Spot is an enormous storm system, wider than Earth. The origin of the red color (greatly enhanced in the image below) is not known, but it is believed to come from chemicals in the gases that make up the clouds, especially phosphorus.

Saturn

Earth

Saturn

Saturn is well known as the ringed planet. While it is not the only planet that has rings, Saturn's are by far the brightest and most spectacular in the Solar System. Like Jupiter, Saturn has no solid surface.

Saturn, Roman god of agriculture

Saturn

ORIGIN OF NAME
SATURNUS, THE ROMAN GOD OF AGRICULTURE

DISCOVERED
KNOWN SINCE ANTIQUITY

DISTANCE FROM THE SUN
890.7 MILLION MILES (1,434 MILLION KM)

DIAMETER AT THE EQUATOR
74,898 MILES (120,536 KM)

MASS
95 X EARTH'S MASS

MOONS
AT LEAST 57

LENGTH OF YEAR
29.5 EARTH YEARS

North Polar Region

Far Northern Temperate Belt

Northern Temperate Belt

Northern Equatorial Belt

Southern Equatorial Belt

Southern Temperate Belt

Far Southern Temperate Belt

South Polar Region

Tilted rings

These photos, taken by the Cassini probe in orbit around Saturn, show the planet's ring system from two slightly different angles. The rings are so thin that, when seen edge on, they all but disappear.

Encke Division

Cassini Division

Saturn

D   C   B   A   F   G   E

Rings of Saturn

Saturn has seven main rings, seen here from above, named after letters of the alphabet. But each of these is in turn made up of thousands of ringlets. They are very bright and made largely of water ice.

Far Northern Temperate Zone

Northern Temperate Zone

Northern Tropical Zone

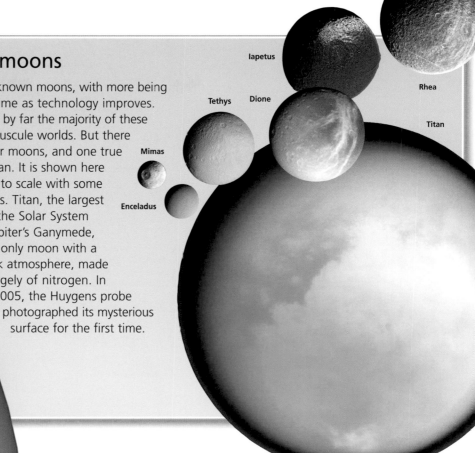

Saturn's moons

Saturn has 57 known moons, with more being found all the time as technology improves. As with Jupiter, by far the majority of these moons are minuscule worlds. But there are a few larger moons, and one true giant called Titan. It is shown here approximately to scale with some of the others. Titan, the largest moon in the Solar System after Jupiter's Ganymede, is the only moon with a thick atmosphere, made largely of nitrogen. In 2005, the Huygens probe photographed its mysterious surface for the first time.

Iapetus

Rhea

Tethys Dione

Titan

Mimas

Enceladus

Equatorial Zone

If Saturn were placed where Earth is, its brightest rings would easily stretch more than a third of the way to the Moon.

Forming Saturn's rings
We do not know how Saturn got its rings. It is likely that they are the remains of a moon that strayed too close to the planet in the relatively recent past and was torn apart by Saturn's gravity. Or they might be the outcome of a collision between two moons, long ago.

Southern Tropical Zone

Southern Temperate Zone

Far Southern Temperate Zone

Cassini
The most recent probe to visit Saturn is Cassini. It arrived there in 2005, after a journey of eight years, and is still in orbit around Saturn, helping to uncover the planet's secrets.

High-speed crash!
Two of Saturn's moons collide at great speed in orbit high above the planet.

Caught in gravity
Some fragments from the collision escape to space, while others orbit the planet.

Thinning out
The orbiting fragments spread out above the planet. Further collisions between them grind the particles down.

Saturn today
The rings as they are today. Very likely, similar collisions regularly inject fresh ring particles into the system.

Mimas
Saturn's moon Mimas, a world about 250 miles (400 km) across, is dominated by a huge crater. This covers almost a third of the visible surface.

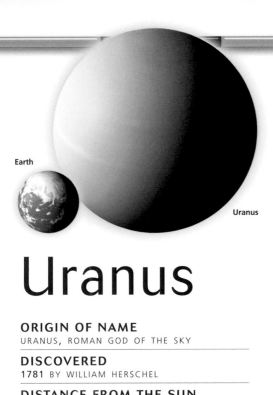

Earth

Uranus

Uranus,
Roman god
of the sky

Uranus

Uranus is a pale blue-green world, a vast globe of liquefied gas about four times the size of our Earth. Like the other gas planets it has a system of rings but no solid surface. It has many satellites. Its atmosphere is made of a gas called methane.

Uranus

ORIGIN OF NAME
URANUS, ROMAN GOD OF THE SKY

DISCOVERED
1781 BY WILLIAM HERSCHEL

DISTANCE FROM THE SUN
1,785 MILLION MILES (2,872 MILLION KM)

DIAMETER AT THE EQUATOR
31,763 MILES (51,118 KM)

MASS
14 x EARTH'S MASS

MOONS
AT LEAST 27

LENGTH OF YEAR
84.04 EARTH YEARS

Uranus is tipped on its side. Each pole sees the Sun for 42 years, then does not see sunlight for another 42 years.

Miranda

Ariel

Umbriel

North Pole

Moons of Uranus

Uranus has 27 known moons to date, although more will no doubt be discovered. Most of these are minuscule, irregularly shaped chunks of ice and rock, between a few miles and a few dozen miles across. One of them, Miranda, is slightly bigger at 294 miles (472 km), while the largest four (Umbriel, Ariel, Oberon, and Titania) are substantial and almost spherical, measuring from 716 to 980 miles (1,158 to 1,578 km). All of these relatively big moons are made from a mixture of water ice and rock.

Oberon

Titania

Verona Rupes on Miranda

Miranda may be a fairly small moon, but it still boasts the tallest cliff in the Solar System. Known as Verona Rupes, it is 12 miles (20 km) high. If Miranda were scaled up to the size of Earth, Verona Rupes would be about 320 miles (520 km) high!

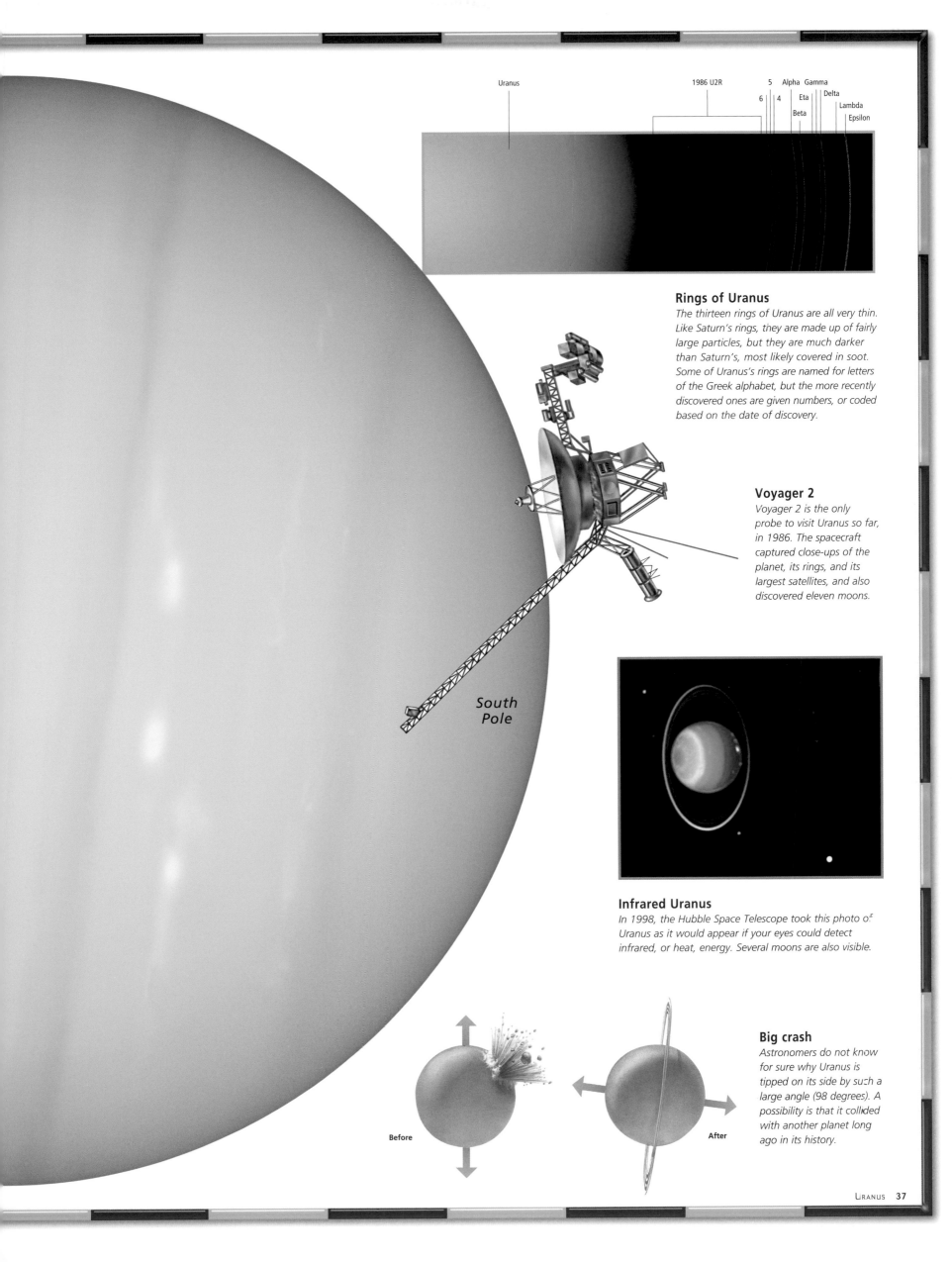

Uranus

1986 U2R   5   Alpha Gamma
6   4   Delta
          Eta   Lambda
        Beta   Epsilon

Rings of Uranus

The thirteen rings of Uranus are all very thin. Like Saturn's rings, they are made up of fairly large particles, but they are much darker than Saturn's, most likely covered in soot. Some of Uranus's rings are named for letters of the Greek alphabet, but the more recently discovered ones are given numbers, or coded based on the date of discovery.

Voyager 2

Voyager 2 is the only probe to visit Uranus so far, in 1986. The spacecraft captured close-ups of the planet, its rings, and its largest satellites, and also discovered eleven moons.

South Pole

Infrared Uranus

In 1998, the Hubble Space Telescope took this photo of Uranus as it would appear if your eyes could detect infrared, or heat, energy. Several moons are also visible.

Big crash

Astronomers do not know for sure why Uranus is tipped on its side by such a large angle (98 degrees). A possibility is that it collided with another planet long ago in its history.

Before   After

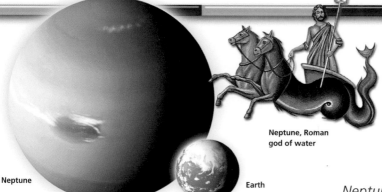

Neptune, Roman
god of water

Neptune

Neptune
Neptune is very similar to Uranus. The two planets have virtually identical sizes and chemical makeup. But Neptune is the more colorful world, with its stripy blue atmosphere and the occasional dark storm systems that dot its face.

Earth

Neptune

ORIGIN OF NAME
NEPTUNUS, THE ROMAN GOD OF WATER

DISCOVERED
1846 BY JOHANN GALLE AND HEINRICH D'ARREST

DISTANCE FROM THE SUN
2,793 MILLION MILES (4,495 MILLION KM)

DIAMETER AT THE EQUATOR
30,775 MILES (49,528 KM)

MASS
17 X EARTH'S MASS

MOONS
AT LEAST 13

LENGTH OF YEAR
164.79 EARTH YEARS

Neptune is warmer than its great distance from the Sun would suggest. It must have an unknown internal heat source.

Cloudy Neptune
Neptune's atmosphere is very lively and changeable. This photo, taken by Voyager 2 in 1989, shows streaks of white clouds very much like cirrus clouds on Earth.

Neptune and Triton
Neptune (top right in the above photo) and its largest moon, Triton (lower left), appear together in this portrait, which was taken from the Voyager 2 probe at a distance of 47 million miles (76 million km).

Geysers
Neptune's largest moon, Triton, is volcanically active. In 1989, scientists observed several dark streaks on its surface, which were left by geysers. Unlike the hot geysers found on Earth, Triton's are driven by nitrogen gas rather than boiling water.

Neptune   Galle   Lassell   Adams
           Le Verrier Arago

Rings of Neptune

Neptune has five rings, very dark like those of Uranus, probably made of particles of rock and ice covered in a sootlike dirt. The rings are named for the scientists whose early work shaped our understanding of Neptune.

Passing through

The Voyager 2 probe took this image of Neptune's rings as it passed the planet in 1989. This photograph had to be overexposed in order to bring out the rings, which are otherwise very dark.

Moons of Neptune

Proteus

Nereid

Larissa

Neptune has fewer moons than the other giant planets, at only thirteen. But this may simply be because the planet is farther from Earth than the others, so its moons are difficult to see. The smallest known satellites are up to 260 miles (418 km) in diameter. Of these, the largest three are Larissa, Nereid, and Proteus. There is only one very large moon, which is called Triton. At 1,682 miles (2,707 km) in diameter, Triton is the seventh-largest moon in the Solar System, ranking just smaller than Europa, a large moon of Jupiter.

Triton

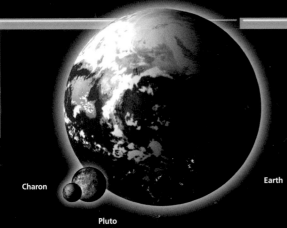

Charon

Pluto

Earth

Pluto, Greek god
of the underworld

Beyond Neptune
This diagram illustrates how far away several large objects in the Kuiper Belt are from the Sun. Close to Neptune, the Kuiper Belt is quite flat, but it flares up farther out. This second region is called the scattered disk, because the objects within it have been scattered by Neptune's gravity to high above that planet's orbit.

Neptune

Pluto and Beyond

There are no major planets beyond Neptune. Instead, the space around and outside of Neptune's orbit is home to the dwarf planets Pluto and Eris, and a whole family of icy worlds just like them. These worlds are known as Kuiper Belt Objects (KBOs) because they inhabit a donut-shaped region of space beyond Neptune called the Kuiper Belt. About a thousand are known, but the total number is probably measured in billions. Like asteroids, the KBOs are ancient fragments—leftovers from the formation of the Solar System. But KBOs tend to be rich in ice, while asteroids are rocky or metallic.

Pluto is so distant that it takes sunlight between four and seven hours to reach it, depending where it is in its orbit.

This shows the typical path of a comet around the Sun—it is very elongated.

The Sun is at the center of the Oort Cloud

Oort Cloud

The Sun's influence extends far beyond the planets and Kuiper Belt. Bound by the Sun's gravity, frozen comets surround our star in their trillions, perhaps out as far as one light-year—that's 60,000 times farther from the Sun than Earth. These comets occupy a region of space known as the Oort Cloud. The Cloud is probably almost spherical at its outermost edge, but it may be slightly warped by the gravity of the countless stars that lurk at the center of the Milky Way.

The inner regions of the Oort Cloud are flat, merging with the edge of the Kuiper Belt.

Comets develop tails only when they approach close to the Sun. The tail here is only shown for clarity.

The outer regions of the Oort Cloud are more spherical, but the shape may be a bit distorted.

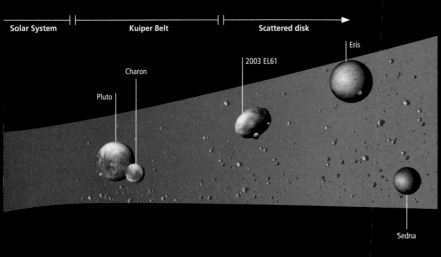

Solar System | Kuiper Belt | Scattered disk

Pluto
Charon
2003 EL61
Eris
Sedna

Pluto
Charon
Nix
Hydra

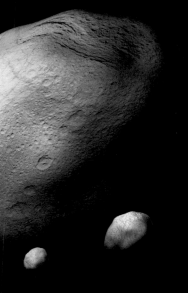

2003 EL61

Pluto and its moons

Until 2006, icy Pluto was considered a planet. But astronomers relabeled it a dwarf planet because of its small size. At 1,440 miles (2,320 km) across, it is far smaller than a true planet. Pluto has one large moon, called Charon, almost half its size, and two much smaller satellites called Nix and Hydra.

Sedna

Sedna is a large KBO about 750–1,120 miles (1,200–1,800 km) across. It has no known moons. Sedna has an extremely long, 12,000-year orbit, which takes it almost 1,000 times farther from the Sun than Earth.

2003 EL61 and its moons

2003 EL61 is a large KBO that has yet to be officially named. It is almost 100 times farther from the Sun than Earth. It is oval in shape, measures almost 1,200 miles (2,000 km) across, and is accompanied by two small nameless moons, which are about 110 miles (170 km) and 190 miles (310 km) in diameter.

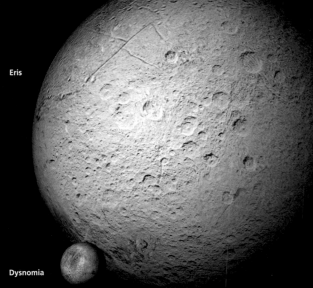

Eris

Dysnomia

New Horizons

No probe has ever visited a KBO. But that is set to change with the launch in 2006 of NASA's New Horizons spacecraft. The craft encountered Jupiter in February 2007, and that planet's powerful gravity slingshotted it to increase its speed. Still, Pluto is so distant that New Horizons is not scheduled to arrive there until 2015. Once there, the craft will fly past Pluto at a distance of 6,200 miles (10,000 km), photographing it and its largest moon Charon and then, hopefully, moving on to another KBO.

This artist's impression shows the New Horizons probe in front of the dwarf planet Pluto, with Charon and the Sun beyond.

Eris and Dysnomia

The largest KBO and dwarf planet found to date is Eris (previously nicknamed Xena). The latest measurements show that at 1,490 miles (2,400 km) across, Eris is probably slightly bigger than Pluto. Eris has a small moon, Dysnomia, which orbits Eris about once every 14 days.

Comets

Comets are among the most attractive objects in the Solar System. These small lumps of ice and rock, only a few miles across, would be all but invisible from Earth were it not for their brilliant tails, which can stretch for tens of millions of miles across space. The tails are made from gas and dust, which evaporate from the comet as it approaches the Sun and heats up. Like planets, comets move around the Sun not in circles, but in oval paths called ellipses. But comet orbits tend to be more elongated than those of the planets and also more highly tilted relative to Earth's path around the Sun.

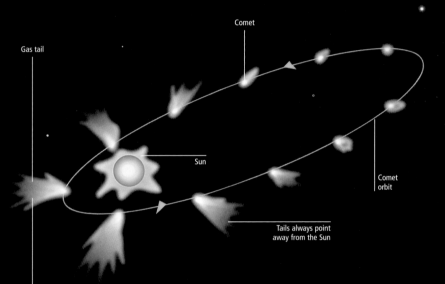

Gas tail

Comet

Sun

Comet orbit

Tails always point away from the Sun

Dust tail

Comet orbits
When a comet is far from the Sun, it is cold and frozen solid, with no tail. The tail develops only as the comet approaches the heat of the Sun, then gradually disappears again as the comet moves away. Repeated visits to the warmth of the Sun eventually boil away all the comet's ice.

Up close to Wild 2
This photo of the surface of Wild 2, taken by NASA's Stardust probe in 2004, is one of the clearest views we have of the heart, or nucleus, of a comet. The nucleus is about 3 miles (5 km) across.

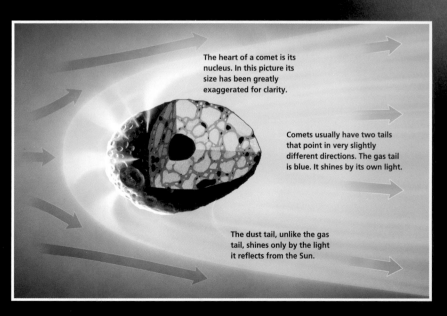

The heart of a comet is its nucleus. In this picture its size has been greatly exaggerated for clarity.

Comets usually have two tails that point in very slightly different directions. The gas tail is blue. It shines by its own light.

The dust tail, unlike the gas tail, shines only by the light it reflects from the Sun.

Inside a comet
Comets are dirty snowballs—chunks of ice mixed together loosely with dust and other debris. This diagram shows what one might look like inside. At the center there may be a solid core of rock, but this is not known for sure. Comets are porous and full of holes, a little like sponges.

Comet McNaught

The brightest comet to visit earthly skies since 1965 was Comet McNaught, discovered in 2006. In January 2007 it was a very interesting naked-eye object, but only those people living in the Southern Hemisphere were able to appreciate its true beauty. In the Northern Hemisphere it was too close to the Sun to be seen well and could be spotted only just after sunset. At its best it was brighter than the planet Venus.

This photograph was taken at Swifts Creek in Victoria, Australia.

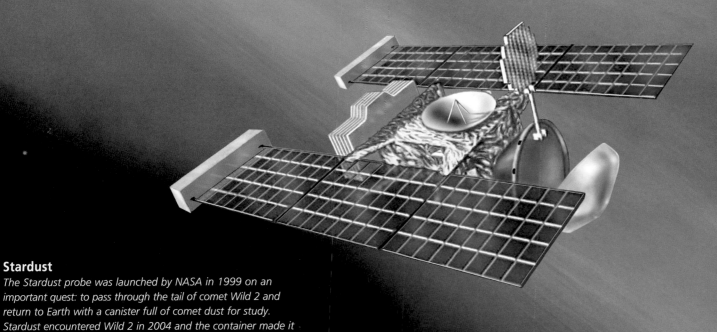

Stardust

The Stardust probe was launched by NASA in 1999 on an important quest: to pass through the tail of comet Wild 2 and return to Earth with a canister full of comet dust for study. Stardust encountered Wild 2 in 2004 and the container made it home safely in early 2006. Scientists are now analyzing its contents.

The Outer Solar System

Neptune takes 163.7 Earth years to orbit the Sun.

Saturn takes 29.4 Earth years to orbit the Sun.

Jupiter takes 11.9 Earth years to orbit the Sun.

Uranus takes 83.8 Earth years to orbit the Sun.

Jupiter has more moons than any other planet—and no doubt more are waiting to be discovered.

WHAT'S OUT THERE?

Gas giants
Jupiter, Saturn, Uranus, and Neptune are called the gas giants because of their great size and because they are rich in hydrogen, helium, and other gases. They formed from the same sorts of materials that made up the Sun.

Comets
Comets, made of ice and dust, may be only a few miles in diameter, but they can have spectacular tails that stretch for millions of miles. Comets spend most of their time in the far parts of the Solar System.

Kuiper Belt
This cutaway view shows planet orbits and the Kuiper Belt, a region beyond Neptune populated by millions of small, icy bodies. Some comets come from the Kuiper Belt.

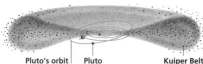

Pluto's orbit | Pluto | Kuiper Belt

Pluto and other dwarf planets
The Kuiper Belt is home to not only many smaller bodies, but also to larger worlds called dwarf planets. These include Pluto and Eris, both of which also have their own satellites.

PLANET SIZES

Jupiter Diameter 88,846 miles (142,984 km)

Saturn Diameter 74,898 miles (120,536 km)

Uranus Diameter 31,763 miles (51,118 km)

Neptune Diameter 30,775 miles (49,528 km)

Earth | Jupiter | Saturn | Uranus | Neptune

SIZE COMPARED WITH EARTH

Jupiter 11 times

Saturn 9.5 times

Uranus 4 times

Neptune 3.9 times

NUMBER OF MOONS

Jupiter 63

Saturn 57

Uranus 27

Neptune 13

INSIDE AND OUTSIDE

Jupiter KING OF THE PLANETS
Jupiter is distinguished by its great size and its colorful, banded atmosphere. Storms on Jupiter can last for centuries.

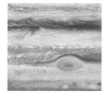

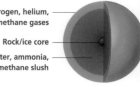
Hydrogen gas
Liquid hydrogen
Rocky core
Metallic hydrogen

Saturn THE RINGED GIANT
Saturn has no solid surface and is almost all hydrogen and helium. Its famous, beautiful rings are made of fragments of ice and rock.

Hydrogen gas
Liquid hydrogen
Rocky core
Metallic hydrogen

Uranus THE SIDEWAYS PLANET
Uranus is the only planet that is tipped on its side. It has a system of dark rings, and its atmosphere is bland, with a green tinge.

Hydrogen, helium, and methane gases
Rock/ice core
Water, ammonia, and methane slush

Neptune PLANET OF WINDS
Neptune is an icy gas giant, similar in mass to Uranus. Unlike Uranus, it has an internal source of heat that keeps the atmosphere stormy.

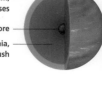
Hydrogen, helium, and methane gases
Rock/ice core
Water, ammonia, and methane slush

Pluto THE ICY DWARF
Pluto's surface is covered in ice, and it probably has a large rocky core. It has never been seen up close, but a probe is on its way there.

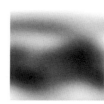
Water, methane, and nitrogen crust
Rocky core
Water ice mantle

Distance from the Sun

Jupiter 484 million miles (779 million km)

Saturn 891 million miles (1,434 million km)

Uranus 1,784 million miles (2,871 million km)

Neptune 2,795 million miles (4,498 million km)

NOTABLE NUMBERS

1610 Year Galileo Galilei discovered the rings of Saturn. His telescope lens was not very sharp, so he thought the planet had "ears" or "handles."

24 Age of astronomer Clyde Tombaugh when he discovered Pluto in 1930.

6 Years it took the Galileo spacecraft to reach Jupiter.

1997 The year the Cassini-Huygens mission was launched to study Saturn. The Cassini orbiter reached Saturn in 2004.

1,321 Number of Earths that could fit inside Jupiter.

248 Earth years it takes Pluto to travel around the Sun.

63 Number of known moons in orbit around Jupiter.

30,000,000 Years it can take some comets on the edge of our Solar System to travel around the Sun.

40 Years it took to find the Kuiper Belt after scientists predicted that it was out there somewhere.

59 Minutes NASA's Galileo probe survived before it was crushed by the pressure of Jupiter's atmosphere.

16 Earth hours in a Neptunian day.

Cassini orbiter

Since Neptune was first seen from Earth in 1846, it still has not made a full orbit around the Sun. The trip takes 163.7 Earth years, so it will complete it in 2011.

Naming Pluto

In 1930, after a long search, Pluto was discovered. The new world, then labeled a planet, captured the world's imagination, and it was called Pluto, after the Roman god of the underworld. It was a fitting name for this dark, frozen world. The following year, seemingly inspired by the new discovery, Disney named Mickey Mouse's lovable dog Pluto. In 2006, astronomers voted to demote Pluto. It is no longer a "true" planet, but a dwarf planet.

OUTER SOLAR SYSTEM RECORDS

Triton

Coldest place in the Solar System
This is Triton, Neptune's largest moon. When the Voyager 2 probe passed by in 1989, it found a freezing surface, with a temperature of –391°F (–235°C).

Flattest planet in the Solar System
Saturn is the Solar System's flattest planet. Its rapid spin makes it bulge visibly at the equator.

Largest planet in the Solar System
Eleven times the diameter of Earth and 318 times the mass of Earth, Jupiter contains more mass than all the rest of the planets, comets, asteroids, and moons put together. Yet, it is only about a hundredth as massive as the smallest star.

Earth   Jupiter

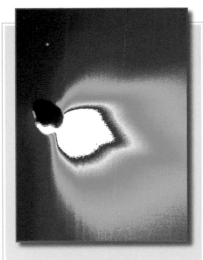

Mission to a Comet
On July 4, 2005, NASA's Deep Impact probe collided with a comet. Its mother ship took photographs from a safe distance. The images and data collected by this mission will reveal what lies beneath a comet's surface. Because comets have barely changed since our Solar System began, this could help us to understand how the Solar System formed.

Largest Kuiper Belt Object
The largest Kuiper Belt Object (and dwarf planet) is Eris (formerly known as Xena). At 1,440 miles (2,320 km) across, it is about 4 percent larger than Pluto.

Largest moon in the Solar System

Ganymede

Coldest place in the Solar System
Triton, the largest moon of Neptune. When the Voyager 2 probe passed by in 1989, it found a freezing surface, with a temperature of -391°F (-235°C).

Flattest planet in the Solar System
Saturn is the Solar System's flattest planet. Its rapid spin makes it bulge visibly at the equator.

Largest planet in the Solar System
Eleven times the diameter of Earth

DISCOVERING THE OUTER SOLAR SYSTEM

Galileo's telescope

1610
Galileo Galilei becomes the first person to use a telescope for astronomy. His telescopes can magnify by only 20 to 30 times, but he uses them to discover the large moons orbiting Jupiter.

1781
William Herschel, a musician and amateur astronomer, discovers Uranus, the seventh planet in the Solar System and the first to be discovered since prehistoric times.

Herschel's telescope

1846
Johann Galle and Heinrich d'Arrest discover Neptune, the eighth planet. The deep-blue planet is named for the Roman god of water.

1930
Clyde Tombaugh discovers Pluto, after a long search. Pluto is a dwarf planet, much smaller than the other planets. Its large moon, Charon, is discovered in 1978, by James Christy.

1973
The NASA space probe Pioneer 10 becomes the first to reach a gas giant planet, Jupiter. It flies by at a distance of 80,000 miles (130,000 km) and detects powerful radiation belts.

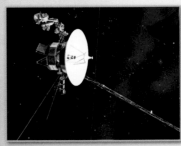
Voyager 2

1979
Voyagers 1 and 2 spacecraft fly past Jupiter and find its rings. From 1979 to 1989 they continue to collect information about the gas giant planets. Pioneer 11 becomes the first probe to reach Saturn and observe its rings and satellites up close.

1994
Fragments from comet Shoemaker-Levy 9 crash into Jupiter. The impacts leave dusty smudges that last for months. This is the first time the collision of two Solar System bodies has been observed from Earth.

1995
The Galileo spacecraft, launched in 1989, sends its probe into Jupiter's atmosphere and begins a tour of Jupiter's moons. Its successful 14-year journey ends in 2003 when it disintegrates in Jupiter's atmosphere.

2005
Launched in 1997, the Cassini probe reaches Saturn in January 2005 and dispatches a smaller craft, Huygens, to land on Saturn's largest moon, Titan. Both Cassini and Huygens provide valuable data for furthering our understanding of the Solar System.

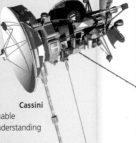
Cassini

The Universe

Other Solar Systems

In 1995, astronomers finally answered the question as to whether or not there were planets out there in space, orbiting other stars, just as the Earth moves around the Sun. The answer is yes—and lots of them, too. Since that initial discovery, the number of stars with known planets has climbed past 170. And because some of those stars have more than one planet, the total number of planets chalked up is now greater than 200. To differentiate them from planets in our Solar System, these new worlds are called "extrasolar" planets, or "exoplanets" for short. So far, while the technology to detect these worlds is improving all the time, we are only just learning how to find small planets, comparable to Earth. Most planets so far found are all huge, much bigger than Earth.

Exoplanet up close
Not all extrasolar planets orbit stars. In this photo, which is one of very few images of an actual exoplanet, the planet (red) orbits a faint object called a brown dwarf (colored blue in this image). Brown dwarfs are heavier than planets but not as massive as true stars. They shine only very feebly. The photo was taken in 2004 using a telescope at the European Southern Observatory in Chile.

Discovering exoplanets

Exoplanets are too faint to be seen directly. When a massive planet moves around a star, the planet's gravity pulls on the star and drags it in a tiny orbit. When this wobbling orbital motion is directed toward Earth, its light appears slightly bluer than otherwise. And when the star moves away, its light reddens. Astronomers use these tiny shifts as the main method of finding planets next to their overwhelmingly bright stars.

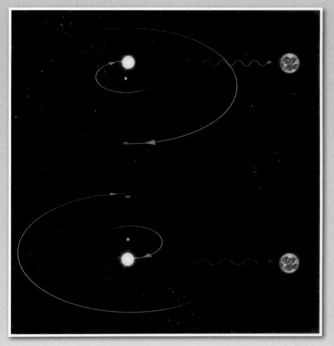

As a planet orbits a star, the star's light is alternately blueshifted (top) and redshifted (bottom). These changes tell astronomers that a planet must be present.

Asteroids
Our Solar System is probably not unique in having a belt of asteroids. In 2005, using the Spitzer Space Telescope, astronomers discovered signs of a heavy ring of dusty rubble circling a star called HD69830, some 41 light-years from Earth. It could be an extrasolar asteroid belt, about 20 times more massive than our Solar System's own. This illustration imagines the scene looking toward the star HD69830 from one of its planets, of which three are currently known.

Comparing planetary systems

Our Solar System is not very much like those that astronomers are finding around other stars. For reasons that we do not yet fully understand, most extrasolar planets are massive and in very small orbits, right up close to their suns. In our own Solar System, though, the massive planets (such as Jupiter and Saturn) are found much farther from the Sun. This diagram shows how the planets are arranged in some well-known systems, with the inner region of the Solar System shown at the top.

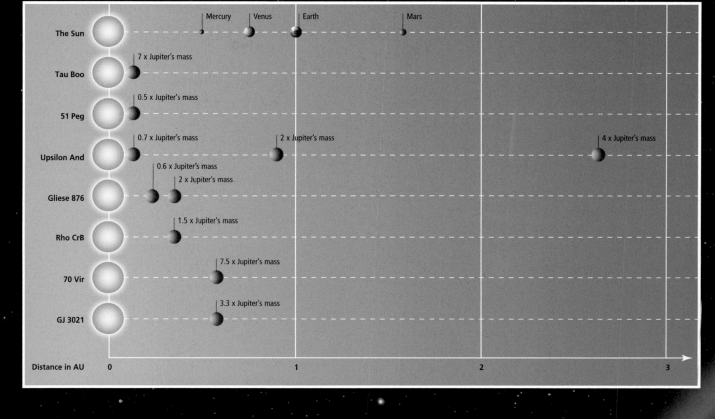

The Sun	Mercury	Venus	Earth	Mars
Tau Boo	7 x Jupiter's mass		
51 Peg	0.5 x Jupiter's mass		
Upsilon And	0.7 x Jupiter's mass	2 x Jupiter's mass	4 x Jupiter's mass
Gliese 876	0.6 x Jupiter's mass / 2 x Jupiter's mass		
Rho CrB	1.5 x Jupiter's mass		
70 Vir	7.5 x Jupiter's mass		
GJ 3021	3.3 x Jupiter's mass		

Distance in AU   0   1   2   3

The most distant star with a confirmed planet is 17,000 light-years away. Most known planets are much closer than that.

16 Cygni B

One of the very first stars to be found with an exoplanet is called 16 Cygni B. It is a yellow star that is in turn in orbit around another star, called 16 Cygni A. This artist's impression imagines the planet as a blue gas giant with a possible moon orbiting it.

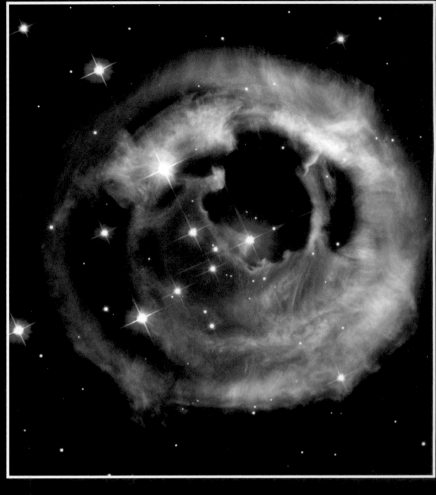

Nebulas

Our galaxy is filled with beautiful clouds of glowing gas and dust called nebulas. They are the stuff stars are made of and the place some stars scatter their remains into space as they die. Nebulas glow either because they are illuminated by nearby stars, or because stars within them heat them up. Still other nebulas are dark—they emit no light, and we see them only if they block the light of stars or bright nebulas behind them.

Reflection nebula NGC 1999
This is an example of a reflection nebula. It glows not because stars within it are heating it up, but because stars off to the side are shining on it, in the same way that the Sun shines on the Moon. Reflection nebulas such as these are usually blue in color.

V838 Monocerotis
V838 Monocerotis is an unusual star about 20,000 light-years from the Sun. Over several months in 2002, the Hubble Space Telescope took a series of photos showing billowing shells of gas around the central star. The shells were thrown off the star in the past. The most recent outburst is lighting them up, as seen in this October 2002 image.

The tops of the columns are lit by the ultraviolet light from nearby stars

Radiation from this hot star is hollowing out the side of the largest dust column

The tallest pillar towers 4 light-years high

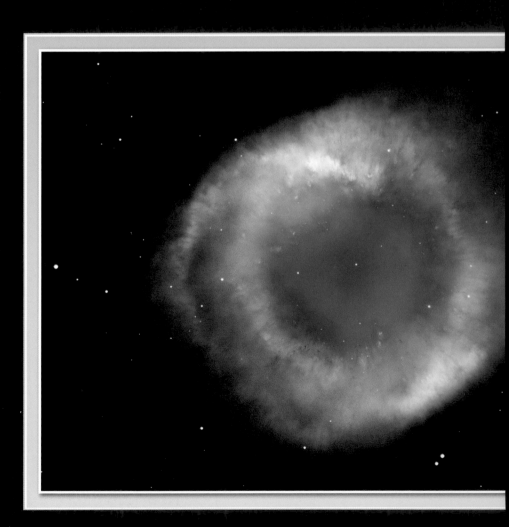

Pillars of creation
This strange gas sculpture, a small part of the Eagle Nebula, is a star factory. Its shape has been molded by the light of hot, young stars nearby. The light has melted away the wispier parts of the nebula to leave behind relatively clumpy regions called fingers. Portions of the fingers are very dense and gravity causes them to collapse. As they contract they eventually break away to form cocoons that will one day create stars.

EAGLE NEBULA
TYPE: EMISSION; DISTANCE: **7,000** LIGHT-YEARS;
DIAMETER: **15** LIGHT-YEARS

NGC 1999
TYPE: REFLECTION; DISTANCE: **1,500** LIGHT-YEARS;
DIAMETER: **1** LIGHT-YEAR

HORSEHEAD NEBULA
TYPE: DARK; DISTANCE: **1,300** LIGHT-YEARS;
DIAMETER: **4** LIGHT-YEARS

HELIX NEBULA
TYPE: PLANETARY; DISTANCE: **680** LIGHT-YEARS;
DIAMETER: **5** LIGHT-YEARS

Horsehead Nebula
As its name suggests, this nebula is famed for its odd resemblance to the head of a horse. The horsehead itself is dark and cold, emitting little or no light. We can see it only because of the brighter nebula that lies behind it.

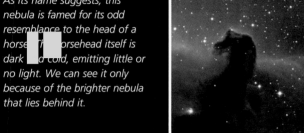

If you were inside a nebula it would appear as if you were in empty space, as they are so thin and wispy.

Death of a star

The Helix Nebula (left) is an example of what scientists call a planetary nebula. However, these sculptures of gas and light have nothing to do with planets. When seen through a small telescope, many planetary nebulas (but not the Helix) appear as tiny, round disks, similar to viewing the planets Uranus and Neptune—hence the name. The Helix Nebula is one of the closest known examples. A nebula like this is created when a relatively lightweight star dies. At the end of its life, the star puffs off its atmosphere like a giant smoke ring. The gas glows while it is illuminated by the light of the dying star at the center. But as the nebula expands, it grows fainter, and fades from view after about 10,000 years.

This portrait of the Helix Nebula was made by combining photos from the Hubble Space Telescope with those taken from a telescope on the ground.

Eagle Nebula
Some 7,000 light-years from the Earth in the constellation of Serpens lies the Eagle Nebula. This is a close-up of part of the region taken in 2005 by the Hubble Space Telescope. It reveals a vast column of cold, dense gas and dust that will one day form stars. The column is about 9.5 light-years long, or twice the distance from the Sun to the nearest star.

Stars

The stars are brilliant globes of radiating gas, just like the Sun, but very far away. Although most look white in the night sky, if you look carefully you will see that some are slightly red or orange, while others are a steely blue. This is because different stars have different temperatures. Hot ones are blue or white; average ones like the Sun are yellow; cooler ones are orange; and the coolest of all are red. Stars also come in many different sizes: from neutron stars, barely larger than a city, to supergiants, which can be hundreds of times bigger than the Sun.

Proxima Centauri
Proxima Centauri (below), the closest star to the Sun, is a red dwarf, the most common star in existence. It is 20,000 times dimmer than the Sun and only one-seventh its size. So, despite its distance of only 4.22 light-years, it can only be seen through a telescope.

Sirius B
Sirius B (right, below Proxima Centauri) is a very compact star called a white dwarf, which is in orbit around Sirius A. White dwarfs are not normal stars. They are the remains of stars that have grown old and thrown off their outermost layers. Sirius B is less than 1/100th the size of the Sun—even smaller than Earth.

Sirius B

Antares
Antares is a huge red supergiant star—10,000 times brighter than our Sun and 700 times as large. Surrounding Antares is a cloud of gas and dust that the violent supergiant has thrown off. This red star can be easily seen in the constellation Scorpio.

Sirius A
Sirius A, or the "Dog Star," is one of the closest stars to us. It is only 8.6 light-years away from Earth, and it is also the brightest star in the night sky. Sirius A is not alone—its tiny white dwarf companion, Sirius B, can just be seen as a white fleck below and to the left of Sirius A.

Life of a star
Although the stars are not really alive, astronomers still like to speak about their "life cycles." What happens to a star during its "life" depends on its size. Once a fairly small star, like our own Sun, runs out of fuel, it expands to become a giant and then puffs off its atmosphere to leave behind its core, a tiny star called a white dwarf, about the size of Earth (sequence 1). More massive stars, however, explode violently, leaving behind an even more compact neutron star (sequence 2) or a black hole (sequence 3). A black hole is an object whose gravity is so powerful that not even light can escape it.

THE SUN
TYPE: YELLOW MAIN SEQUENCE; DIAMETER: **865,000** MILES (**1,392,000** KM)

SIRIUS B
TYPE: WHITE DWARF; DIAMETER: **1%** OF THE SUN

PROXIMA CENTAURI
TYPE: RED DWARF; DIAMETER: **15%** OF THE SUN

SIRIUS A
TYPE: BLUE MAIN SEQUENCE; DIAMETER: **1.7** X THE SUN

RIGEL
TYPE: BLUE SUPERGIANT; DIAMETER: **50** X THE SUN

BETELGEUSE
TYPE: RED SUPERGIANT; DIAMETER: **800** X THE SUN

The Sun

The Sun is shown here to compare with other smaller dwarf stars (left page). It is also shown on the right, but it is scaled down for comparison with the larger stars shown on this page.

The Sun

Sirius A

Sirius, the brightest star in the sky as seen from Earth, is actually two stars, orbiting each other as Earth orbits the Sun. The bigger of the two is called Sirius A. It is about 1.7 times the size of the Sun and is much hotter.

Rigel

Rigel is a very bright and large star called a blue supergiant, fully 50 times the diameter of our Sun. It lies in the constellation of Orion. Despite being approximately 800 light-years away, Rigel is the seventh-brightest star in the sky, shining with the light of 40,000 Suns.

Arcturus

This star, 37 light-years away in the constellation of Boötes (the Herdsman), is the fourth-brightest in the entire sky. It is a very large star called an orange giant, 25 times the size of the Sun but 1,800°F (1,000°C) cooler. It appears orange because of its cooler temperature.

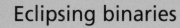

Variable Stars

The stars may seem to shine steadily, but in fact a great many of them are variable, changing their light output with time. Some variables are actually binary stars—two stars revolving around each other, each one periodically blocking the other's light. From Earth, they appear as a single variable star—even in the most powerful telescopes—whose light levels go up and down with time. Other stars, such as the Cepheids or Mira stars, change their brightness regularly as they pulsate in and out. Astronomers have catalogued about 40,000 confirmed variable stars.

Eclipsing binaries

Many stars come in pairs, called binaries. Sometimes, when seen from Earth, one star goes in front of its partner and blocks its light. These systems are called eclipsing binaries. The diagram shows how light levels change as the stars revolve around each other. We receive more light when the two stars are seen (middle), less when the white star eclipses its dimmer yellow partner (bottom), and even less light when the yellow star eclipses the bright white one (top).

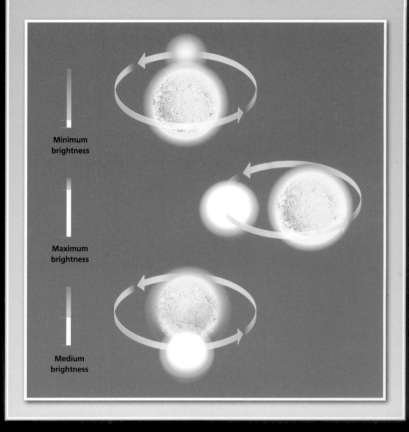

Minimum brightness

Maximum brightness

Medium brightness

Caught in the act
These two false-color images, which were taken with the Hubble Space Telescope, show the change in brightness of a Cepheid variable in a nearby galaxy. The variable star—the large red dot in the image bottom left—is noticeably fainter in the photo on the left, which was taken 22 days earlier.

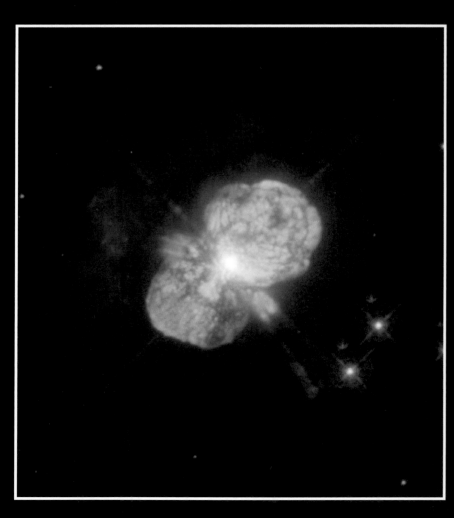

Eta Carinae
In 1841, the star known as Eta Carinae suffered a violent outburst and blew off two giant clouds of dust. Since then, the clouds have been expanding. This strong cataclysmic variable recently doubled in brightness. It will explode as a supernova sometime in the next few thousand years.

Cataclysmic binaries

This is an illustration of a cataclysmic binary (right). The red star on the left is orbiting a much smaller white dwarf, whose powerful gravity has pulled some of the red star's gas around itself to form a gigantic disk. These binary star systems often erupt violently as a result of this transfer of material, ejecting a shell of bright gas to produce what astronomers call a nova explosion.

Astronomers did not notice that some stars are variable until around 1600. They thought the stars were constant and unchanging.

Mira

The most common variable stars are called Mira variables. They are named after the first such object found—Mira in the constellation of Cetus. They are red giants or supergiants, pulsating in and out and varying their light as they do. Mira is the larger blob on the right of this X-ray image, and its white dwarf companion lies to its left.

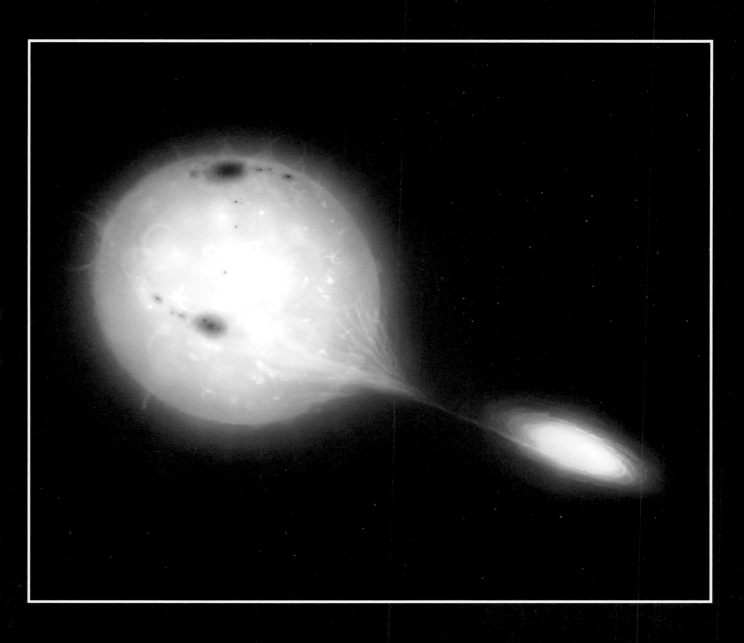

MIRA
TYPE: PULSATING VARIABLE; MAGNITUDE: VARIES FROM **3.4** TO **9.3**; PERIOD: **332** DAYS

ALGOL
TYPE: ECLIPSING BINARY; MAGNITUDE: VARIES FROM **2.1** TO **3.4**; PERIOD: **2** DAYS **21** HOURS

DELTA CEPHEI
TYPE: CEPHEID VARIABLE; MAGNITUDE: VARIES FROM **3.6** TO **4.3**; PERIOD: **5** DAYS **8** HOURS

POLARIS A
TYPE: CEPHEID VARIABLE; MAGNITUDE: VARIES FROM **1.92** TO **2.07**; PERIOD: **4** DAYS

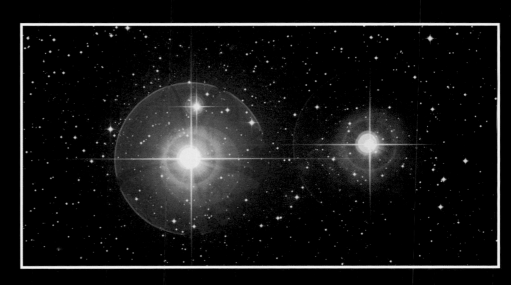

Variable stars

The photograph above shows two stars in the constellation of Lupus (the Wolf). The red star is a variable called RX Leporis. Its brightness varies by a factor of almost 100 over an irregular length of time.

Supernovas

When a massive star dies, it does so in a spectacular explosion known as a supernova. Through much of a star's existence, its central region, the core, generates thermonuclear reactions like those inside a hydrogen bomb. This heat creates a great outward pressure, preventing the star from collapsing in on itself. But when the thermonuclear fuel runs dry, the core shrinks, finally collapsing until it rebounds, generating a violent blast that blows away the outer layers of the star. What is left is either a tiny, dense object called a neutron star, only the size of a city but weighing more than the Sun, or a black hole—an object whose gravity even sucks in light.

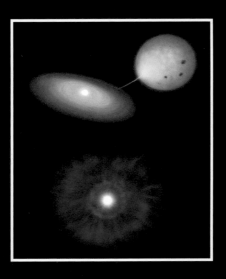

Binary star supernovas

Supernovas can happen in some binary systems, too, where a dense star called a white dwarf sucks in gas from its orbiting neighbor (top). As the stolen gas piles up, the white dwarf becomes unstable and eventually explodes (bottom).

Bang!

A supernova explodes (below, in this artist's impression), scattering starstuff into the depths of space and shining briefly with the power of an entire galaxy of tens, or even hundreds, of billions of stars. But while devastating, supernovas also serve an important purpose, for their remains provide the raw material from which more stars can later form.

A blast close to home: SN1987A

In 1987, astronomers were given a rare treat when a star went supernova in a nearby galaxy, the Large Magellanic Cloud. Without warning, on February 24 of that year, a blue supergiant star, about 18 times the mass of the Sun, exploded. This photo shows the rings surrounding the site. The star probably ejected shells of gas tens of thousands of years before its doom. Then, when it went supernova, the light from the explosion illuminated the gas, sculpting the bright rings seen in this photograph.

The Hubble Space Telescope captured this image of SN1987A's pair of gas "hoops" in April 1994—some seven years after the star went supernova.

Before and after

These photos (right) were taken by the Anglo-Australian Telescope. They show the region of sky around the star that eventually exploded as SN1987A (Supernova 1987A) in the Large Magellanic Cloud. On the left is the scene before detonation, the doomed star just one among thousands. On the right is the supernova just after the explosion.

Supernovas are very rare. Of the roughly 200 billion stars in our galaxy, only one explodes per century on average.

SUPERNOVA 1987A
SEEN EXPLODING: FEBRUARY 23, 1987; NOW: A YOUNG SUPERNOVA REMNANT; DISTANCE: 179,000 LIGHT-YEARS; DIAMETER: 0.2 LIGHT-YEAR

CRAB NEBULA
SEEN EXPLODING: 1054; NOW: A SUPERNOVA REMNANT AND PULSAR; DISTANCE: 6,300 LIGHT-YEARS; SIZE: 8.8 BY 13.7 LIGHT-YEARS

SAX J1808.4-3658
SEEN EXPLODING: IN PREHISTORIC TIMES; NOW: A PULSAR; DISTANCE: 13,000 LIGHT-YEARS

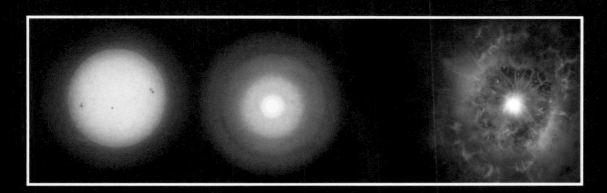

Buildup to a supernova

This image demonstrates how a supernova unfolds. On the left is a red supergiant, the fuel in its core completely spent. Within a short time, just a few thousandths of a second, the core collapses in on itself or "implodes" (middle). The core then rebounds, generating an outward blast that rips the star to pieces (right), leaving behind only a tiny neutron star or black hole.

Star Clusters

Since the giant gas clouds from which stars are formed can be so massive, they often give rise not just to single stars, but to entire families of them, called clusters. There are two types. The smallest are known as open clusters, each of them hosting anywhere between a few dozen and several hundred members. Open clusters are found mainly in the spiral arms of the Milky Way. Globular clusters, the second type, are much larger and older. Some of them boast up to a million individual stars and span several hundred light-years. These clusters swarm around our Galaxy in a huge halo.

Omega Centauri

This photo (above) shows Omega Centauri, a true monster of a globular cluster. It measures 600 light-years side to side, and is home to well over a million stars. It is the largest and brightest globular cluster belonging to our Galaxy, the Milky Way.

Star clusters in the Milky Way

The illustration below shows the positions of globular (yellow) and open (blue) star clusters in the Milky Way. Open clusters are in the spiral arms, while globular clusters surround our galaxy above and below its disk in a spherical region known as the galactic halo. They orbit the Milky Way in the same way that comets orbit the Sun.

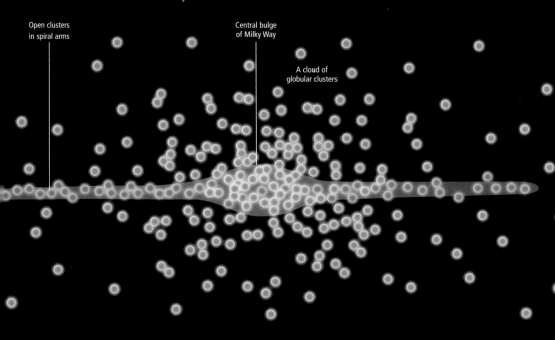

Open clusters in spiral arms

Central bulge of Milky Way

A cloud of globular clusters

The Seven Sisters

The Pleiades is an open star cluster in the constellation of Taurus. It is one of the closest and brightest clusters in the night sky. Even though the cluster is also known as the "seven sisters," it contains about 500 stars, fourteen of which can be seen without a telescope.

It is quite possible that the Sun was formed in an open cluster, 4.6 billion years ago. If so, the cluster has long since dissolved.

Globular clusters

Globular clusters (illustrated right) are many billions of years old. Because stars turn redder as they age, this means globular clusters usually have a distinctly yellowish tinge.

Open clusters

Open clusters (illustrated left) tend to break apart relatively quickly in astronomical terms—within a few hundred million years or less. This is less than the time it takes the stars, like the Sun, to age and redden. However, larger stars will die long before they escape the cluster.

Comparing open clusters

While stars may live for billions of years, the open clusters in which they are born exist only for a fraction of that time. As they travel around the galaxy, they experience the gravitational pull from other stars and gas clouds and, one by one, stars are wrenched free. For this reason, open clusters come in a variety of appearances depending largely (but not entirely) on age. Some harbor a few dozen stars, while others may be much more dense. These photos show some examples.

The Butterfly Cluster (M6) is a loose scattering of stars in the constellation Scorpius.

M35 is a larger cluster of several hundred stars in the constellation Gemini.

NGC 2516 in Carina is larger, richer in stars, and more dense than either M6 or M35.

Stars

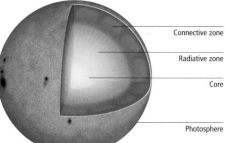

WHAT'S OUT THERE?

Dwarf stars
Dwarf stars are those that are in the longest-lived period of their lives, during which they produce energy by converting hydrogen into helium via a series of nuclear reactions. The Sun is a dwarf star.

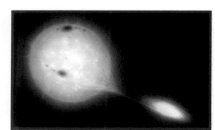

The Sun

Red dwarfs
Red dwarfs are very cool and dim dwarf stars. They are the most common stars in the entire Universe. Some, like Proxima Centauri, are many thousands of times dimmer than the Sun.

Giants and supergiants
These are stars that have grown old, swelling up to tens or even hundreds of times the size of a normal star. Many giants are red, but there are blue giants too. Supergiants are the biggest and brightest stars of all.

White dwarfs
White dwarfs are the dead cores of old stars that have been very compressed. They are formed after the star has turned into a red giant. The Sun will become a white dwarf at the end of its life, more than six billion years from now.

A very close binary system

Binary and multiple stars
Single stars are in the minority, for most have at least one companion in orbit around them. These are called binaries. Sometimes three or more stars may orbit each other, forming multiple systems.

Open star cluster

Star clusters
Because the gas clouds from which stars form are so huge, stars tend to form in clusters, dozens or hundreds at once.

STRUCTURE OF THE SUN

Connective zone

Radiative zone

Core

Photosphere

There are several layers inside the Sun. In the middle is the core, where nuclear reactions produce energy to make the Sun shine. Outside this are the radiative and convective zones. Each transports energy to the surface in a different way. Lastly there is the photosphere. It can be thought of as the Sun's "surface," although it is made of gas.

STAR SIZES

Sirius B: 0.08 x the Sun

Alpha Centauri: 1.2 x the Sun

Vega: 2 x the Sun

Capella: 13 x the Sun

Aldebaran: 46 x the Sun

Betelgeuse: 230 x the Sun

INSIDE A RED SUPERGIANT

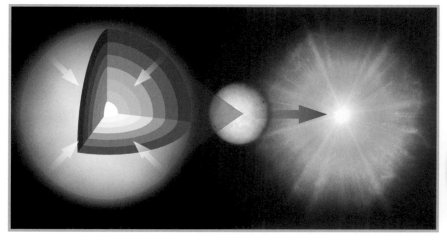

A red supergiant's core is tiny in relation to the rest of the star. Just before it collapses and then explodes as a supernova, it has a layered structure, each layer burning a different element to produce energy. Heavier elements accumulate in the core.

Star color and temperature

Red: The coolest stars of all are distinctly red in color. They have surface temperatures of around 5,800°F (3,200°C).

Orange: Orange stars are slightly warmer than red stars. They have surface temperatures of about 8,800°F (4,900°C).

Yellow: Yellow stars, such as the Sun, are medium–hot. These stars have temperatures of around 10,800°F (6,000°C).

White: White or blue–white stars have surface temperatures up to 18,000°F (10,000°C).

Blue: The hottest stars of all are very blue, and have surface temperatures of up to 54,000°F (30,000°C) or more.

FORMATION OF A STAR

Stage 1
A cloud of gas shrinks under gravity and its center warms up. As it shrinks it starts to flatten and forms a vast spinning structure called a protoplanetary disk.

Stage 2
The center of the disk is much warmer than the rest. After a million years or so, it develops into a blob about the size of the Solar System, known as a protostar.

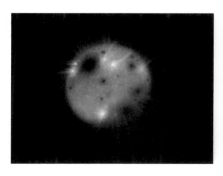

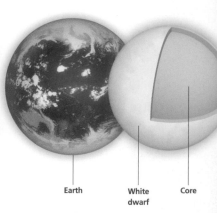

Stage 3
After another million years, the protostar has shrunk to only a few times the size of the Sun. It has gigantic dark star spots on it. This is called a T Tauri star.

Stage 4
T Tauri stars are not stable. They are still shrinking under gravity and warming up as they contract. They won't become "true" stars for another few million years.

INSIDE A WHITE DWARF

Although they may weigh as much as a star like the Sun, white dwarfs are comparable to the size of Earth. Some may have cores of solid crystallized carbon, or diamond.

Earth

White dwarf

Core

8.6 *Distance in light-years to Sirius, the brightest star in the night sky.*

1,300,000 *Number of Earths that could be squeezed into the Sun.*

266,000 *Number of times closer to Earth the Sun is than the next nearest star, Proxima Centauri.*

1,000 *The estimated number of open star clusters so far found throughout the Milky Way Galaxy.*

5,000 *The approximate number of stars you can see with the naked eye.*

47,200,000 *Number of years it would take to travel to the nearest star, Proxima Centauri, at 60 miles per hour (97 km/h).*

150 *The approximate number of globular clusters in orbit around the Milky Way Galaxy.*

12 *Total number of stars, including the Sun, found within 10 light-years of the Earth. There may well be more, very dim stars awaiting discovery.*

8,000,000,000 *Number of Suns needed to completely fill VY Canis Majoris, possibly the largest known star.*

Omega Centauri, a globular star cluster.

The largest stars, called red supergiants, are many millions of times larger in diameter than the smallest, which are known as neutron stars.

Celestial sphere

We know now that the distance to stars varies greatly—some are relatively distant, while others are much closer to home. But in ancient times, it was thought that the stars were all at the same distance, somehow "glued" to the inside of a gigantic dome that enclosed the Earth, Sun, Moon, and the planets known at the time. This was known as the celestial sphere.

Betelgeuse

This is an image of a red supergiant star called Betelgeuse, which is found in the constellation of Orion. Betelgeuse is so enormous, being well over 200 times the diameter of the Sun, and yet so close to Earth, at only 430 light-years away, that it appears as a disk using special techniques and a big enough telescope. Unlike Betelgeuse, most stars are so far away, or small, that they only ever appear as points of light when viewed by a telescope.

STAR RECORDS

The closest star beyond the Sun
The closest star beyond the Sun is a dim red dwarf called Proxima Centauri, in the constellation Centaurus. It is only 4.22 light-years away.

Proxima Centauri

The biggest star
The star with the largest known diameter is believed to be the red supergiant VY Canis Majoris, at 1,800 to 2,100 times the size of the Sun. If placed at the center of the Solar System, it would stretch almost to the orbit of Saturn.

The hottest star
The hottest known star is a white dwarf, comparable to the size of Earth, inside the planetary nebula NGC 2440. At 360,000°F (200,000°C) its surface is more than 30 times hotter than the Sun.

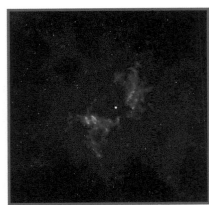

Planetary nebula NGC 2440

The smallest star
The smallest types of stars are called neutron stars. They are no larger than a city but are nothing like normal stars.

Brightest and most massive star
The heaviest and most brilliant known star is probably LBV 1806-20. Compared to the Sun it weighs 150 times as much and shines an incredible 40 million times more brightly.

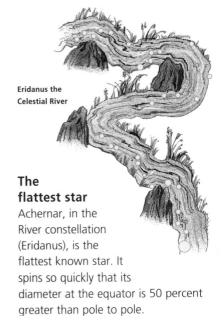

Eridanus the Celestial River

The flattest star
Achernar, in the River constellation (Eridanus), is the flattest known star. It spins so quickly that its diameter at the equator is 50 percent greater than pole to pole.

The coolest star
The coolest true star is a red dwarf called Gliese 105C. Its surface temperature is only around 4,200°F (2,300°C), less than half that of the Sun. Brown dwarfs are cooler, but not true stars.

4TH CENTURY BC
The world's first known star catalog is compiled in China by astronomer Gan De.

AD 185
Chinese astronomers record the first exploding star, an event known now as a supernova. Today, this supernova's remains are called RCW 86.

RCW 86

1667
Geminiano Montanari discovers the first eclipsing binary star, Algol, two stars that eclipse one another as they revolve around each other.

1764
Frenchman Charles Messier discovers the first planetary nebula (M27), the discarded atmosphere of a dying star. It was later named the Dumbell Nebula.

Helix nebula

1838
Friedrich Wilhelm Bessel becomes the first astronomer to accurately measure the distance to a star, called 61 Cygni. His result is close to the actual figure of 11.4 light-years.

1908–12
Henrietta Leavitt discovers how the so-called Cepheid variable stars can be used to accurately measure the scale of the Milky Way Galaxy.

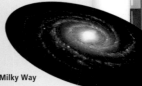

Milky Way

1915–24
Annie Jump Cannon publishes a catalog of 225,300 stars. The system of classification she invented is still in use today.

1938
German physicist Hans Bethe explains that nuclear reactions might be the energy source that sustains stars.

1967
Jocelyn Bell and her colleagues discover the first pulsar. It is only realized a short time later that pulsars are rapidly spinning dead stars called neutron stars.

Black hole

1971
Cygnus X-1 is identified as the first strong candidate for a black hole. Modern astronomers are still sure that there is a black hole there.

1995
Michael Mayor and Didier Queloz announce the discovery of the first planet orbiting a star other than the Sun, a star called 51 Pegasi.

The Milky Way

The Sun, the planets, and all the stars and nebulas that you can see in the night sky—these are all part of the Milky Way Galaxy. It is a vast island of gas, dust, and 200 billion stars, flat like a disk and spinning slowly, surrounded by a faint spherical halo of stars. The Milky Way is an incredibly large place. It takes light, traveling at 186,000 miles per second (300,000 km/s), about 100,000 light-years to cross from one edge to the other. And it is just one of billions of other galaxies, far beyond our own.

The Milky Way
Our Galaxy is a dusty place. A long exposure photograph shows the band of black clouds of gas and dust that lies within the disk of the Milky Way. Bright blue young stars and older red stars shine in front of the more distant clouds.

SIZE OF MILKY WAY
AT LEAST **100,000** LIGHT-YEARS IN DIAMETER

STARS IN MILKY WAY
ABOUT **200** BILLION

STAR CLUSTERS IN MILKY WAY
ABOUT **150** GLOBULAR CLUSTERS;
ABOUT **1,000** OPEN CLUSTERS

DUST AND GAS IN MILKY WAY
ONLY ABOUT **5** PERCENT OF THE MILKY WAY'S VISIBLE MATTER IS GAS AND DUST

The Milky Way at night
Because we live inside our Galaxy's disk, we can only ever see it edge on, no matter where we go on Earth. If you gaze upward on a clear night not too close to a city, you should be able to make it out, a ghostly band of light stretching across the sky, as in this photograph.

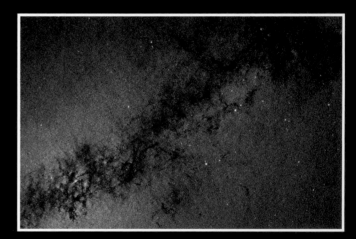

Infrared view
When the Milky Way is viewed in infrared, you can see many more stars than with the naked eye. This is because the stars that are usually clouded by dust and gas can shine through. These appear reddish in the photo. To the lower left lies a yellowish glow of densely packed stars—our Galaxy's core.

Edge on

If seen from the outside, the flat shape of the Milky Way would be obvious. It is shaped a little like two fried eggs glued back-to-back. The disk, which is 100,000 light-years across, is only 3,000 light-years thick on its outermost edges, but it gets thicker toward the middle, where the nucleus is. The dark lane dividing the Milky Way in two is dust and gas, the raw material for new stars. Surrounding the Galaxy is a "halo" scattered with gigantic, glistening balls of stars called globular clusters. Each contains hundreds of thousands of members.

This artist's impression of the Milky Way reveals the Galaxy's central glowing nucleus and the distinct region of dust and gas that bisects the Galaxy.

Our Solar System takes around 225 million years to make a complete trip around the Milky Way Galaxy.

Heart of the Galaxy

Near the heart of the Milky Way lies the massive and very compact Arches Cluster, seen here in an artist's impression. All of the stars in this cluster, around 100 of them, are squeezed into a region of space just one light-year across. The cluster is only about 25 light-years from the very center of the galaxy where, astronomers suspect, lies a very massive black hole, gobbling up stars and gas.

Galactic proportions
The Milky Way is so big that the fastest thing in the Universe, a beam of light, takes 100,000 years to get from one side to the other.

Spiral arms
These are bands of brilliant stars and nebulas. The gaps between the arms have dimmer stars and fewer nebulas.

Black hole
A massive black hole lurks at our Galaxy's center. A swarm of stars and gas swirls around the hole, feeding it with new material.

Our Galaxy

If you could see our Galaxy from the outside, it would look something like this illustration. Its most obvious feature is its spiral pattern within the flat disk. The stars that make the spiral pattern are young and hot, so the curved arms tend to have a blue color. In the center is the small nucleus—which is roughly spherical—with a central bar running through it. The stars in the bar and nucleus are mainly old, so they have a distinctly yellow color.

Inner core
This is packed with stars. If we could view it from near the core, the night sky would be thick with white, yellow, and red lights.

Solar System
The Sun is about halfway between the Milky Way's bright core and its dark, remote edge.

Galaxies

The Milky Way is huge, yet it is just one galaxy among many millions. In fact, there are probably as many galaxies in the Universe as there are stars in the Milky Way. Galaxies are the basic building blocks of the Universe, gigantic islands of stars, gas, and dust. Spirals are the most famous galaxies, because of their beauty, but they share the Universe with other galaxies called ellipticals and irregulars. Galaxies come in various sizes. The smallest—called "dwarfs"—are the most common.

The smallest dwarf galaxies harbor about one million stars; the largest galaxies, called giant ellipticals, may contain more than a million million.

Andromeda Galaxy (M31)
The Andromeda Galaxy, situated in the constellation of Andromeda from which it takes its name, is a large spiral galaxy somewhat like our own Milky Way. At a distance of 2,900,000 light-years, it is the farthest object most people are likely to see with the naked eye. Several dwarf galaxies are in orbit around Andromeda. Two of the brightest are shown in this illustration. They are called M32 and M110.

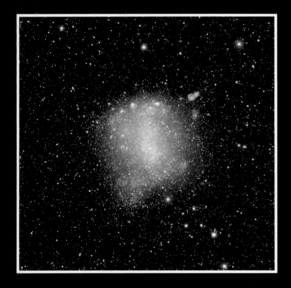

Irregular galaxies
Some galaxies, neither elliptical nor spiral, are known as irregulars, such as Barnard's Galaxy, shown here. The word "irregular" does not mean that they are all shapeless. Some, such as Type I irregulars, are flat like spirals, but they are wobbly or warped and have little or no spiral pattern. The Type II irregulars truly are "irregular," though. They are simply misshapen "clouds" of stars of various sizes.

BARNARD'S GALAXY
TYPE: BARRED IRREGULAR; DISTANCE: 1.6 MILLION LIGHT-YEARS;
DIAMETER: 7,000 LIGHT-YEARS

ANDROMEDA GALAXY (M31)
TYPE: SPIRAL; DISTANCE: 2.5 MILLION LIGHT-YEARS;
DIAMETER: 140,000 LIGHT-YEARS

WHIRLPOOL GALAXY (M51)
TYPE: SPIRAL; DISTANCE: 23 MILLION LIGHT-YEARS;
DIAMETER: 38,000 LIGHT-YEARS

M87
TYPE: ELLIPTICAL; DISTANCE: 52 MILLION LIGHT-YEARS;
DIAMETER: 120,000 LIGHT-YEARS

Spiral galaxies
Probably the most beautiful galaxies are the spirals, named for their shapes. This example is known as the Whirlpool Galaxy (M51). Spiral galaxies are flat like disks but with a ball-shaped central hub. Their spiral arms are crammed with dust and young stars, while their centers are home to much older generations of stars.

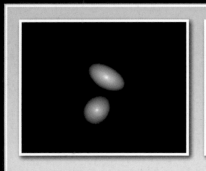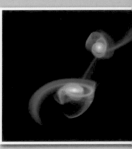

Elliptical galaxies

The largest galaxies of all are the giant elliptical galaxies. They are gigantic swarms of stars, some spherical in shape and others a flat, elliptical shape. These galaxies have no gas clouds within them, so they lack the brightly colored nebulas that dot the arms of their spiral cousins. And because they have no gas, they cannot make new stars. They are full of old, reddish stars. This photograph shows M87, a huge elliptical galaxy in the Virgo Cluster, about 52 million light-years from Earth.

M32 Galaxy

Andromeda's distinct blueish spiral arms are seen clearly in this illustration.

M110 Galaxy

Andromeca's nucleus

Dark lanes of dust appear between the spiral arms

Future of the Milky Way

The Milky Way and Andromeda galaxies are approaching each other at a speed of about 300,000 miles per hour (500,000 km/h). In about three billion years, there is going to be a huge cosmic crash, as this sequence shows. Many stars will be flung far into deep space. Finally, the galaxies will merge into one.

Galaxy Clusters

Only a few galaxies live in isolation. Just as stars tend to bunch together to form clusters, so do galaxies. Most of them gather into galaxy clusters, held together by gravity. The size of galaxy clusters varies enormously. Some, like the Local Group, which is the cluster that our own Milky Way Galaxy calls home, have only a few dozen members. But some galaxy clusters can contain thousands of individual galaxies.

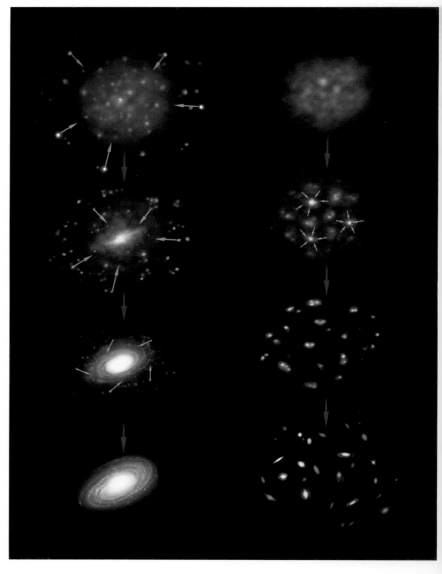

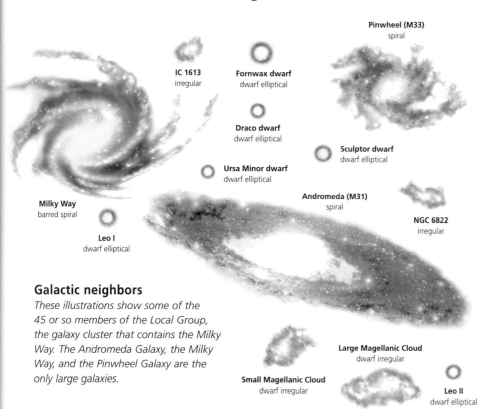

IC 1613
irregular

Fornwax dwarf
dwarf elliptical

Pinwheel (M33)
spiral

Draco dwarf
dwarf elliptical

Sculptor dwarf
dwarf elliptical

Ursa Minor dwarf
dwarf elliptical

Andromeda (M31)
spiral

NGC 6822
irregular

Milky Way
barred spiral

Leo I
dwarf elliptical

Galactic neighbors

These illustrations show some of the 45 or so members of the Local Group, the galaxy cluster that contains the Milky Way. The Andromeda Galaxy, the Milky Way, and the Pinwheel Galaxy are the only large galaxies.

Large Magellanic Cloud
dwarf irregular

Small Magellanic Cloud
dwarf irregular

Leo II
dwarf elliptical

Bottom-up scenario (left stream)

Galaxies are born in one of two ways. In the bottom-up scenario, they form from smaller building blocks, in the same way that a model is built from many smaller parts. The building blocks are clouds of gas or smaller galaxies. Gradually these collide with each other to create a single massive galaxy with stars forming inside it.

Top-down scenario (right stream)

The other way galaxies can form is from the top down, in which many galaxies are born from a single, gigantic cloud of gas. Currents within the cloud cause it to break up into smaller cloudlets, and these in turn disintegrate even more.

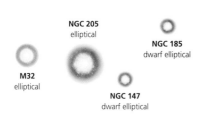

NGC 205
elliptical

NGC 185
dwarf elliptical

M32
elliptical

NGC 147
dwarf elliptical

Virgo Cluster

The Virgo Cluster, a part of which is shown in this photograph, is a large group of more than 1,000 galaxies, and possibly as many as 2,000. It is the closest large cluster to the Milky Way, about 60 million light-years away, and measures 7 to 9 million light-years across. The bright glow on the left of the photograph is a giant elliptical galaxy called M87.

Coma Cluster
The Coma Cluster is a group of about 1,000 galaxies. This photo shows the cluster's two main galaxies, which are called NGC 4889 (left) and NGC 4874 (right). Most of the objects in the photograph are galaxies, not stars.

SIZE OF THE LOCAL GROUP
ABOUT **8** MILLION LIGHT-YEARS IN DIAMETER

MEMBERS IN THE LOCAL GROUP
AT LEAST **45**

MAGELLANIC CLOUDS
LARGE CLOUD—SIZE: **34,000** LIGHT-YEARS
SMALL CLOUD—SIZE: **17,000** LIGHT-YEARS

ANDROMEDA GALAXY (M31)
DIAMETER: AT LEAST **140,000** LIGHT-YEARS

Superclusters

Galaxy clusters are big, but they are not the largest structures in the Universe. Superclusters are bigger still: quite simply, they are clusters of galaxy clusters! The size of superclusters is mind-boggling. They can contain between 10 and 100 entire clusters of galaxies, and may measure as much as 300 million light-years across. They are part of a larger structure of galaxies that spans the Universe.

This illustration shows how clusters of galaxies clump together. The orange regions represent galaxy clusters and superclusters; the blue regions are mostly empty space.

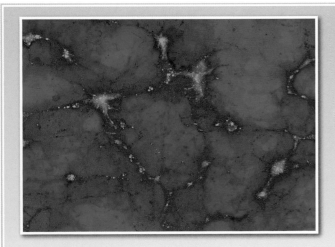

Although a similar size, the Virgo Cluster has many more galaxies than the Local Group.

Looking back in time
The Hubble Space Telescope stared at a tiny region of sky for eleven days, revealing young galaxies near the edge of the visible Universe.

Bullet Cluster
Astronomers think that this galaxy cluster, known as 1ES 0657-558 or the Bullet Cluster, is two neighboring galaxy clusters in the process of merging. The Bullet Cluster is in the southern constellation of Carina (the Keel). This photograph was taken using the Very Large Telescope (VLT), in Chile.

Black Holes

Black holes are probably the most puzzling and fascinating of all astronomical phenomena. They are regions of space where gravity is so intense, so powerful, that nothing can escape them—not even light. Astronomers have observed two main types of black holes. There are the so-called stellar black holes, which are created when massive stars die. And then there are supermassive black holes. These are much, much bigger, weighing in at a few hundred thousand to hundreds of billions of Suns.

Down a black hole
This illustration shows how Earth would suffer if it ventured too close to a black hole. The side closest to the hole gets pulled more strongly than the other, stretching Earth until it finally crumbles and gets sucked in.

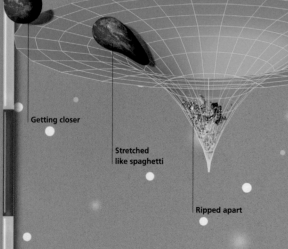

Getting closer

Stretched like spaghetti

Ripped apart

Jet-set M87
The giant elliptical galaxy M87 is the subject of this composite photograph. The blue streak is a jet of high-energy, fast-moving particles that are being ejected from the heart of the galaxy. A vast black hole, lurking at the center of M87, is responsible for blasting the jet out of the galaxy.

The smaller an object is, the more powerful its gravity. If Earth were compressed to the size of a pea, it would become a black hole.

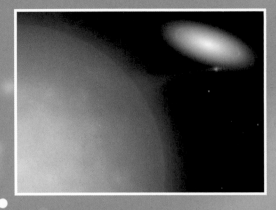

Stealing from a neighbor
This is an artist's impression of a binary star called Cygnus X-1—two stars in orbit around each other, one of which is almost certainly a black hole. The suspected black hole, at right in the illustration, pulls gas from the giant blue star on the left and forms a brightly glowing disk around the hole.

Active galaxies

While many galaxies have black holes, in most cases they behave as if the black hole were absent, probably because the accretion disk around the hole has been largely "eaten," and there is nothing for the black hole to devour. But when the accretion disk is full, gas on its inside edges can fall into the hole. Just before it goes in, it heats up and glows, and astronomers call the galaxy "active" because it appears to have a bright, active core with jets emerging. What we call it— blazar, quasar, or radio galaxy—depends on the angle of the galaxy to our view.

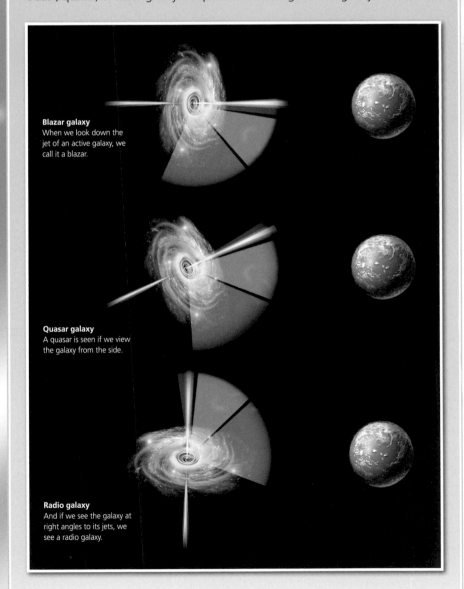

Blazar galaxy
When we look down the jet of an active galaxy, we call it a blazar.

Quasar galaxy
A quasar is seen if we view the galaxy from the side.

Radio galaxy
And if we see the galaxy at right angles to its jets, we see a radio galaxy.

Supermassive black holes
The most impressive black holes are the supermassive ones. Astronomers think that these lie at the cores of many, if not most, galaxies—including our own Milky Way. These black holes are surrounded by giant donuts of shredded nebulas and stars called accretion disks, which can be hundreds of light-years across.

CYGNUS X-1
TYPE: STELLAR MASS BLACK HOLE; MASS: 10 X THE SUN; DIAMETER: 36 MILES (60 KM); DISTANCE: 7,000 LIGHT-YEARS

V404 CYGNI
TYPE: STELLAR MASS BLACK HOLE; MASS: 12 X THE SUN; DIAMETER: 44 MILES (72 KM); DISTANCE: 10,000 LIGHT-YEARS

SAGITTARIUS A*
TYPE: SUPERMASSIVE BLACK HOLE; MASS: 3.7 MILLION X THE SUN; DIAMETER: 0.002 LIGHT-YEAR; DISTANCE: 25,000 LIGHT-YEARS

CENTER OF M87
TYPE: SUPERMASSIVE BLACK HOLE; MASS: 2–3 BILLION X THE SUN; DIAMETER: 1.6 LIGHT-YEARS; DISTANCE: 52 MILLION LIGHT-YEARS

DISTANCE TO THE EDGE OF THE VISIBLE UNIVERSE
12 TO 15 BILLION LIGHT-YEARS

AGE OF THE UNIVERSE
13.7 BILLION YEARS

AGE OF THE SUN
4.6 BILLION YEARS

FAINTEST GALAXIES DETECTED
30TH MAGNITUDE, WHICH IS 4 BILLION TIMES FAINTER THAN YOU CAN SEE BY EYE ALONE

The Universe

The Universe is all around us. Every star, planet, galaxy, tree, person, and microbe—all of them are part of the visible Universe. Early in the twentieth century, astronomers realized that the Universe is expanding. And from this, cosmologists— astronomers who study the Universe—have concluded that 13.7 billion years ago the entire Universe exploded into being in an event called the Big Bang.

Structure arises in the distribution of matter, building on seeds hidden in the fog of the early Universe and leading to the formation of galaxies.

First stars and galaxies form, processing the early gas into fuel for later generations of stars.

13.7 billion years ago the Big Bang marks the beginning of the expansion of space.

Electrons combined with nuclei to form atoms, lifting the foggy veil of the cosmic background radiation.

Matter formed within seconds, and combined into hydrogen and helium nuclei within the first few minutes.

The Big Bang

The origin and history of the Universe around us is described by the remarkably successful Big Bang theory. For 13.7 billion years, space itself has expanded while matter and radiation have cooled from their incredibly hot, dense beginnings to the cool, sparse Universe today.

The name "Universe" is derived from the Latin term unis— meaning "one."

0   380,000 years   1 billion years

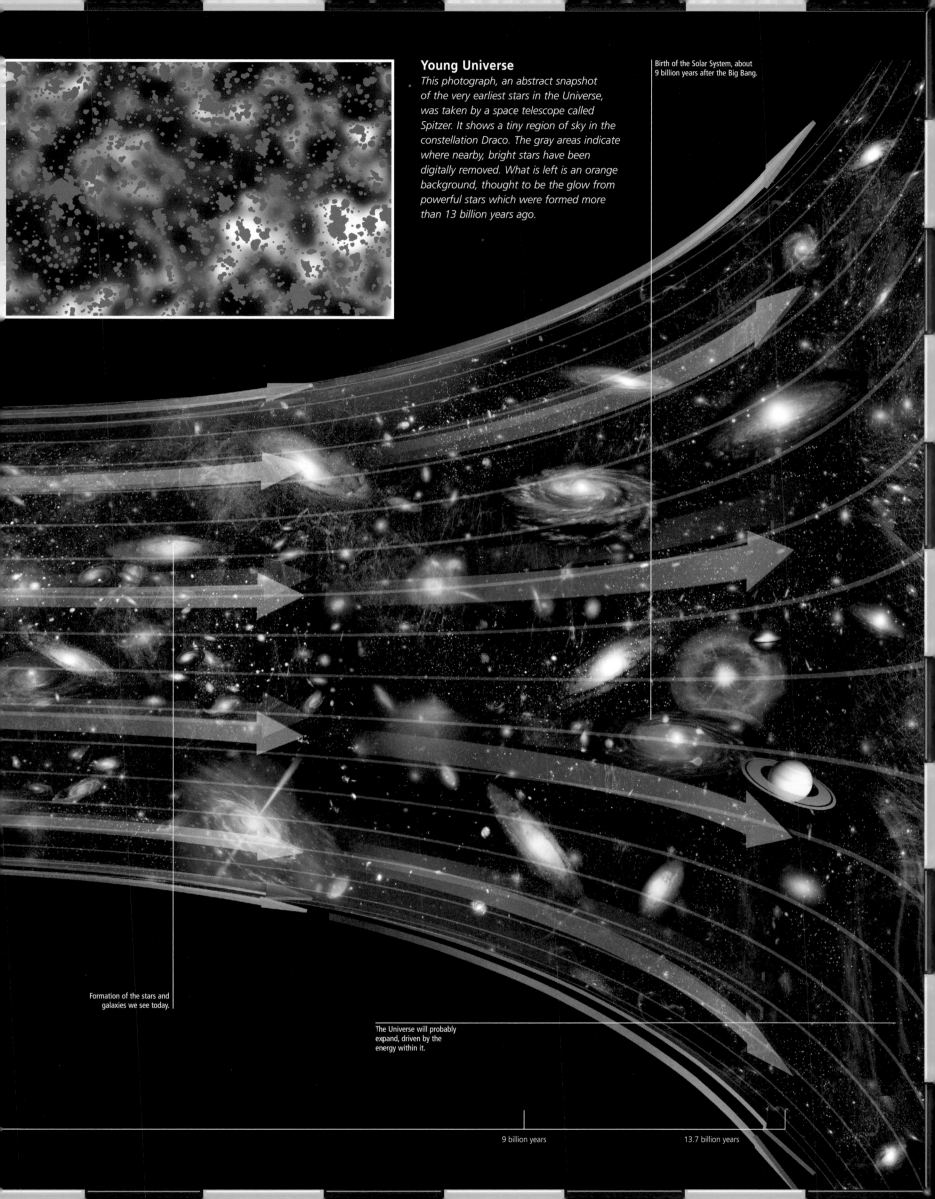

Young Universe

This photograph, an abstract snapshot of the very earliest stars in the Universe, was taken by a space telescope called Spitzer. It shows a tiny region of sky in the constellation Draco. The gray areas indicate where nearby, bright stars have been digitally removed. What is left is an orange background, thought to be the glow from powerful stars which were formed more than 13 billion years ago.

Birth of the Solar System, about 9 billion years after the Big Bang.

Formation of the stars and galaxies we see today.

The Universe will probably expand, driven by the energy within it.

9 billion years

13.7 billion years

At least twelve galaxies are known to orbit around the Milky Way. But they are all very small compared to the Milky Way.

The Universe

WHAT'S OUT THERE?

Galaxies
There may be more galaxies in the visible Universe than there are stars in the Milky Way—the number is measured in hundreds of billions.

Active galaxies
Active galaxies are those that emit much more powerful radiation than normal galaxies. The power is driven by supermassive black holes.

Galaxy clusters
Galaxies are clumped together into groups or much larger gatherings called clusters. The Milky Way, for example, belongs to the Local Group.

Superclusters and voids
Superclusters are the largest known structures in the Universe—clusters of clusters of galaxies—containing many thousands of individual galaxies. Between superclusters are vast regions called voids, containing almost no visible material.

Superclusters and voids

Dark matter
As well as the bright stuff in the Universe, there is also a lot of other material that we cannot see at all, and about which we know very little. This dark matter outweighs visible matter by about six to one.

Dark energy
Even stranger than dark matter is dark energy, a kind of anti-gravity energy field causing the Universe's expansion to accelerate. If converted into matter, it would outweigh visible stars and gas by eighteen times.

SIZE OF FAMOUS GALAXIES

Canis Major Dwarf: 5,000 light-years

M32: 6,800 light-years

Small Magellanic Cloud: 18,000 light-years

Large Magellanic Cloud: 30,000 light-years

Pinwheel Galaxy (M33): 60,000 light-years

Whirlpool Galaxy (M51): 65,000 light-years

Sombrero Galaxy (M104): 80,000 light-years

Milky Way: 100,000 light-years

M87: 120,000 light-years

Andromeda Galaxy (M31): 140,000 light-years

Centaurus A: 200,000 light-years

SIZE COMPARED TO THE MILKY WAY

Canis Major Dwarf: 5%

M32: 7%

Small Magellanic Cloud: 18%

Large Magellanic Cloud: 30%

Pinwheel Galaxy (M33): 60%

Whirlpool Galaxy (M51): 65%

Sombrero Galaxy (M104): 80%

M87: 1. 2 x Milky Way

Andromeda Galaxy (M31): 1.4 x Milky Way

Centaurus A: 2 x Milky Way

CENTER OF MILKY WAY

The center of the Milky Way is a busy place, where a suspected supermassive black hole lurks. This illustration shows the view looking toward the Arches Cluster, which is a compact group of 100 stars found very close to the galactic core.

Arches Cluster in the Milky Way

Spiral galaxy
Spiral galaxies generally have a flat disk, often with a distinct bulge in the center. The disks are rich in clouds of gas and dust from which new stars can form.

Elliptical galaxy
The most common galaxies are the ellipticals. They are made almost entirely of stars. They contain almost no gas and dust, so few new stars can form.

Barred spiral galaxy
These galaxies have two large arms twisting out from the ends of a straight bar of stars, which is attached to a small bright core. The Milky Way is a barred spiral.

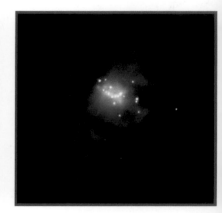

Lenticular galaxy
These lens-shaped galaxies look much like elliptical galaxies but are surrounded by a flat disk of stars that resembles a spiral galaxy, without the prominent arms.

Irregular galaxy
Irregular galaxies are those that do not have a clear spiral or elliptical shape. Some can be flat like spirals, while others have no obvious shape.

NOTABLE NUMBERS

2.73 *The temperature of space in Kelvin, equivalent to -454.76°F or -270.42°C. The Kelvin temperature scale is used by astronomers. Zero Kelvin, also called absolute zero, is the coldest possible temperature.*

73 *The percentage of the Universe's mass that is composed of the invisible and mysterious "dark energy."*

74 *The percentage of the Universe's visible mass made up of hydrogen—the most abundant element in existence.*

6,000,000 *The size of the largest known galaxy, IC 1101, measured in light-years across. This is up to 80 times larger than our own galaxy.*

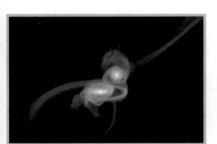

The Milky Way and Andromeda galaxies collide

As you approach a black hole, the view of a universe around you would get distorted as the light bends.

Gamma-ray bursts

Gamma-ray bursts, or GRBs, are the most powerful explosions in the known Universe, almost always witnessed in very distant galaxies. They are not fully understood, but one possible explanation is that they are extra-powerful supernovas, exploding stars in which some of the material is beamed outward in a narrow jet. Whatever the cause, astronomers are fairly sure that all GRBs mark the births of black holes.

380,000 *Number of years it took for the Universe to become transparent after its fiery birth in the Big Bang.*

47 *Current number of confirmed members of the Local Group, the galaxy cluster that includes our Milky Way Galaxy. There are almost certainly more.*

3,000,000,000 *Number of years before the Milky Way and Andromeda galaxies collide.*

1 *Approximate number of stars per year swallowed by a supermassive black hole at the center of an active galaxy.*

1,500 *The approximate number of galaxies belonging to the Virgo Galaxy Cluster. The actual number could be higher still.*

UNIVERSE RECORDS

The Pinwheel Galaxy (M33) as seen through a telescope

Most distant naked-eye object

The Pinwheel Galaxy (M33) in the constellation of Triangulum is probably the most distant object visible to the naked eye, at about three million light-years, but you need very good eyesight and a very dark sky to see it.

Largest galaxy

The largest galaxy in terms of diameter is probably IC 1101, about one billion light-years away. At six million light-years across, it is some 60–80 times larger than the Milky Way. IC 1101 shines brighter than two trillion Suns.

Brightest galaxy in the sky

The brightest galaxy in the night sky is the Large Magellanic Cloud, which is seen in the Southern Hemisphere. It only appears bright because it is close; it is actually relatively small and dim.

Colliding galaxies

The distances between galaxies in a typical galaxy cluster are of course mind-boggling, measured in millions of light-years. But at the same time, these distances are not so great compared to the sizes of galaxies themselves. Consequently, galaxies frequently collide and merge, forming new ones. Stars, on the other hand, almost never do this—the gulfs that separate stars are much, much greater than the diameter of a typical star.

Closest galaxy to the Milky Way

The Canis Major dwarf galaxy is the closest galaxy to the Milky Way—in fact, it is in orbit around it. The Canis Major galaxy is only about 25,000 light-years from the Solar System.

Most globular clusters

M87 contains probably the most globular clusters—ball-shaped groups of stars found on the outskirts of galaxies. There are around 12,000 globular clusters orbiting M87, compared to no more than 200 for the Milky Way.

M87

Most distant galaxy

This record changes all the time, as astronomical instruments become more sensitive. But at present, the farthest known galaxy is Abell 1835 IR1916, which was spotted an incredible 13.2 billion light-years away.

Largest stellar black hole

The most massive black hole formed from the death of a star is probably in the binary system GRS 1915+105. It is fourteen times heavier than the Sun.

HISTORY AT A GLANCE

KEY EVENTS

1845
Lord Rosse describes the first spiral galaxy, M51 or the Whirlpool. It was not known at the time how galaxies differed from nebulas, and M51 was at first called a spiral nebula.

1905
Albert Einstein publishes his *Special Theory of Relativity*, which says, among other things, that the speed of light is the fastest possible speed in the entire Universe.

Albert Einstein

1916
Einstein goes farther, now publishing a *General Theory of Relativity*. In it, Einstein describes gravity not so much as a force, but as a curvature of space and time.

1927
Georges Lemaître, a Belgian priest, proposes that the Universe began as a tiny speck called a "primeval atom." This is the origin of the modern Big Bang theory.

Edwin Hubble

1929
American astronomer Edwin Hubble discovers that the Universe is expanding, as predicted by Lemaître, and that more distant galaxies are moving away faster than closer ones.

1933
Bulgarian-born Swiss astronomer Fritz Zwicky deduces that the Universe contains unseen material, now known as dark matter.

1948
British astronomer Fred Hoyle proposes the "Steady State Theory." As the Universe expands, he said, new matter is created to take the place of old matter. The theory is now disregarded.

1965
Two communications scientists, Arno Penzias and Robert Wilson, discover the cosmic microwave background, interpreted as an "echo" of the Big Bang.

1981
Cosmologist Alan Guth describes the inflation theory, in which the Universe's expansion during its first few instants was extremely rapid.

1989
The NASA probe COBE (Cosmic Background Explorer) is launched. COBE observed the cosmic background radiation and found that its smoothness across the Universe was as expected according to theory.

COBE

1998
Astronomers discover that the Universe's expansion is speeding up. They say that it is because of a mysterious "dark energy" that acts like anti-gravity, pushing the Universe apart ever faster.

Stargazing

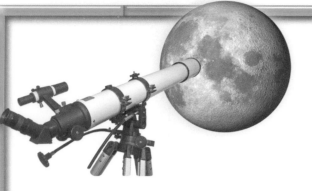

Beginning Astronomy

Astronomy can be a rewarding hobby. On a good, dark night, depending where you live, you can see not just stars and the Moon, but up to five planets, the Milky Way, the Magellanic Clouds (small galaxies that orbit our own), several beautiful star clusters and nebulas, even a very distant galaxy—all without aid. Of course, binoculars or a telescope will improve your viewing enormously, and each has its own purpose.

Light exits

Eyepiece

Prism

Prism

Lens

Light enters

Refracting telescope
Refracting telescopes like this one use lenses to produce the final image. There is a lens at the front of the tube and an eyepiece at the back. This is similar to the telescope that was used by the Italian astronomer Galileo to discover the moons of Jupiter, among other things.

Binoculars
Although they cannot get you as close to the heavens as a telescope, a good pair of binoculars can still be invaluable for stargazing. Some objects, such as star clusters, are simply too big to fit entirely within a telescope's highly magnified view. Binoculars are also much more portable and lighter than a telescope. Just pick them up and away you go.

Stargazing
This woman is enjoying the sky without any optical aid. A laptop computer is a useful tool to look up the positions of objects in the sky on a computerized star map. Without a laptop, however, you can easily use the star maps supplied in this book (see pages 88–103).

Big binoculars

You don't need a big telescope to make an impression in astronomy. These giant binoculars belong to the amateur Japanese astronomer Yuuji Hyakutake, seen in this photograph. Binoculars like these are great for hunting down objects that are faint but fairly large, such as comets or nebulas. The large lenses let a lot of light in, ensuring a nice, bright image. With these big binoculars, Hyakutake discovered a comet in 1997, before it became very bright in earthly skies. The comet was named after him.

Yuuji Hyakutake stands next to the large set of binoculars that made him famous.

| 2° |

| 10° |

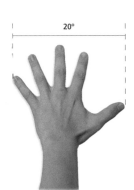
| 20° |

Measuring the sky

Astronomers talk about degrees when measuring the size of objects on the sky. The Moon, for example, is half a degree across on the sky. To help understand these measurements, you can use your outstretched hands. Your thumb extends across about two degrees of sky, your fist ten degrees, and your open hand twenty degrees.

Several ancient civilizations observed and studied the skies centuries before the invention of the telescope.

Reflecting telescope

Reflecting telescopes like this one work with a mirror at the back of the telescope. Light enters the open front end of the telescope and travels down the tube. It is reflected off the mirror, back up to the eyepiece near the top of the tube. A telescope like this was used by famous British astronomer Sir Isaac Newton.

Light pollution

If you live in a city you will suffer from light pollution because the city's lights illuminate the sky and blot out the stars. Try to find a place shadowed from bright lights, like a park. If you are stargazing in your own garden, turn off all the lights, even those inside the house, and try to block as much other light as possible.

Observing the Moon and Sun

You don't need any special tools to observe the Moon. Ancient stargazers have been appreciating it since long before the invention of the telescope. But a good pair of binoculars or a small telescope will reveal a wealth of detail, such as crisp craters and mountain ranges. The Sun is harder to study without help because it is dangerously bright. Never look at the Sun directly with any optical instrument, unless you have filters and know how to use them.

Annular eclipse

Sometimes, even when the Moon is directly in front of the Sun, it does not block it completely. This is called an annular eclipse, and you can see one in this photo. The Moon's orbit is not perfectly circular, so its distance from Earth varies by 10 percent. Because the Moon is smaller when farther away, it cannot fully cover the Sun at this time.

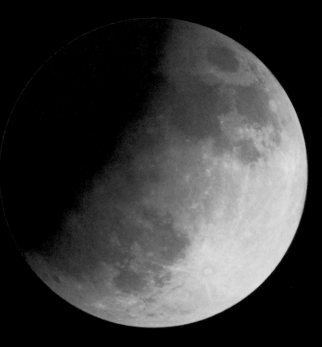

Lunar eclipse

Because the Sun constantly shines onto Earth, our planet casts a shadow in space. When the Moon, moving around Earth, passes into this shadow, part or all of it goes very dark. This is called a lunar eclipse. This photo shows a partial lunar eclipse, in which part of the Moon is partly in shadow.

Total solar eclipse

Sun

Moon's orbit

Moon

Total eclipse seen here

Earth

Moon's shadow

Lunar eclipse

Sun

Earth

Eclipsed Moon

Moon's orbit

Earth's shadow

Eclipses

Eclipses of the Sun and Moon happen when the Sun, Earth, and Moon are all lined up, as seen above (not to scale). If the Moon is exactly between Earth and the Sun, it blocks the Sun's light and we see a solar eclipse. Depending how much of the Sun is hidden, the eclipse may be partial, annular, or total. If the Earth is exactly between the Sun and the Moon, we see a lunar eclipse.

Viewing a solar eclipse

Eclipses are unforgettable sights that we would all like to see, but the Sun is very dangerous to look at without proper protection for your eyes. Permanent blindness can result from the shortest look through binoculars or telescopes. The eyepiece filters that are often supplied with small telescopes are not safe either. The girl in this picture is safely viewing an eclipse without a telescope. With the Sun behind her, she holds a piece of card with a hole through it. The light passes through the hole and projects an image of the eclipse onto another piece of card in front of her.

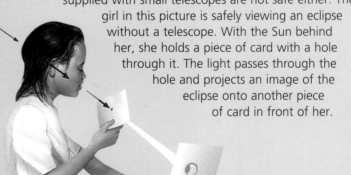

Projecting the Sun's image onto a piece of card like this is a great way to see the Sun's surface without damaging your eyes.

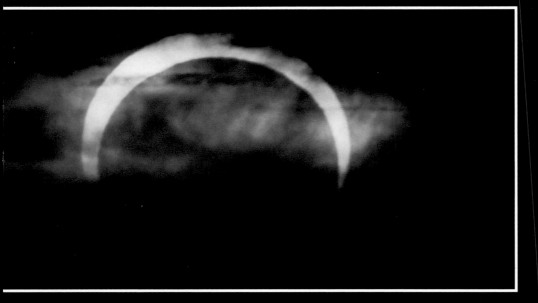

Phases of the Moon

From Earth, the Moon cycles through a series of changes, called phases. When Earth is between the Sun and Moon, we see a full Moon because the part of the Moon's face we can see from Earth is fully lit by the Sun. At other times, the phase differs depending on how much of the Moon's lit surface we can see.

New Moon

Waxing crescent

First quarter

Waxing gibbous

Full Moon

Waning gibbous

Last quarter

Waning crescent

New Moon

The ancient Chinese thought that solar eclipses were caused by a dragon eating the Sun. They made a lot of noise to scare it away.

Total solar eclipse captured

This time-lapse photo shows how the Sun's appearance changes during a total solar eclipse. As the Sun and Moon move in the sky, the Moon gradually covers more of the Sun's disk until the moment of "totality," when the Sun is fully hidden. Only its glowing corona, the Sun's outer atmosphere, can be seen. Afterward, the Moon slowly moves away again, until the Sun is fully uncovered.

Groovy glasses

You should never look directly at the Sun, even during an eclipse. If you are still looking when the eclipse ends, you risk damaging your eyes when the Sun's light returns to full brightness. One way to appreciate these magical moments is to use a special pair of eclipse spectacles.

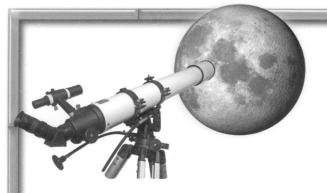

Observing the Planets

The planets are among the brightest objects in the night sky. Five of them are clearly visible to the naked eye: Mercury, Venus, Mars, and the giants Jupiter and Saturn. Venus is particularly bright—more brilliant than any star. With binoculars, you can make out the largest moons of Jupiter. But you need a small telescope to really appreciate the planets. Only then can you marvel at the phases of Venus and Mercury, the rings of Saturn, or the clouds on Jupiter.

Viewing Venus

All five of the naked-eye planets appear at different sizes on the sky, depending where they are in relation to Earth in their orbits around the Sun. Let's take Venus as an example. When Venus and Earth are on opposite sides of the Sun, Venus is farthest from Earth. It then appears about 180 times smaller than the apparent size of the full Moon. But when Venus and Earth are both on the same side of the Sun, Venus appears almost six times bigger. These images illustrate how Venus's size changes with time during its orbit. Its phase changes too, being crescent when closest, and full when farthest away.

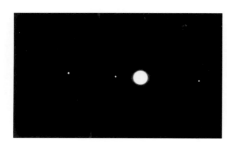
Closest to Earth

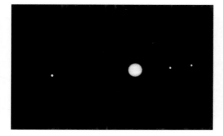
Mid-distance from Earth

Farthest from Earth

Observing Jupiter's moons

The image on the right shows how Jupiter might appear through a small telescope. Its cloud bands are clearly visible, as well as its four largest moons. The sequence below shows how the moons change position from night to night, as they orbit Jupiter.

Where to look

Finding planets is not very difficult. If you know the night sky well enough, it will be quite obvious to you where the planets are, because they will drift from week to week against the background of stars. Once you find them, a telescope will reveal details of their disks, moons, and even rings.

Five planets on show

Five planets are seen in this photograph (left), which was taken just after sunset on April 30, 2002. Venus is the brightest, just above the horizon. Mercury, quite a bit fainter, is below it to the right. Above and left of Venus is Mars, and just left of Mars is Saturn. The fifth planet is Jupiter—the bright speck in the top left corner.

If you have keen eyesight, a dark sky, and you know where to look, you might be able to see Uranus.

The Moon and Venus

This photo shows a conjunction. This occurs when two objects appear close together on the sky. In this case, the two objects are Venus (left) and the Moon (right).

MERCURY
DISTANCE FROM EARTH: **48–138** MILLION MILES (**77–222** MILLION KM)
MAXIMUM MAGNITUDE: **-1.9**; VISIBILITY: NAKED EYE

VENUS
DISTANCE FROM EARTH: **24–162** MILLION MILES (**38–261** MILLION KM)
MAXIMUM MAGNITUDE: **-4.7**; VISIBILITY: NAKED EYE

MARS
DISTANCE FROM EARTH: **34–249** MILLION MILES (**55–401** MILLION KM)
MAXIMUM MAGNITUDE: **-2.9**; VISIBILITY: NAKED EYE

JUPITER
DISTANCE FROM EARTH: **366–602** MILLION MILES (**588–968** MILLION KM)
MAXIMUM MAGNITUDE: **-2.8**; VISIBILITY: NAKED EYE

SATURN
DISTANCE FROM EARTH: **0.75–1.03** BILLION MILES (**1.20–1.66** BILLION KM)
MAXIMUM MAGNITUDE: **0.7**; VISIBILITY: NAKED EYE

URANUS
DISTANCE FROM EARTH: **1.60–1.96** BILLION MILES (**2.58–3.16** BILLION KM)
MAXIMUM MAGNITUDE: **5.5**; VISIBILITY: NAKED EYE/BINOCULARS

NEPTUNE
DISTANCE FROM EARTH: **2.68–2.91** BILLION MILES (**4.31–4.69** BILLION KM)
MAXIMUM MAGNITUDE: **7.7**; VISIBILITY: BINOCULARS

Constellations

People have always seen patterns in the stars. The Mesopotamians, living in what is now Iraq, created the earliest recorded constellations about 8,000 years ago, including Leo, Scorpius, and Taurus. Many famous constellations, such as Perseus, Orion, and Andromeda, are from Greek myths. Others are more recent, such as Microscopium, Telescopium, and Horologium, which were named in the 18th century. Today, there are 88 officially recognized constellations.

Stars in motion

The stars are actually moving through space, and quite quickly too. But they are so far away that it takes tens or even hundreds of thousands of years for the motion to become obvious in the sky. This changes the shape of the constellations, as this sequence of the Big Dipper shows. Our descendants will see very different constellations from those we see.

100,000 years ago

Present day

100,000 years in the future

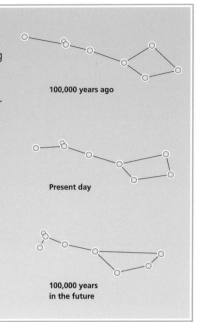

A map of the constellations
This map shows the Northern Hemisphere constellations, including those of the zodiac. It is one of 29 star maps drawn by Dutch-German mathematician Andreas Cellarius (1596–1665). Curiously, Cellarius shows Cancer as a lobster (bottom right), although it is traditionally seen as a crab.

Star distances
Although all the stars may appear to be the same distance from Earth, this is not the case. This diagram shows how the stars in the constellation Orion are strung out in space. Bellatrix, for example, is much closer to Earth than Alnilam.

Bellatrix

Betelgeuse

Mintaka

The stars that we think of as the Big Dipper were seen by the Sioux people of North America as a skunk.

Alnitak

Rigel

Saiph

Alnilam

Orion
Orion is one of the sky's brightest and most spectacular constellations, shown on his side in this photo. He represents a mythical Greek hunter. The cactus is pointing almost directly at Betelgeuse, a red supergiant star that marks Orion's shoulder. To the right of this is his belt, marked by three bright stars in an almost perfectly straight line.

The zodiac
As the year passes, the Sun appears in the sky in a total of thirteen constellations. Twelve of these belong to the so-called zodiac, by which astrologers claim to tell your future. The thirteenth constellation, Ophiuchus, is not counted as one of the astrological signs.

Aries the Ram

Taurus the Bull

Gemini the Twins

Cancer the Crab

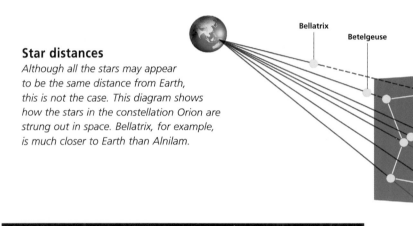

Leo the Lion   Virgo the Maiden   Libra the Scales   Scorpius the Scorpion   Sagittarius the Archer   Capricornus the Goat   Aquarius the Water Carrier   Pisces the Fish

Mapping the Stars

These charts divide the sky into two hemispheres to show all 88 constellations in the sky. They are centered on the celestial poles—the points about which the sky seems to turn. The maps have been simplified to make your stargazing easier. The main stars in the constellations have been joined to help you recognize patterns. The larger the star is on the map, the brighter it appears is in the sky.

Columba the Dove

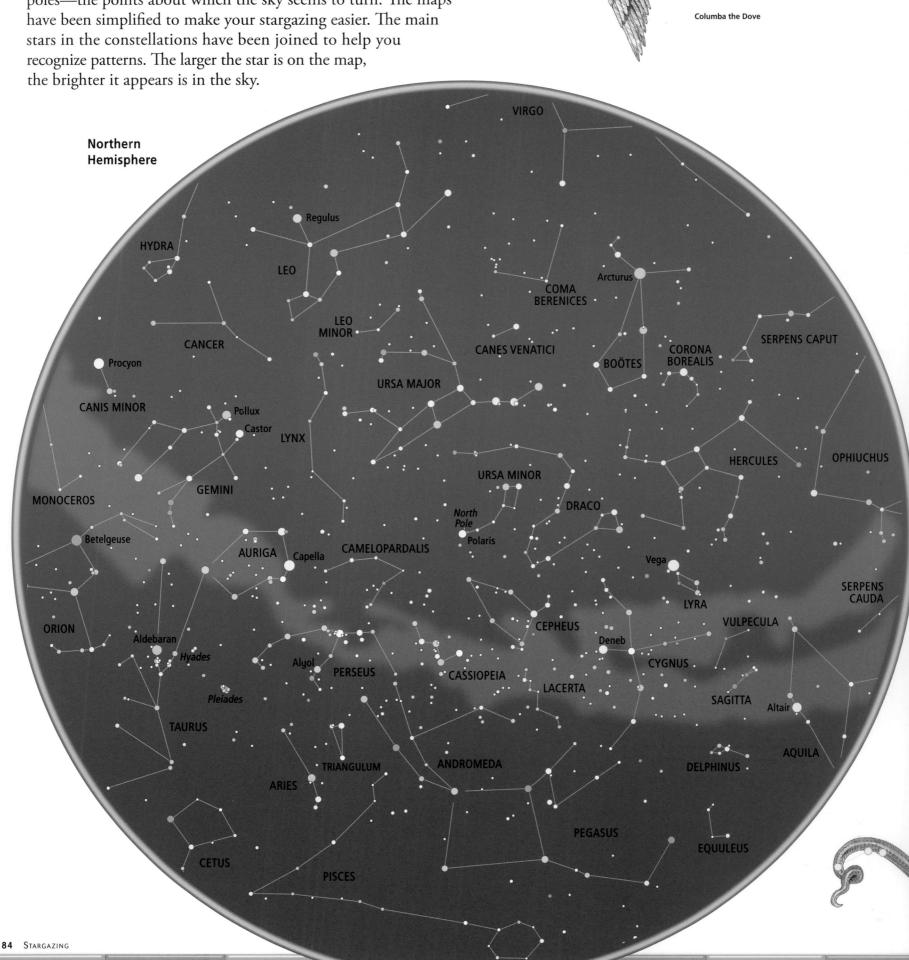

Northern Hemisphere

VIRGO

Regulus

HYDRA

LEO

COMA BERENICES

Arcturus

LEO MINOR

CANCER

CANES VENATICI

SERPENS CAPUT

BOÖTES

CORONA BOREALIS

Procyon

URSA MAJOR

CANIS MINOR

Pollux

Castor

LYNX

HERCULES

OPHIUCHUS

GEMINI

URSA MINOR

MONOCEROS

DRACO

North Pole

Polaris

Betelgeuse

AURIGA

Capella

CAMELOPARDALIS

Vega

LYRA

SERPENS CAUDA

ORION

CEPHEUS

VULPECULA

Aldebaran

Deneb

Hyades

Algol

PERSEUS

CASSIOPEIA

CYGNUS

LACERTA

SAGITTA

Altair

Pleiades

TAURUS

DELPHINUS

AQUILA

TRIANGULUM

ANDROMEDA

ARIES

PEGASUS

EQUULEUS

CETUS

PISCES

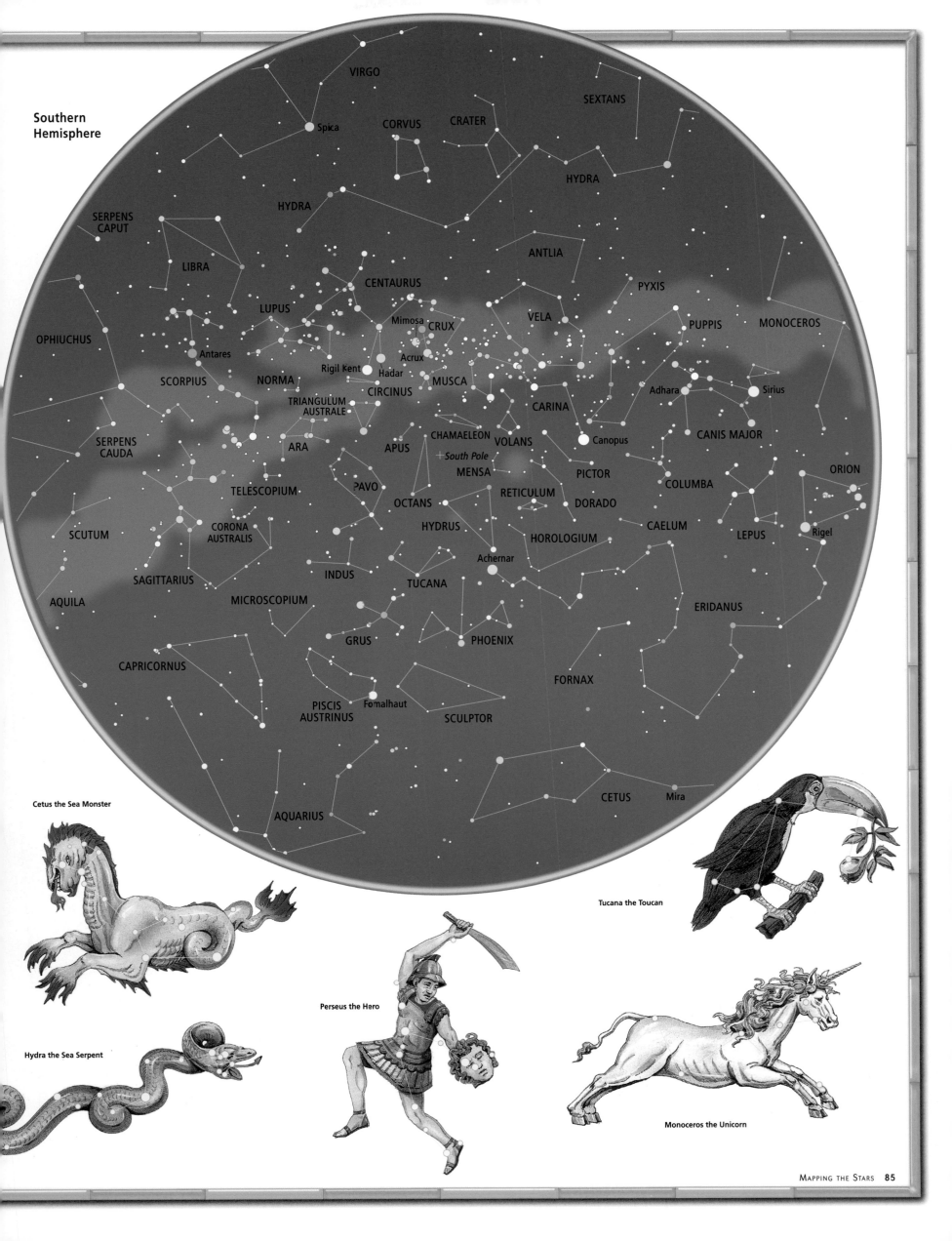

Southern Hemisphere

VIRGO

SEXTANS

Spica

CORVUS

CRATER

SERPENS
CAPUT

HYDRA

HYDRA

LIBRA

ANTLIA

CENTAURUS

PYXIS

OPHIUCHUS

LUPUS

Mimosa CRUX

VELA

PUPPIS MONOCEROS

Antares

Acrux

Rigil Kent Hadar

SCORPIUS

NORMA

MUSCA

Adhara Sirius

CIRCINUS

CARINA

TRIANGULUM
AUSTRALE

CANIS MAJOR

SERPENS
CAUDA

ARA

CHAMAELEON VOLANS

Canopus

APUS

ORION

South Pole

TELESCOPIUM

PAVO

MENSA

PICTOR

COLUMBA

SCUTUM

OCTANS

RETICULUM

Rigel

CORONA
AUSTRALIS

HYDRUS

DORADO

CAELUM

LEPUS

SAGITTARIUS

INDUS

HOROLOGIUM

Achernar

AQUILA

MICROSCOPIUM

TUCANA

ERIDANUS

GRUS

PHOENIX

CAPRICORNUS

FORNAX

PISCIS
AUSTRINUS Fomalhaut

SCULPTOR

CETUS Mira

AQUARIUS

Cetus the Sea Monster

Tucana the Toucan

Hydra the Sea Serpent

Perseus the Hero

Monoceros the Unicorn

Using a Star Map

It can be a bit difficult finding your way around the sky at first. As Earth rotates, some stars will set and others will rise. And the stars will also change depending on the season. The star charts in this book will help. They will show you what you can expect to see depending on which hemisphere you live in, the time of night, the season, and even which way you are looking. Bigger dots on the maps mean brighter stars, and we have also emphasized the colors of the stars—but in practice, you might find that most stars appear to be white, with the exception of a few that are slightly orange or blue.

Stars moving across the sky

Depending on where in the world you live, the stars will appear to rise and set differently. If you are on the equator (left), the stars will rise and set in a straight line up and down. At the poles (center) they neither rise nor set, but merely move around the sky, centered on the celestial pole overhead. And elsewhere (right), most stars will rise and set at an angle to the horizon.

Equator

North/South Pole

Mid-latitudes

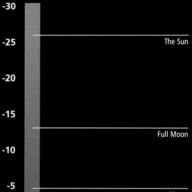

Magnitude scale

Astronomers use the magnitude scale to express the brightness of astronomical objects. Perhaps strangely, objects with larger magnitudes are the faintest. The brightest stars and planets have small or even negative magnitudes. So, for example, the full Moon is magnitude -12.7, but the faintest stars you can see with your eye will be about magnitude +6.

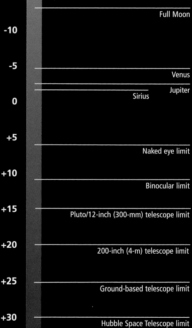

Magnitude	
-30	
-25	The Sun
-20	
-15	
-10	Full Moon
-5	
0	Venus / Jupiter / Sirius
+5	Naked eye limit
+10	Binocular limit
+15	Pluto/12-inch (300-mm) telescope limit
+20	200-inch (4-m) telescope limit
+25	Ground-based telescope limit
+30	Hubble Space Telescope limit

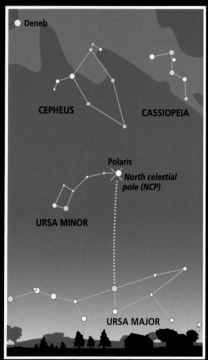

North

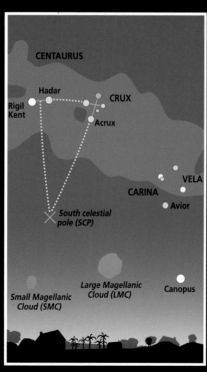

South

Finding north

If you live in the Northern Hemisphere, finding the north is fairly easy. First look for the distinctive shape of the Big Dipper. It looks a little like a saucepan. Locate the two stars that mark the left side of the saucepan, then follow them to the north celestial pole and the pole star, Polaris. Drop down from there to north on the horizon.

Finding south

Finding south in the Southern Hemisphere can be a little trickier, because there is no bright star to clearly mark it. If you bisect the line joining the two "pointers," Alpha Centauri and Hadar, it will cross the line extended from the Southern Cross (Crux) near the south celestial pole. Where these two lines cross is the south celestial pole.

A star with a magnitude of +1 is 2.5 times brighter than one with a magnitude of +2, which in turn is 2.5 times brighter than +3, and so on.

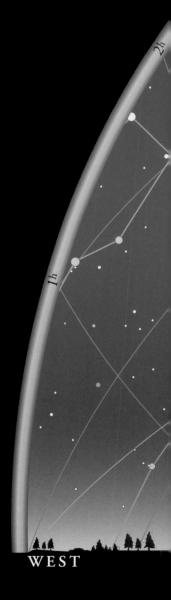

WEST

Open
star cluster

Globular
star cluster

Bright
nebula

Planetary
nebula

Galaxy

Large faint
galaxy

Deep-sky objects
Deep-sky objects
are identified
by this key.

−0.5 and brighter

0.0 to −0.4

Magnitude scale
Star sizes correspond
to their apparent
magnitude—the
brightness of stars as
seen from Earth. The
following star maps
indicate stars to a
magnitude of +6.

0.1 to 0.5

0.6 to 1.0

1.1 to 1.5

True star color is indicated.

Celestial objects are indicated by
their most common name—Messier
or NGC catalog number.

The Milky Way Galaxy is indicated
on the star maps by a light blue band
across the sky.

Constellations are indicated
by an unbroken line.

6h

5h

7h

4h

−30°

CANIS MAJOR

Adhara   Aludra

⊕ *M79*

Wezen

M41

−20°

3h

LEPUS

Mirzam   Sirius

Saiph

−10°

Rigel

M50

ERIDANUS

*Orion
Nebula*   M42, M43

Alnilam   Alnitak

M78

Mintaka

0°

MONOCEROS

2237
Rosette Nebula

Bellatrix   Betelgeuse

2264

ORION   +10°

Alhena   CANI MIN

Procyon

Mira   *M77*   Menkar

Aldebaran   *M1*
Crab Nebula

Eskimo
Nebula
2392

TAURUS   *Hyades*   M35   +20°

Alnath   GEMINI

M36   *M37*   Pollux

M45
Pleiades   M38   Castor   CA

AURIGA

M74   Hamal   ARIES   PERSEUS   Menkalinan   +40°

CES   Algol   Capella

PISCES   CAMELOPARDALIS   +50°   LYNX

TRIANGULUM

Mirphak

1h   2h   3h   4h   5h   NORTH   7h   8h   9h

Northern Spring: Looking North

The Great Bear (Ursa Major) is easy to spot during spring. In March you can find it at right angles to the northern horizon, but as the season progresses it climbs higher, ending up almost directly overhead (depending where you live) around early May. The Charioteer (Auriga) is also eye-catching during spring, as is the Milky Way's band of light. But both sink closer to the northwestern horizon as summer approaches.

Time*

	From 40° N
Early March	1 am
Late March	Midnight
Early April	11 pm
Late April	10 pm
Early May	9 pm
*Add 1 hour for DST	

Magnitude scale

- −0.5 and brighter
- 0.0 to −0.4
- 0.1 to 0.5
- 0.6 to 1.0
- 1.1 to 1.5
- 1.6 to 2.0
- 2.1 to 2.5
- 2.6 to 3.0
- 3.1 to 3.5
- 3.6 to 4.0
- 4.1 to 4.5
- 4.6 to 5.0
- 5.1 to 5.5
- 5.6 to 6.0

Deep-sky objects

- Open star cluster
- Globular star cluster
- Bright nebula
- Planetary nebula
- Galaxy
- Large faint galaxy

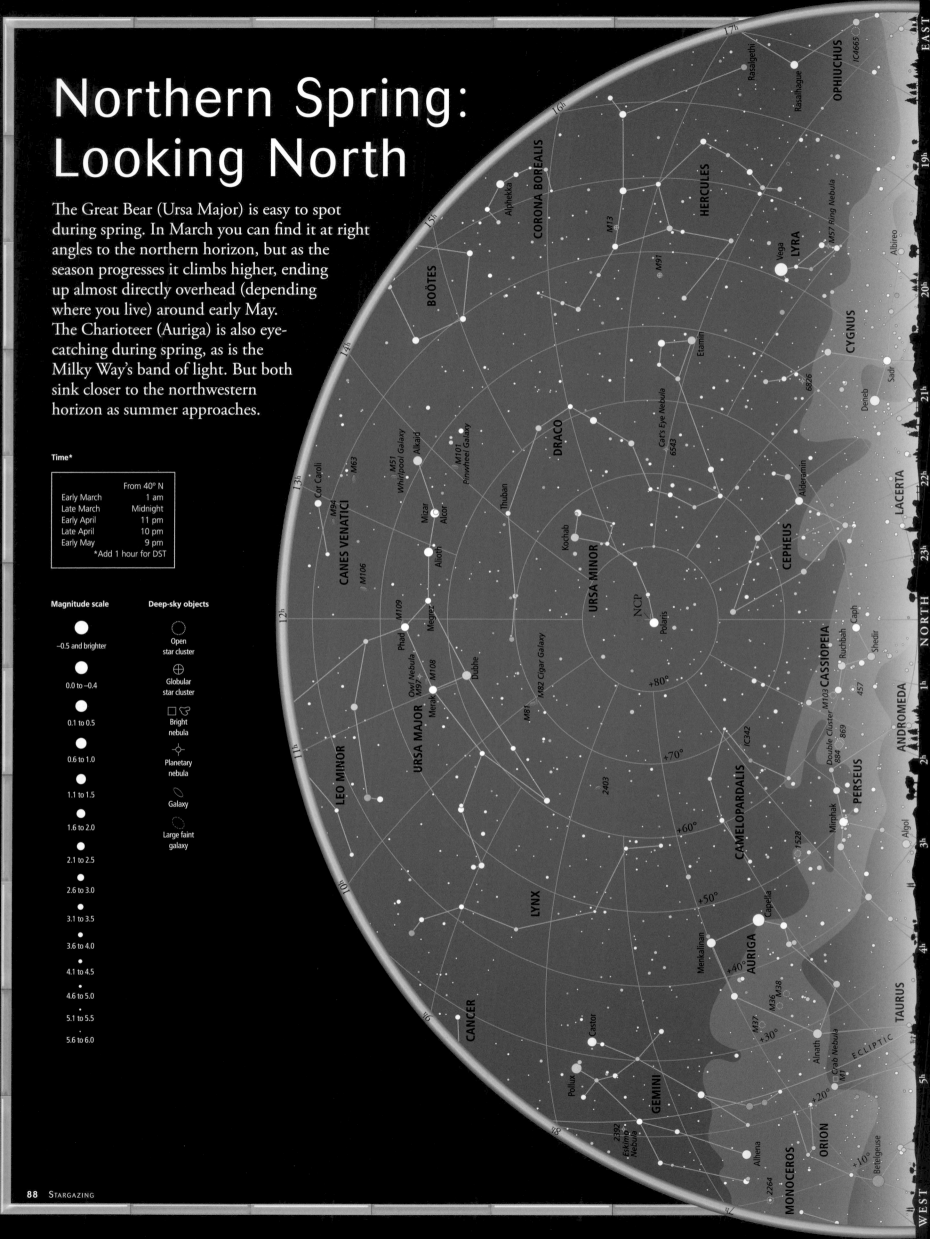

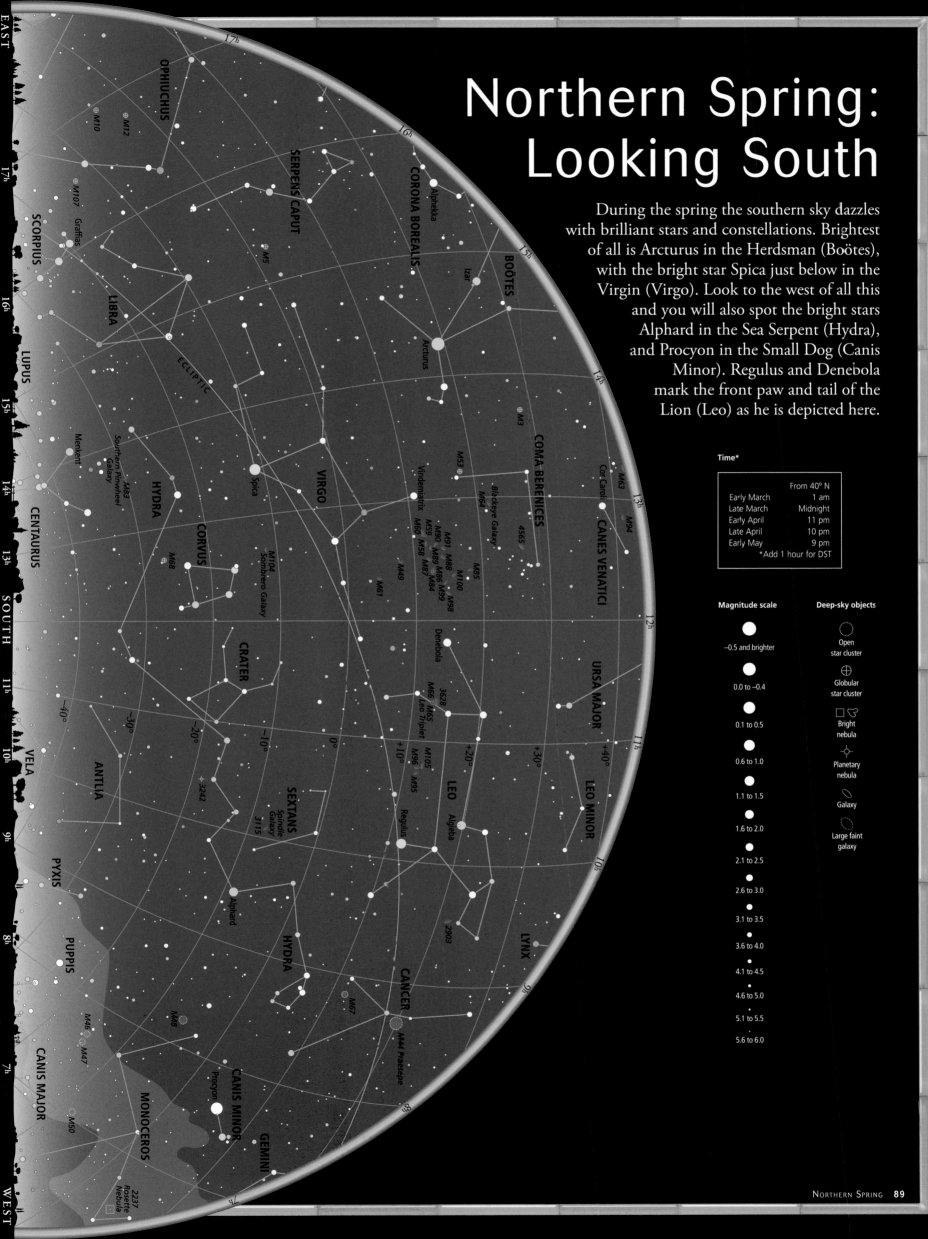

Northern Spring:
Looking South

During the spring the southern sky dazzles with brilliant stars and constellations. Brightest of all is Arcturus in the Herdsman (Boötes), with the bright star Spica just below in the Virgin (Virgo). Look to the west of all this and you will also spot the bright stars Alphard in the Sea Serpent (Hydra), and Procyon in the Small Dog (Canis Minor). Regulus and Denebola mark the front paw and tail of the Lion (Leo) as he is depicted here.

Time*

	From 40° N
Early March	1 am
Late March	Midnight
Early April	11 pm
Late April	10 pm
Early May	9 pm
*Add 1 hour for DST	

Magnitude scale

- −0.5 and brighter
- 0.0 to −0.4
- 0.1 to 0.5
- 0.6 to 1.0
- 1.1 to 1.5
- 1.6 to 2.0
- 2.1 to 2.5
- 2.6 to 3.0
- 3.1 to 3.5
- 3.6 to 4.0
- 4.1 to 4.5
- 4.6 to 5.0
- 5.1 to 5.5
- 5.6 to 6.0

Deep-sky objects

- Open star cluster
- Globular star cluster
- Bright nebula
- Planetary nebula
- Galaxy
- Large faint galaxy

Northern Summer: Looking North

As summer arrives, the Great Bear (Ursa Major) is unmistakable facing north, very high overhead. The characteristic "W" of the Queen (Cassiopeia) is low down on the northern horizon as summer opens, but by early August she is higher in the sky, surrounded by the band of the Milky Way. As summer draws to a close, the Hero (Perseus) puts in an appearance, while the Great Bear skirts above the horizon in the northwest.

Time*

	From 40° N
Early June	1 am
Late June	Midnight
Early July	11 pm
Late July	10 pm
Early August	9 pm
	*Add 1 hour for DST

Magnitude scale

- −0.5 and brighter
- 0.0 to −0.4
- 0.1 to 0.5
- 0.6 to 1.0
- 1.1 to 1.5
- 1.6 to 2.0
- 2.1 to 2.5
- 2.6 to 3.0
- 3.1 to 3.5
- 3.6 to 4.0
- 4.1 to 4.5
- 4.6 to 5.0
- 5.1 to 5.5
- 5.6 to 6.0

Deep-sky objects

- Open star cluster
- Globular star cluster
- Bright nebula
- Planetary nebula
- Galaxy
- Large faint galaxy

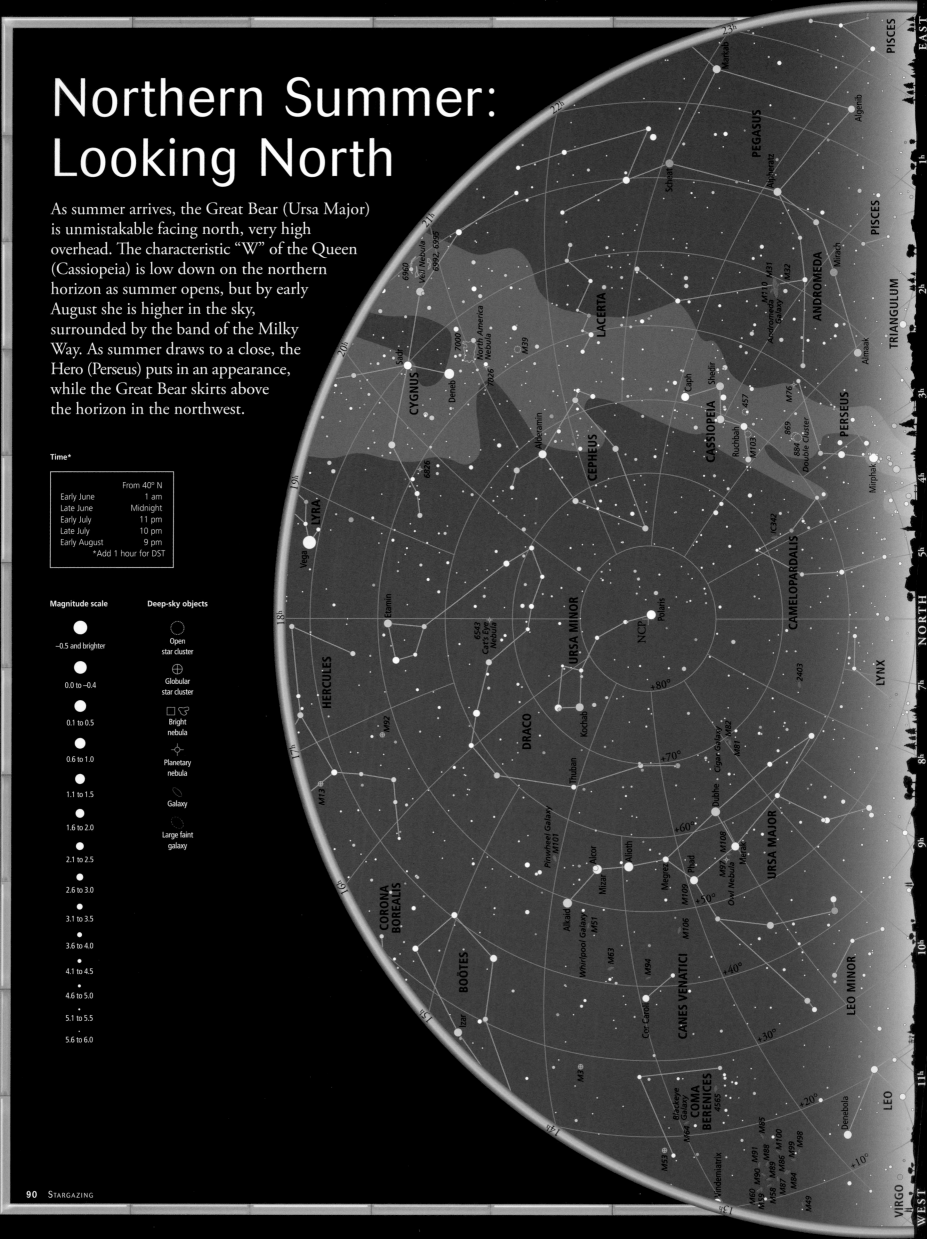

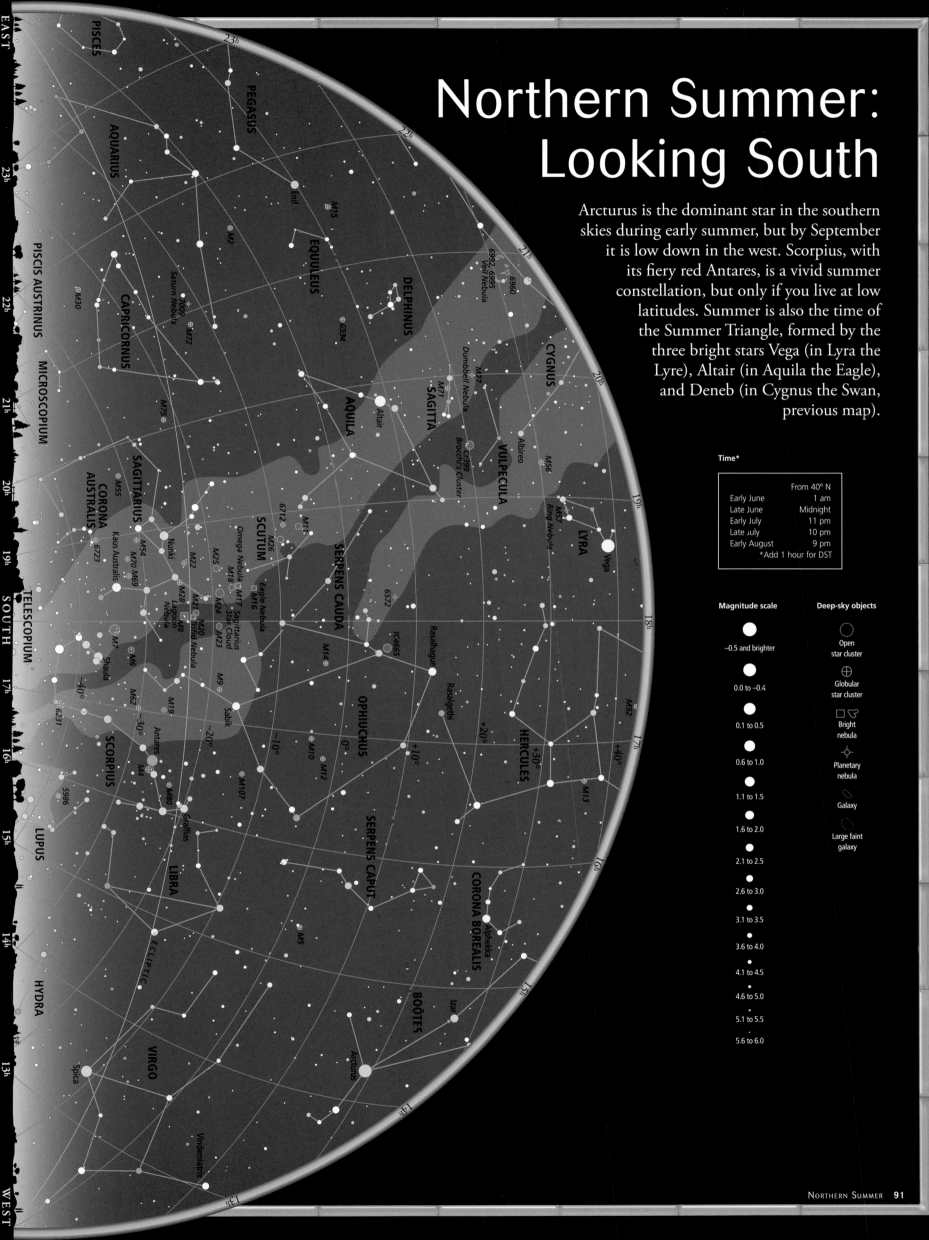

Northern Summer: Looking South

Arcturus is the dominant star in the southern skies during early summer, but by September it is low down in the west. Scorpius, with its fiery red Antares, is a vivid summer constellation, but only if you live at low latitudes. Summer is also the time of the Summer Triangle, formed by the three bright stars Vega (in Lyra the Lyre), Altair (in Aquila the Eagle), and Deneb (in Cygnus the Swan, previous map).

Time*

	From 40° N
Early June	1 am
Late June	Midnight
Early July	11 pm
Late July	10 pm
Early August	9 pm

*Add 1 hour for DST

Magnitude scale

- −0.5 and brighter
- 0.0 to −0.4
- 0.1 to 0.5
- 0.6 to 1.0
- 1.1 to 1.5
- 1.6 to 2.0
- 2.1 to 2.5
- 2.6 to 3.0
- 3.1 to 3.5
- 3.6 to 4.0
- 4.1 to 4.5
- 4.6 to 5.0
- 5.1 to 5.5
- 5.6 to 6.0

Deep-sky objects

- Open star cluster
- Globular star cluster
- Bright nebula
- Planetary nebula
- Galaxy
- Large faint galaxy

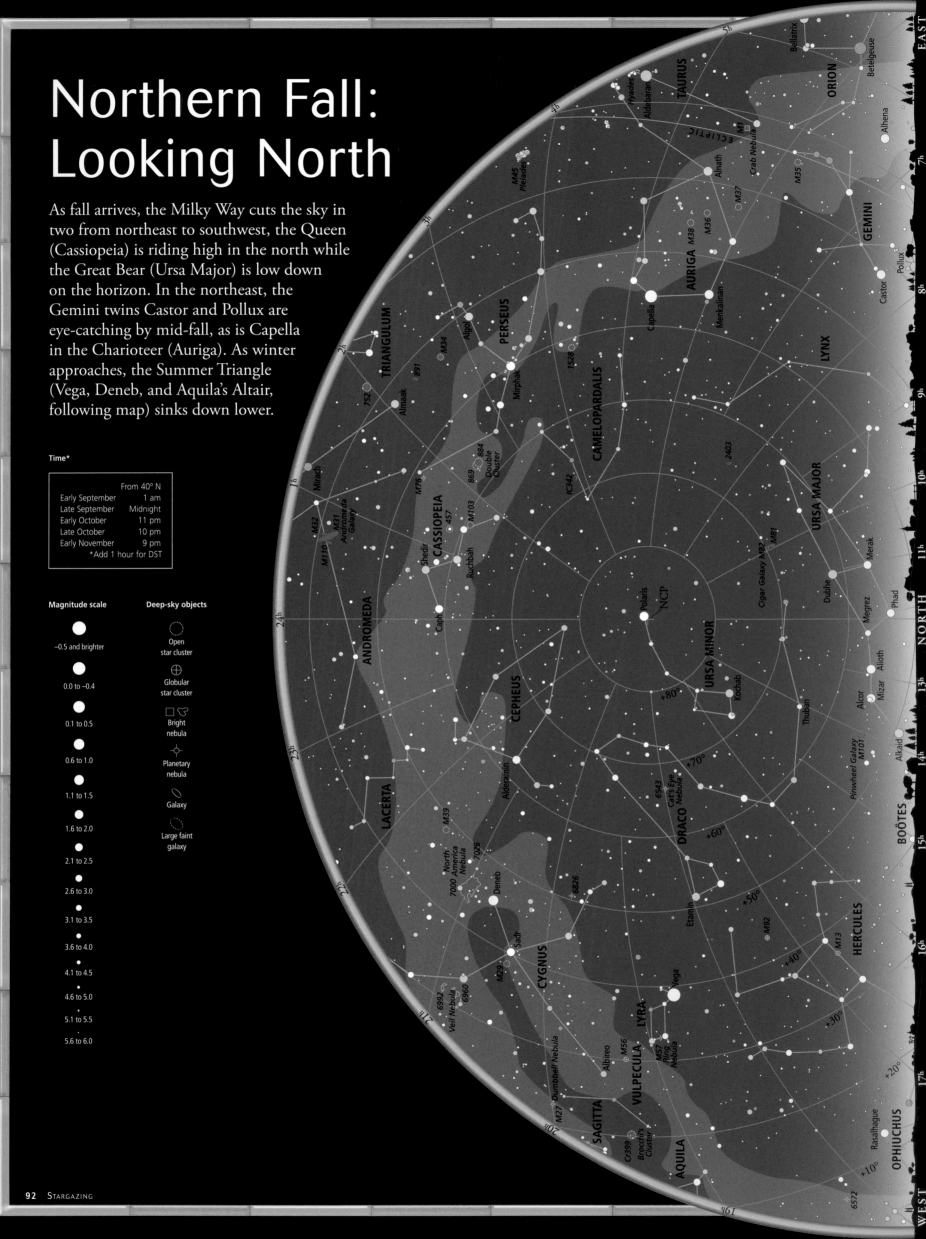

Northern Fall: Looking North

As fall arrives, the Milky Way cuts the sky in two from northeast to southwest, the Queen (Cassiopeia) is riding high in the north while the Great Bear (Ursa Major) is low down on the horizon. In the northeast, the Gemini twins Castor and Pollux are eye-catching by mid-fall, as is Capella in the Charioteer (Auriga). As winter approaches, the Summer Triangle (Vega, Deneb, and Aquila's Altair, following map) sinks down lower.

Time*

	From 40° N
Early September	1 am
Late September	Midnight
Early October	11 pm
Late October	10 pm
Early November	9 pm
*Add 1 hour for DST	

Magnitude scale

- −0.5 and brighter
- 0.0 to −0.4
- 0.1 to 0.5
- 0.6 to 1.0
- 1.1 to 1.5
- 1.6 to 2.0
- 2.1 to 2.5
- 2.6 to 3.0
- 3.1 to 3.5
- 3.6 to 4.0
- 4.1 to 4.5
- 4.6 to 5.0
- 5.1 to 5.5
- 5.6 to 6.0

Deep-sky objects

- Open star cluster
- Globular star cluster
- Bright nebula
- Planetary nebula
- Galaxy
- Large faint galaxy

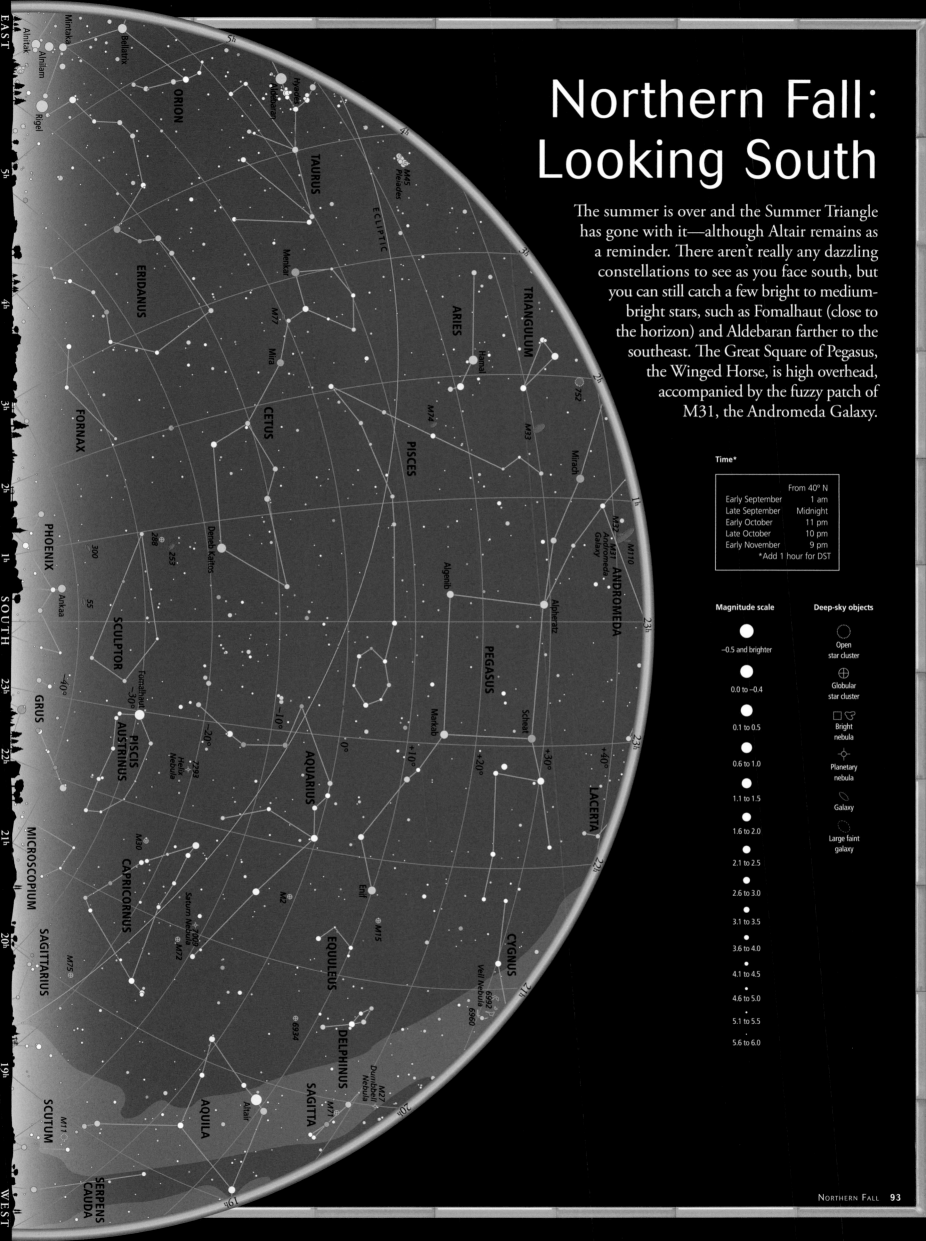

Northern Fall: Looking South

The summer is over and the Summer Triangle has gone with it—although Altair remains as a reminder. There aren't really any dazzling constellations to see as you face south, but you can still catch a few bright to medium-bright stars, such as Fomalhaut (close to the horizon) and Aldebaran farther to the southeast. The Great Square of Pegasus, the Winged Horse, is high overhead, accompanied by the fuzzy patch of M31, the Andromeda Galaxy.

Time*

	From 40° N
Early September	1 am
Late September	Midnight
Early October	11 pm
Late October	10 pm
Early November	9 pm
	*Add 1 hour for DST

Magnitude scale

- −0.5 and brighter
- 0.0 to −0.4
- 0.1 to 0.5
- 0.6 to 1.0
- 1.1 to 1.5
- 1.6 to 2.0
- 2.1 to 2.5
- 2.6 to 3.0
- 3.1 to 3.5
- 3.6 to 4.0
- 4.1 to 4.5
- 4.6 to 5.0
- 5.1 to 5.5
- 5.6 to 6.0

Deep-sky objects

- Open star cluster
- Globular star cluster
- Bright nebula
- Planetary nebula
- Galaxy
- Large faint galaxy

Northern Winter: Looking North

Face north in the winter and you will spot several bright constellations, including the Great Bear (Ursa Major), the Queen (Cassiopeia), and the Charioteer (Auriga). During early winter, the Great Bear is climbing in the northeast while the "W" of the Queen sinks in the northwest, and the Charioteer is high overhead with its bright yellow star Capella. By winter's end, Capella still rides high, and the Great Bear is upside down.

Time

	From 40° N
Early December	1 am
Late December	Midnight
Early January	11 pm
Late January	10 pm
Early February	9 pm

Magnitude scale

- −0.5 and brighter
- 0.0 to −0.4
- 0.1 to 0.5
- 0.6 to 1.0
- 1.1 to 1.5
- 1.6 to 2.0
- 2.1 to 2.5
- 2.6 to 3.0
- 3.1 to 3.5
- 3.6 to 4.0
- 4.1 to 4.5
- 4.6 to 5.0
- 5.1 to 5.5
- 5.6 to 6.0

Deep-sky objects

- Open star cluster
- Globular star cluster
- Bright nebula
- Planetary nebula
- Galaxy
- Large faint galaxy

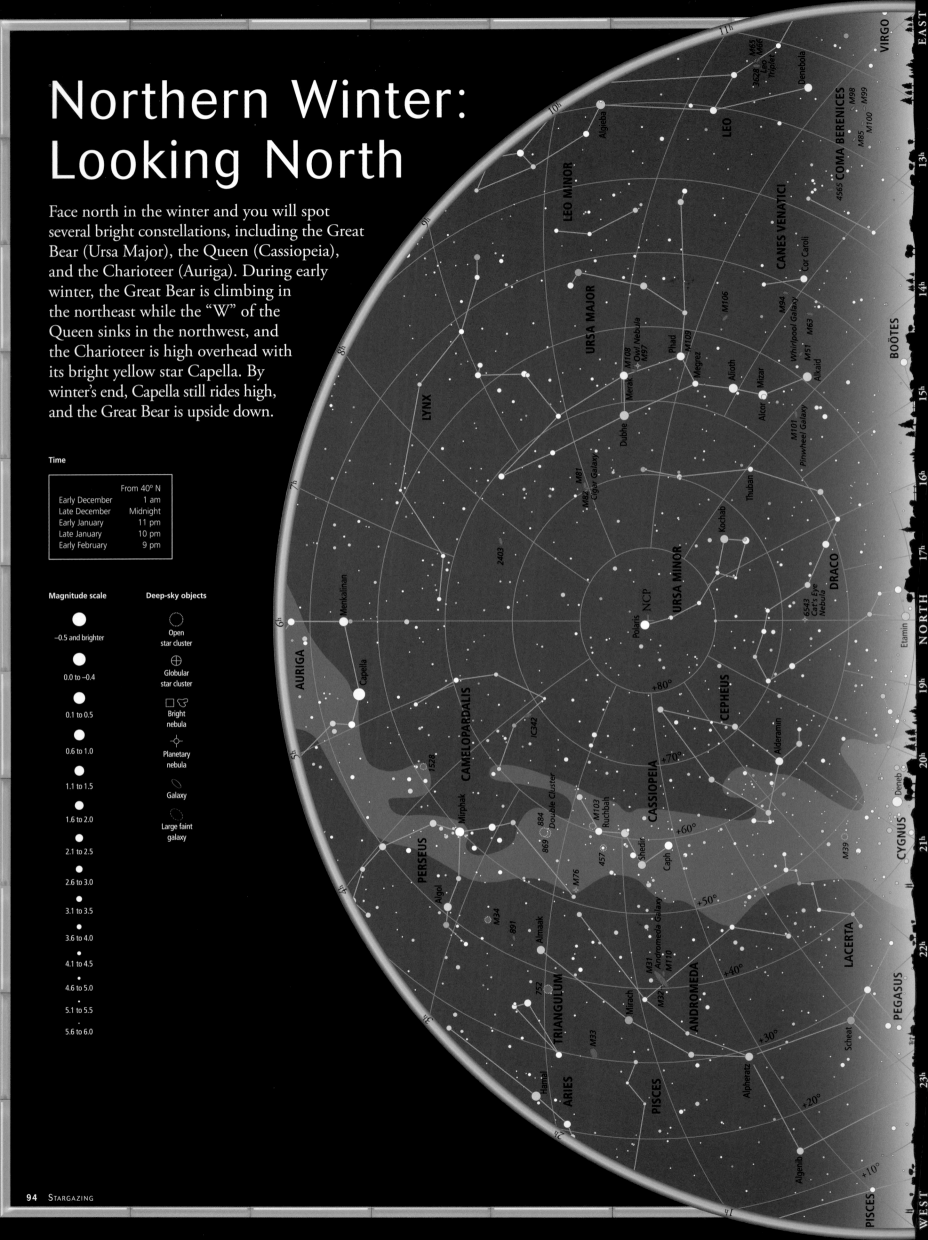

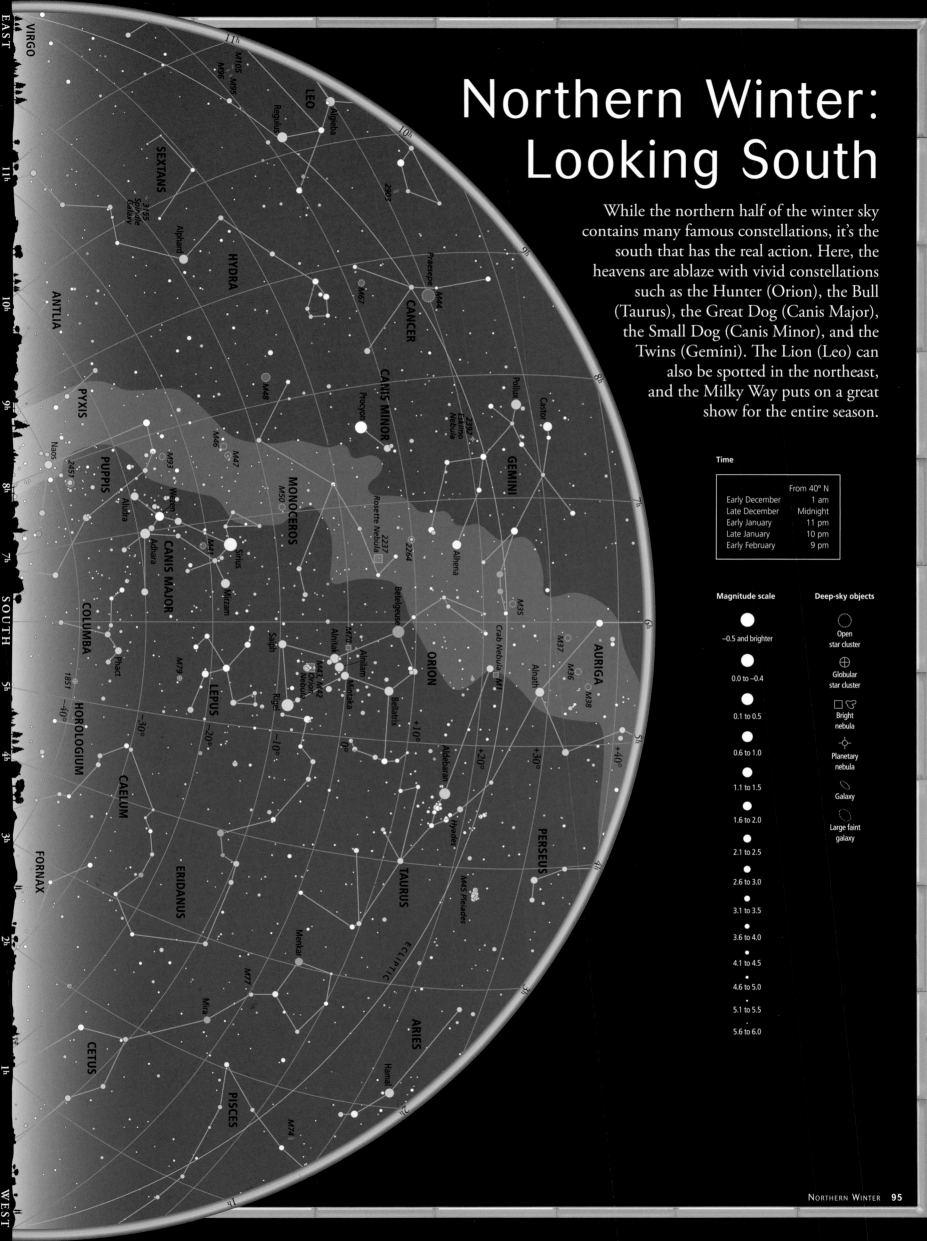

Northern Winter: Looking South

While the northern half of the winter sky contains many famous constellations, it's the south that has the real action. Here, the heavens are ablaze with vivid constellations such as the Hunter (Orion), the Bull (Taurus), the Great Dog (Canis Major), the Small Dog (Canis Minor), and the Twins (Gemini). The Lion (Leo) can also be spotted in the northeast, and the Milky Way puts on a great show for the entire season.

Time

	From 40° N
Early December	1 am
Late December	Midnight
Early January	11 pm
Late January	10 pm
Early February	9 pm

Magnitude scale

- −0.5 and brighter
- 0.0 to −0.4
- 0.1 to 0.5
- 0.6 to 1.0
- 1.1 to 1.5
- 1.6 to 2.0
- 2.1 to 2.5
- 2.6 to 3.0
- 3.1 to 3.5
- 3.6 to 4.0
- 4.1 to 4.5
- 4.6 to 5.0
- 5.1 to 5.5
- 5.6 to 6.0

Deep-sky objects

- Open star cluster
- Globular star cluster
- Bright nebula
- Planetary nebula
- Galaxy
- Large faint galaxy

Southern Spring: Looking North

During spring in the Southern Hemisphere, not many bright stars can be found. However, two exceptions are Altair, a bright star in the Eagle (Aquila), which shines steadily in the north in early spring, and Fomalhaut, the brightest star in the Southern Fish (Piscis Austrinus). By mid-spring, the Great Square of the Winged Horse (Pegasus) dominates the northern sky, and the appearance of Aldebaran promises the bright stars of summer.

Time*

	From 30° S
Early September	1 am
Late September	Midnight
Early October	11 pm
Late October	10 pm
Early November	9 pm
	*Add 1 hour for DST

Magnitude scale

- −0.5 and brighter
- 0.0 to −0.4
- 0.1 to 0.5
- 0.6 to 1.0
- 1.1 to 1.5
- 1.6 to 2.0
- 2.1 to 2.5
- 2.6 to 3.0
- 3.1 to 3.5
- 3.6 to 4.0
- 4.1 to 4.5
- 4.6 to 5.0
- 5.1 to 5.5
- 5.6 to 6.0

Deep-sky objects

- Open star cluster
- Globular star cluster
- Bright nebula
- Planetary nebula
- Galaxy
- Large faint galaxy

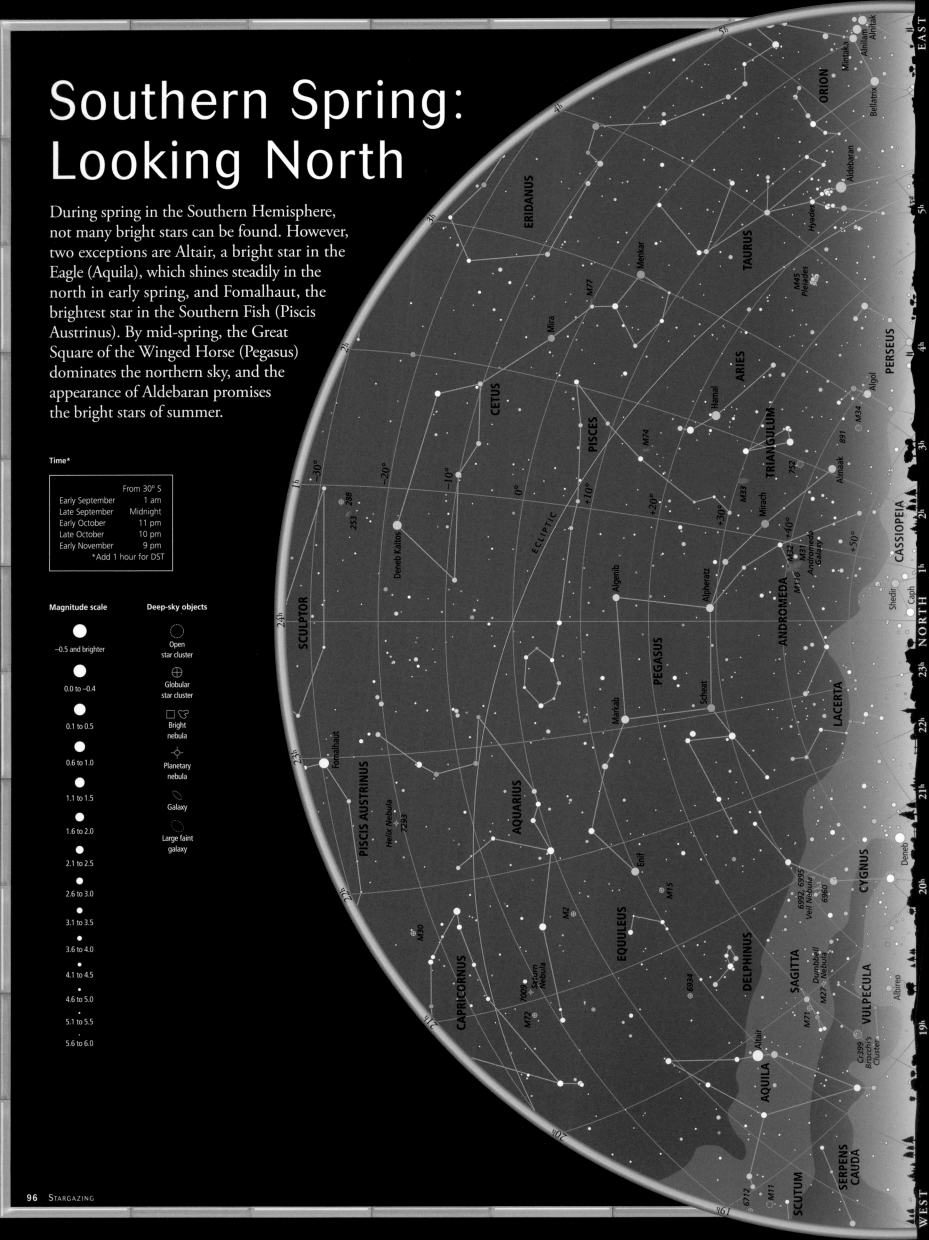

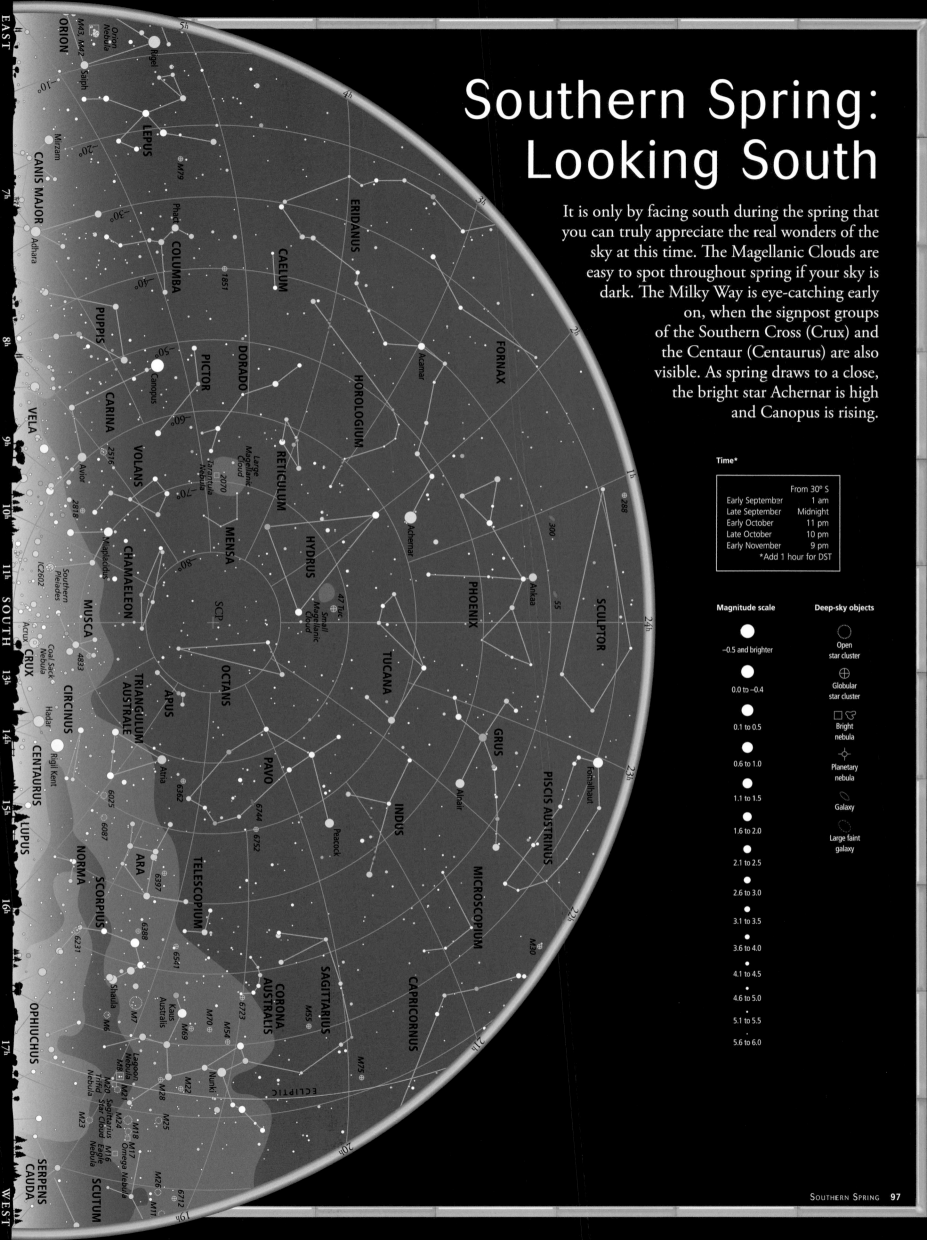

Southern Spring: Looking South

It is only by facing south during the spring that you can truly appreciate the real wonders of the sky at this time. The Magellanic Clouds are easy to spot throughout spring if your sky is dark. The Milky Way is eye-catching early on, when the signpost groups of the Southern Cross (Crux) and the Centaur (Centaurus) are also visible. As spring draws to a close, the bright star Achernar is high and Canopus is rising.

Time*

	From 30° S
Early September	1 am
Late September	Midnight
Early October	11 pm
Late October	10 pm
Early November	9 pm
*Add 1 hour for DST	

Magnitude scale

- −0.5 and brighter
- 0.0 to −0.4
- 0.1 to 0.5
- 0.6 to 1.0
- 1.1 to 1.5
- 1.6 to 2.0
- 2.1 to 2.5
- 2.6 to 3.0
- 3.1 to 3.5
- 3.6 to 4.0
- 4.1 to 4.5
- 4.6 to 5.0
- 5.1 to 5.5
- 5.6 to 6.0

Deep-sky objects

- Open star cluster
- Globular star cluster
- Bright nebula
- Planetary nebula
- Galaxy
- Large faint galaxy

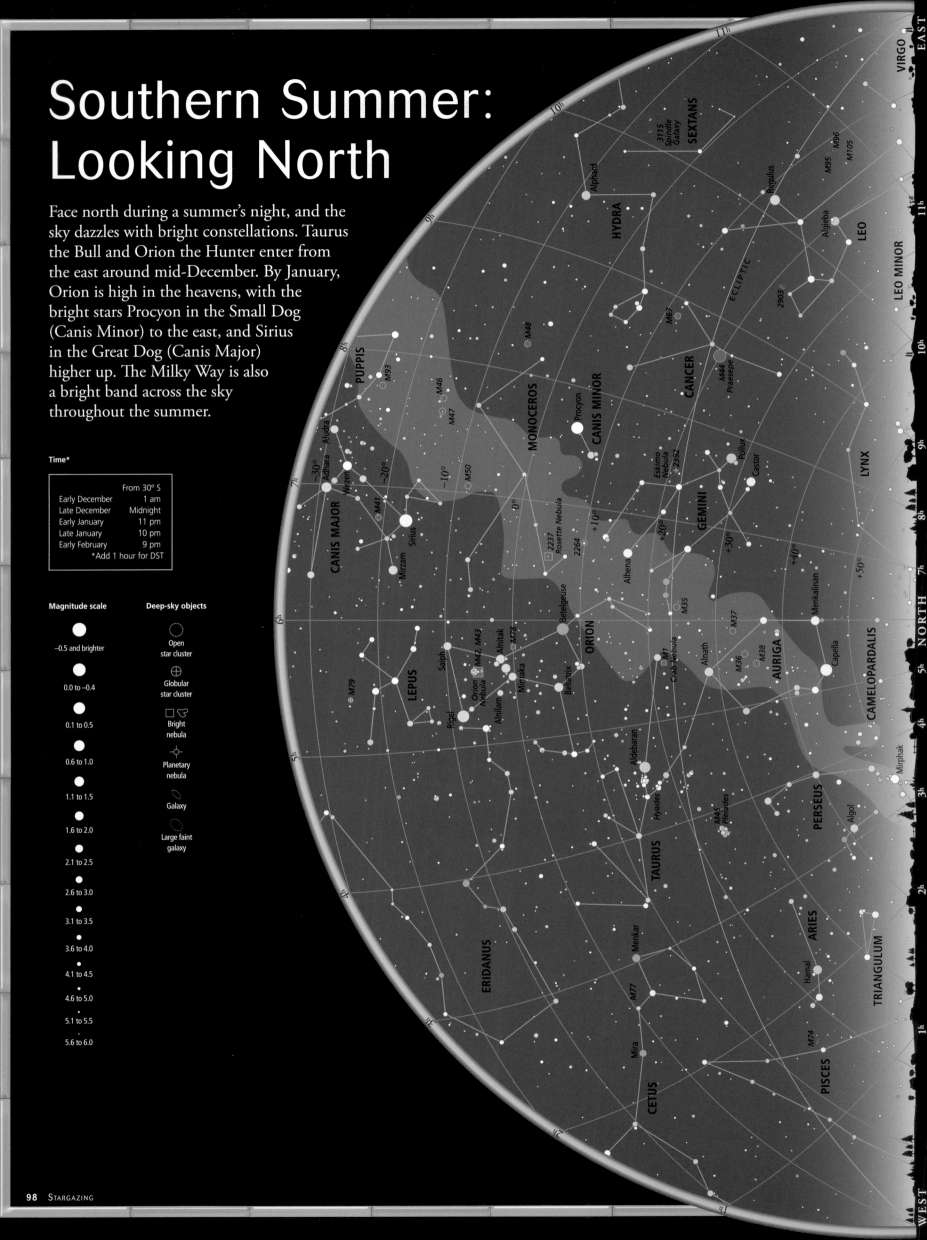

Southern Summer: Looking North

Face north during a summer's night, and the sky dazzles with bright constellations. Taurus the Bull and Orion the Hunter enter from the east around mid-December. By January, Orion is high in the heavens, with the bright stars Procyon in the Small Dog (Canis Minor) to the east, and Sirius in the Great Dog (Canis Major) higher up. The Milky Way is also a bright band across the sky throughout the summer.

Time*

	From 30° S
Early December	1 am
Late December	Midnight
Early January	11 pm
Late January	10 pm
Early February	9 pm
	*Add 1 hour for DST

Magnitude scale

- ● −0.5 and brighter
- ● 0.0 to −0.4
- ● 0.1 to 0.5
- ● 0.6 to 1.0
- ● 1.1 to 1.5
- ● 1.6 to 2.0
- ● 2.1 to 2.5
- ● 2.6 to 3.0
- ● 3.1 to 3.5
- ● 3.6 to 4.0
- · 4.1 to 4.5
- · 4.6 to 5.0
- · 5.1 to 5.5
- · 5.6 to 6.0

Deep-sky objects

- ⬭ Open star cluster
- ⊕ Globular star cluster
- ☐ ⬡ Bright nebula
- ⋄ Planetary nebula
- ⬭ Galaxy
- ⬭ Large faint galaxy

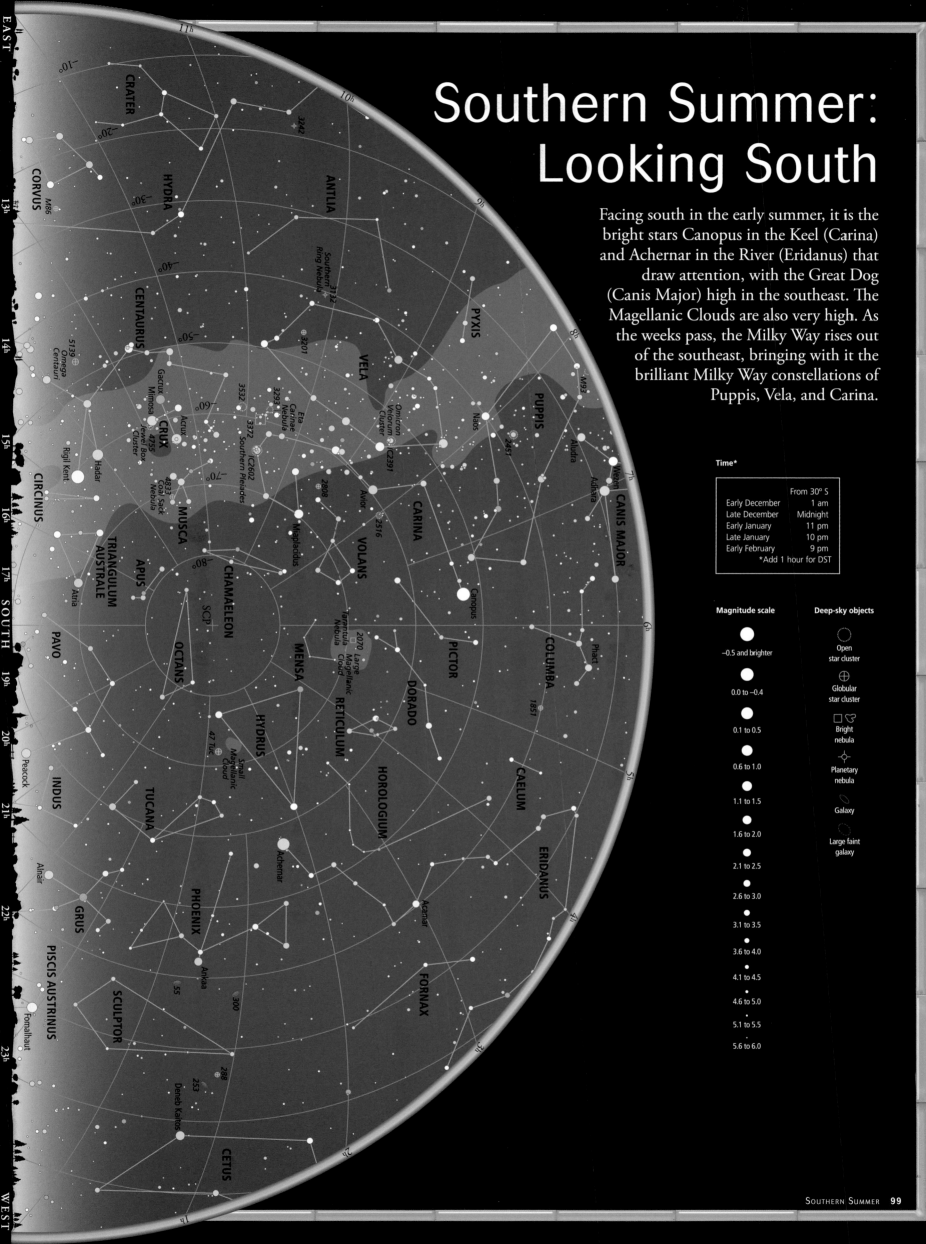

Southern Summer: Looking South

Facing south in the early summer, it is the bright stars Canopus in the Keel (Carina) and Achernar in the River (Eridanus) that draw attention, with the Great Dog (Canis Major) high in the southeast. The Magellanic Clouds are also very high. As the weeks pass, the Milky Way rises out of the southeast, bringing with it the brilliant Milky Way constellations of Puppis, Vela, and Carina.

Time*

	From 30° S
Early December	1 am
Late December	Midnight
Early January	11 pm
Late January	10 pm
Early February	9 pm
	*Add 1 hour for DST

Magnitude scale

- −0.5 and brighter
- 0.0 to −0.4
- 0.1 to 0.5
- 0.6 to 1.0
- 1.1 to 1.5
- 1.6 to 2.0
- 2.1 to 2.5
- 2.6 to 3.0
- 3.1 to 3.5
- 3.6 to 4.0
- 4.1 to 4.5
- 4.6 to 5.0
- 5.1 to 5.5
- 5.6 to 6.0

Deep-sky objects

- Open star cluster
- Globular star cluster
- Bright nebula
- Planetary nebula
- Galaxy
- Large faint galaxy

Southern Fall: Looking North

Once the summer constellations have sunk in the west, the fall sky facing north is not particularly dazzling, but there are still some bright stars. Look for Arcturus in the Herdsman (Boötes), Spica in the Virgin (Virgo), Regulus in the Lion (Leo), and Procyon in the Small Dog (Canis Minor). Also look for the small, distinctive shape of Corvus climbing in the sky.

Time*

	From 30° S
Early March	1 am
Late March	Midnight
Early April	11 pm
Late April	10 pm
Early May	9 pm
	*Add 1 hour for DST

Magnitude scale

- −0.5 and brighter
- 0.0 to −0.4
- 0.1 to 0.5
- 0.6 to 1.0
- 1.1 to 1.5
- 1.6 to 2.0
- 2.1 to 2.5
- 2.6 to 3.0
- 3.1 to 3.5
- 3.6 to 4.0
- 4.1 to 4.5
- 4.6 to 5.0
- 5.1 to 5.5
- 5.6 to 6.0

Deep-sky objects

- Open star cluster
- Globular star cluster
- Bright nebula
- Planetary nebula
- Galaxy
- Large faint galaxy

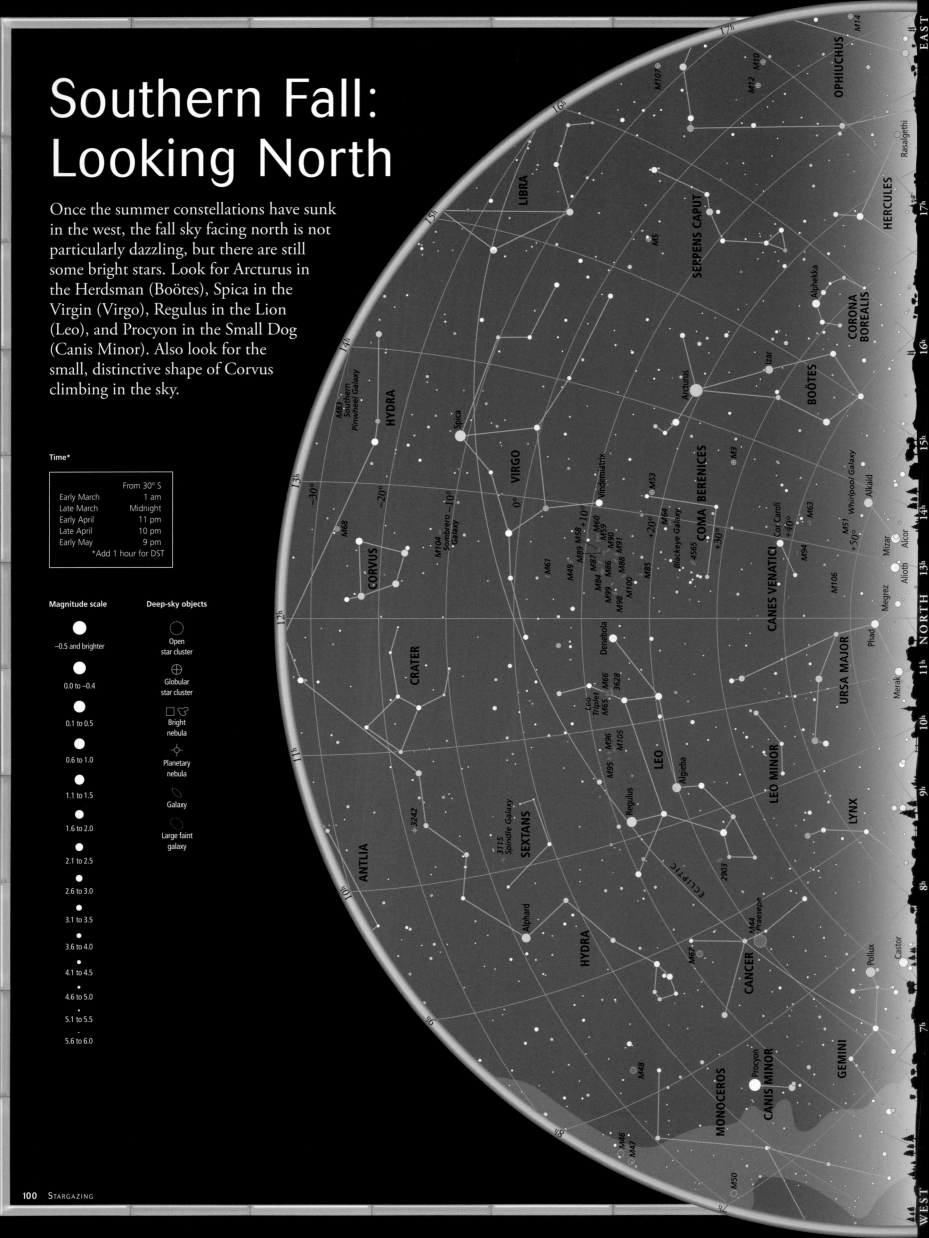

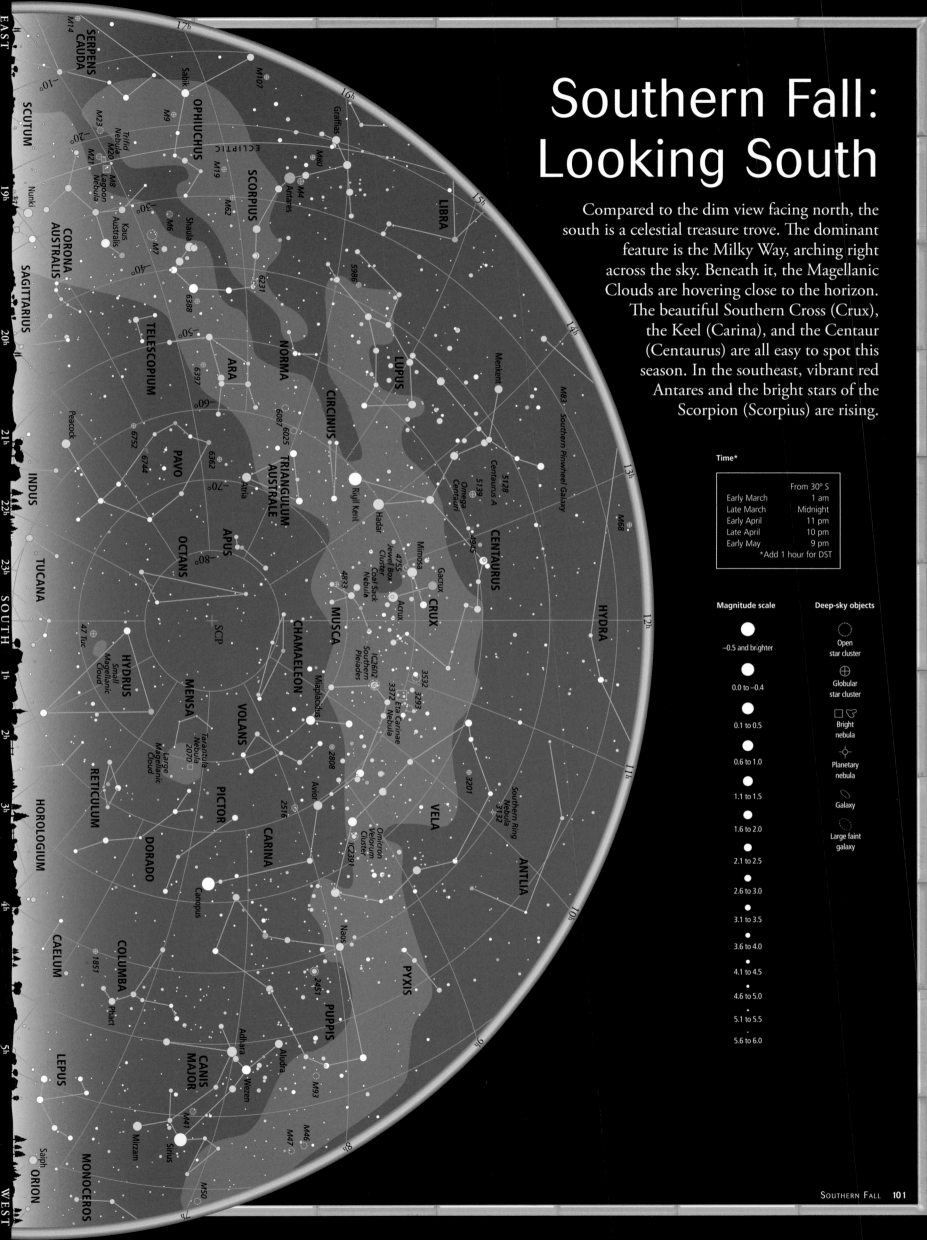

Southern Fall: Looking South

Compared to the dim view facing north, the south is a celestial treasure trove. The dominant feature is the Milky Way, arching right across the sky. Beneath it, the Magellanic Clouds are hovering close to the horizon. The beautiful Southern Cross (Crux), the Keel (Carina), and the Centaur (Centaurus) are all easy to spot this season. In the southeast, vibrant red Antares and the bright stars of the Scorpion (Scorpius) are rising.

Time*

	From 30° S
Early March	1 am
Late March	Midnight
Early April	11 pm
Late April	10 pm
Early May	9 pm
	*Add 1 hour for DST

Magnitude scale

- −0.5 and brighter
- 0.0 to −0.4
- 0.1 to 0.5
- 0.6 to 1.0
- 1.1 to 1.5
- 1.6 to 2.0
- 2.1 to 2.5
- 2.6 to 3.0
- 3.1 to 3.5
- 3.6 to 4.0
- 4.1 to 4.5
- 4.6 to 5.0
- 5.1 to 5.5
- 5.6 to 6.0

Deep-sky objects

- Open star cluster
- Globular star cluster
- Bright nebula
- Planetary nebula
- Galaxy
- Large faint galaxy

Southern Winter: Looking North

At the break of winter facing north, the Herdsman (Boötes) and Virgo, the Virgin, are both high, recognizable by their bright stars Arcturus and Spica. As they drift west, the center of the galaxy in the Archer (Sagittarius) and the adjoining bright stars of the Scorpion (Scorpius) pass overhead. The Northern Hemisphere's Summer Triangle (Vega, Deneb, and Altair) is also the south's Winter Triangle if you are not too far south.

Time

	From 30° S
Early June	1 am
Late June	Midnight
Early July	11 pm
Late July	10 pm
Early August	9 pm

Magnitude scale

⬤ −0.5 and brighter

⬤ 0.0 to −0.4

⬤ 0.1 to 0.5

● 0.6 to 1.0

● 1.1 to 1.5

● 1.6 to 2.0

● 2.1 to 2.5

● 2.6 to 3.0

• 3.1 to 3.5

• 3.6 to 4.0

• 4.1 to 4.5

· 4.6 to 5.0

· 5.1 to 5.5

· 5.6 to 6.0

Deep-sky objects

⭕ Open star cluster

⊕ Globular star cluster

▫ ⧄ Bright nebula

✧ Planetary nebula

⬭ Galaxy

⬭ Large faint galaxy

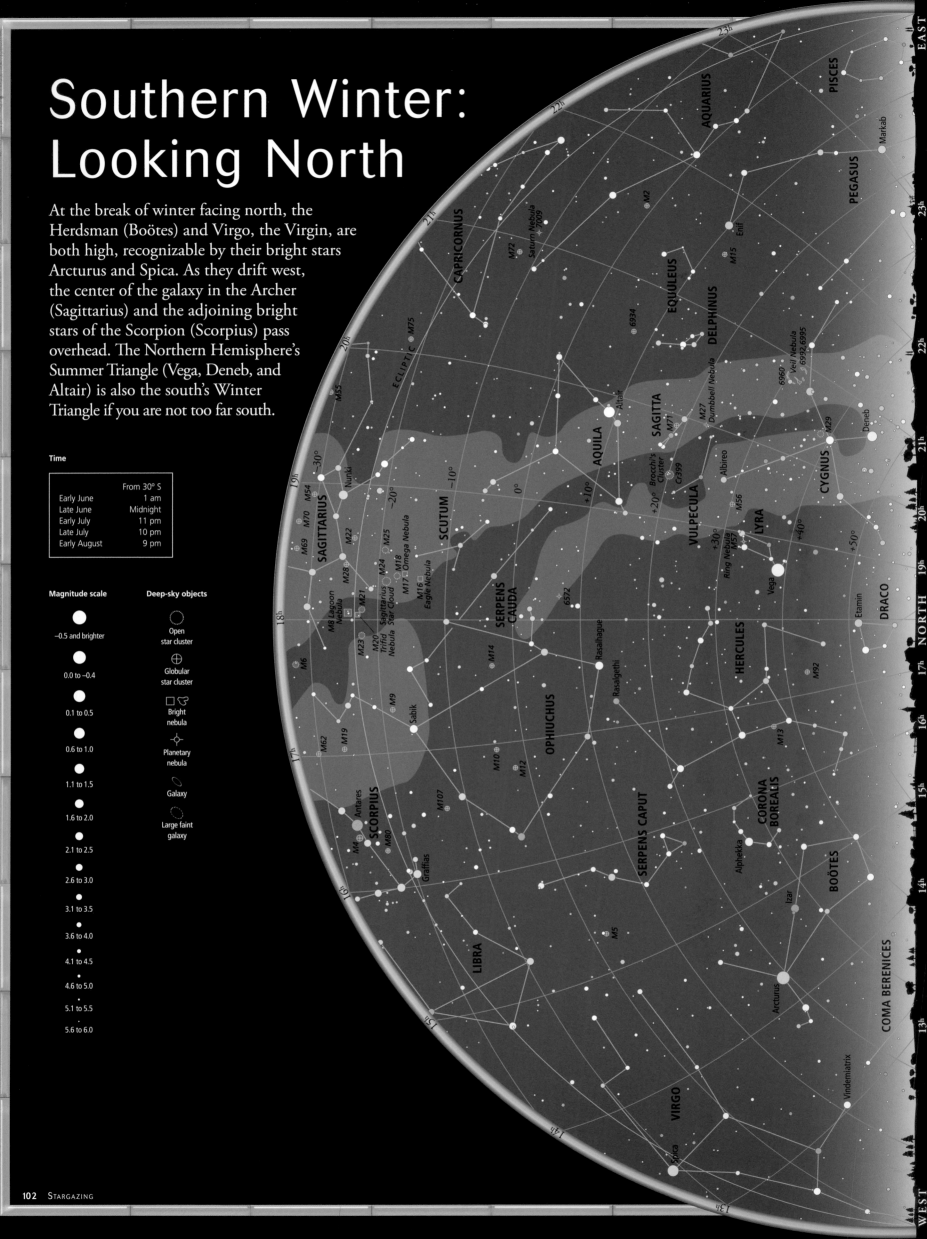

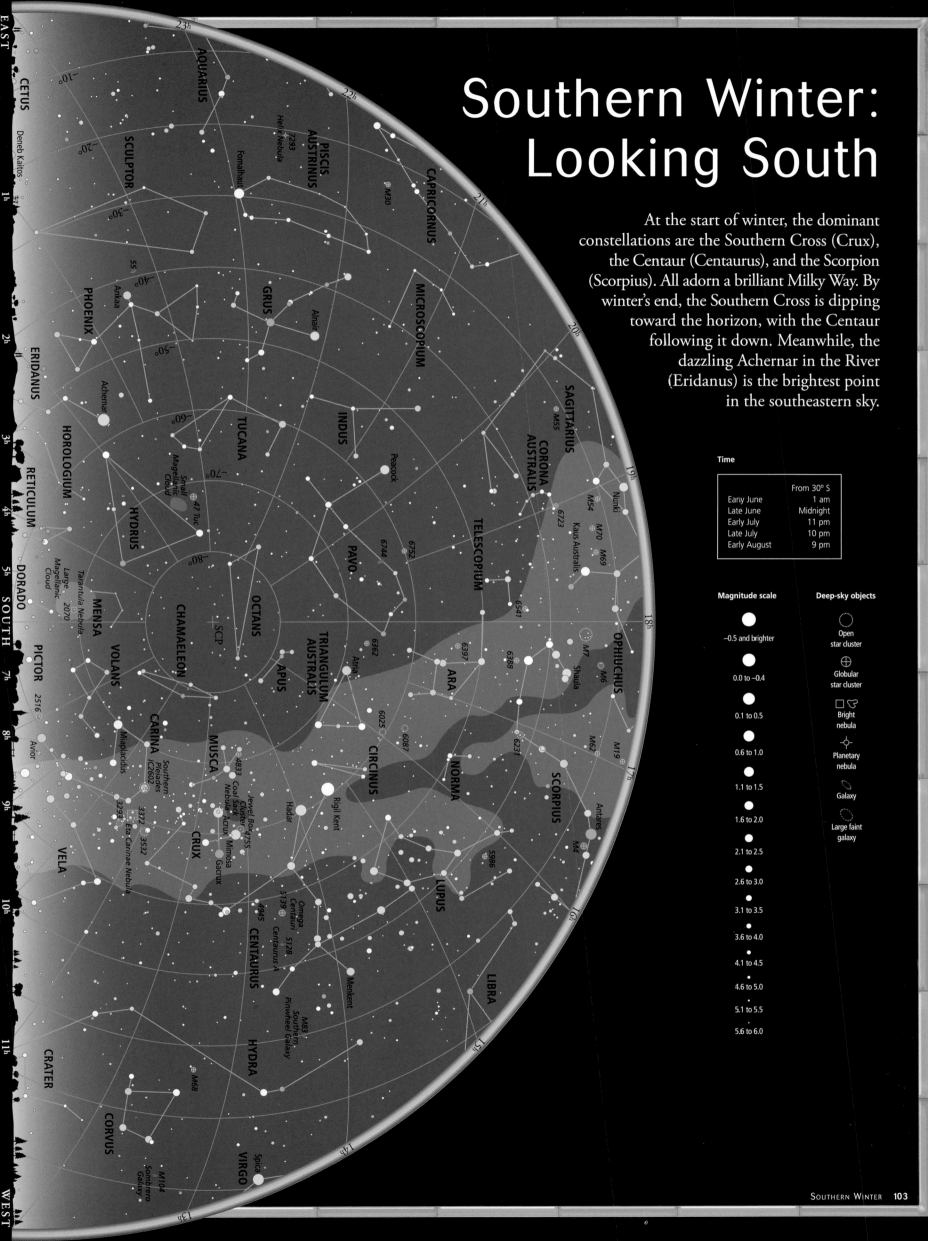

Southern Winter: Looking South

At the start of winter, the dominant constellations are the Southern Cross (Crux), the Centaur (Centaurus), and the Scorpion (Scorpius). All adorn a brilliant Milky Way. By winter's end, the Southern Cross is dipping toward the horizon, with the Centaur following it down. Meanwhile, the dazzling Achernar in the River (Eridanus) is the brightest point in the southeastern sky.

Time

	From 30° S
Early June	1 am
Late June	Midnight
Early July	11 pm
Late July	10 pm
Early August	9 pm

Magnitude scale

- −0.5 and brighter
- 0.0 to −0.4
- 0.1 to 0.5
- 0.6 to 1.0
- 1.1 to 1.5
- 1.6 to 2.0
- 2.1 to 2.5
- 2.6 to 3.0
- 3.1 to 3.5
- 3.6 to 4.0
- 4.1 to 4.5
- 4.6 to 5.0
- 5.1 to 5.5
- 5.6 to 6.0

Deep-sky objects

- Open star cluster
- Globular star cluster
- Bright nebula
- Planetary nebula
- Galaxy
- Large faint galaxy

Into Space

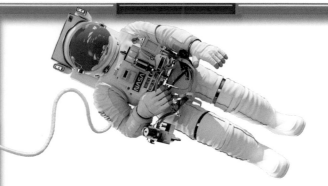

First Observers

Ever since our ancestors lived in caves, the skies have fascinated us. The earliest evidence of that interest dates to the end of the last Ice Age, about 10,000 years ago, when people marked animal bones with what appear to be phases of the Moon. Our ancestors probably named the first constellations thousands of years ago. In those days astronomy was more of a religion than a science, but observations of the stars and how they change with the seasons eventually led to the creation of calendars, which helped greatly with agriculture. These pages mention just some of the astronomical ideas of early civilizations.

Chinese celestial spheres

The Chinese have long been keen astronomers. There are clues that they may have discovered sunspots and other phenomena hundreds of years before they were seen by Western eyes. This Chinese map from the late 18th century shows 1,464 stars arranged into 283 constellations, many more than the 88 modern Western constellations.

Our first known record of a comet comes from the ancient Chinese—in 240 BC.

Stonehenge

Stonehenge is a famous stone monument in Europe, in the heart of the English countryside. Nobody is sure how it was built, by whom, or even why. It was constructed in several stages by different peoples, starting around 5,000 years ago and being completed around 1,500 years later in 1500 BC. The positioning of the stones suggests that it may have been used as an observatory to predict the motion and eclipses of the Moon and Sun.

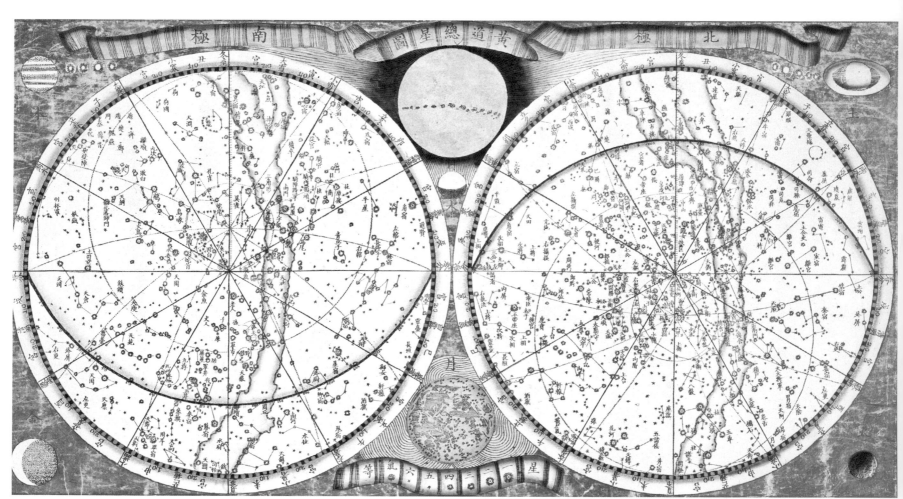

Planet gods

This illustration shows Mercury—not the planet, but the Roman god after whom the planet was named. The Greeks linked the planets with the gods, and the Romans adopted this. It was they who gave the planets the names we use today—except for Uranus, which is a Greek name.

Crab Nebula

In AD 185, ancient Chinese astronomers observed a "guest star" in the sky near the bright star Alpha Centauri. They called it that because the star had not been there before. What they had witnessed, although they did not know it at the time, was the first known exploding star—which we now call a supernova. They found another one in 1054, in the constellation of Taurus. Today, we recognize this as the explosion that produced the famous Crab Nebula (below).

Egyptian constellations

These paintings of constellation figures were found in the tomb of a pharaoh—a ruler of ancient Egypt. But while these constellations are very old, others date back thousands of years earlier, such as Leo and Taurus, which were known in ancient Mesopotamia (modern-day Iraq).

Babylonian astronomy

This Babylonian tablet dates from around 500 BC. It is filled with engravings about the motions of stars and planets. The Babylonians were keen astronomers who learned how to predict eclipses and divided the circle of the sky into the 360 units that we now call degrees.

The Crab Nebula is the remains of a star that blew itself apart almost 1,000 years ago. It is also known as M1, because it was the first of Charles Messier's famous catalog of celestial objects.

Egyptian astronomy

Astronomy was important to the ancient Egyptians, but to them it was closely related to religion. This engraving shows the god of the atmosphere, Shu, separating his daughter Nut, goddess of the sky, from Earth. The Egyptians kept track of the rising and setting of stars such as Sirius, and divided the day and night into the twelve periods from which we get our hours.

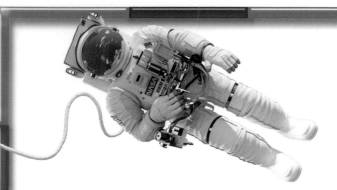

Giant Leaps

Although ancient cultures took a great deal of interest in astronomy, it was almost always associated with religion and mysticism. It was not until around 600 BC, in ancient Greece, that people finally looked at the subject more logically. They deduced that Earth was round and measured its size. They realized the Moon circles Earth and calculated the distances to the Sun and Moon. Although it was suggested that Earth went around the Sun, the prevailing view remained unchanged: that the all-important Earth was at the center of the Universe. But that changed from the 16th century onward, when science took a series of giant leaps.

Galileo Galilei (1564–1642)
Galileo Galilei was an Italian astronomer, physicist, and mathematician. He was the first person to use a telescope for astronomical observation—this painting shows him demonstrating its use to a small crowd in Venice. Galileo found the largest moons of Jupiter, which are named the Galilean satellites in his honor. He also studied the craters of the Moon and the phases of Venus and Mercury.

Ptolemy's universe
Ptolemy believed Earth remained still while the Sun, Moon, and the five other planets then known (Mercury, Venus, Mars, Jupiter, and Saturn) all went around it. The diagram (right) shows a simplified version of his idea. It was accepted for more than a thousand years.

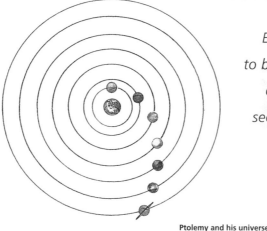

Ptolemy and his universe

Earth was long-thought to be unmoving at the center of the Universe, which seemed sensible, based on everyday experience.

Nicolaus Copernicus (1473–1543)
Nicolaus Copernicus was a Polish churchman and astronomer. He revolutionized astronomy when he dared to suggest, against the religious thinking of the time, that the Sun and not Earth was at the center of the Universe. To avoid persecution he withheld the publication of his work until 1543, the year he died.

Claudius Ptolemy
Claudius Ptolemy lived in Alexandria, Egypt, in the 2nd century AD, and was one of the most influential astronomers of ancient Greece. He is known only through his writings, such as the Almagest, which dates from AD 150.

NICOLAVS COPERNICVS

Brahe and his universe

Brahe's universe
Unlike followers of Ptolemy, Brahe believed that the planets went around the Sun. However, he also thought that the Sun, in turn, went around Earth! Disagreeing with Copernicus, he thought Earth was so important that it had to be in the middle. This was also the belief of the Church at the time.

Tycho Brahe (1546–1601)
Tycho Brahe—who wore a silver nose as his real one was cut off in a duel—was a Danish astronomer whose observations of the planets were the most accurate of his time. His data did not exactly fit the models of Ptolemy or Copernicus, so he invented his own.

Copernicus's universe

According to Copernicus, Earth was just another planet that went around the Sun like the others. The Moon went around Earth, while the stars were placed far beyond the planets, their movement across the sky caused by Earth's rotation. His model was not perfect, but it was much closer to reality than previous explanations had been.

Galileo's telescope

Newton's telescope

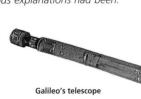

Early telescopes

Telescopes revolutionized the science of astronomy. The first telescopes were perhaps built in Holland around 1600. However, Galileo built his own in 1609, while Sir Isaac Newton used a telescope with quite a different design around 1670. Both designs are still in use today.

Isaac Newton (1642–1727)

Sir Isaac Newton was a brilliant British mathematician and astronomer, and the man credited with the "discovery" of gravity. Newton was the first person to ask what gravity was and to describe it in theory. He showed how two objects attract each other with a force he called gravitation, whose strength depends on how large the objects are, and how far apart they are from each other. The force increases if the objects are more massive or if they are closer together. Gravity, he said, was the reason Earth went around the Sun, and the Moon around Earth.

It is often said, though unlikely to be true, that Isaac Newton started thinking about gravity when an apple fell on his head one day. But this will never be known for sure.

Modern Astronomy

There is a lot more to astronomy than meets the eye—literally. Many objects in space emit all kinds of invisible "light" to which our eyes are not sensitive, including radio waves, infrared, ultraviolet, X-rays, and gamma rays. In the past, astronomy was restricted to what the eyes could see. But modern astronomers, armed with sophisticated equipment, can now study the entire spectrum. The only snag is that some of these radiations cannot be studied on Earth because our atmosphere blocks them. Astronomers get around this by using telescopes in space.

Very Large Array

Many objects in space emit radio waves. Some radio waves are very long—we say that they have long wavelengths. Therefore the dishes of radio telescopes like these, part of the Very Large Array in New Mexico, USA, need to be big to pick them up. The biggest single radio telescope dish, in Puerto Rico, is 1,000 feet (305 m) across!

Chandra X-ray observatory

Chandra is a satellite that is designed to pick up high-energy radiation called X-rays—the same radiation that doctors use to look inside your body. X-rays are emitted by hot objects in space, such as the thin gas in the Sun's corona, its outer atmosphere.

Spitzer Space Telescope

Our atmosphere blocks much of the infrared radiation, which many astronomical bodies (such as gas clouds and very young stars) emit. So infrared is best detected from space. The Spitzer Space Telescope is providing spectacular infrared images from space.

Swift Gamma-Ray Burst Mission

Gamma rays are the most energetic kinds of electromagnetic radiation. They are emitted by powerful objects in space such as gamma-ray bursts, which are caused by exploding stars. Swift is a gamma-ray detector in space dedicated to the study of these phenomena.

Electromagnetic spectrum

The visible light that your eyes can detect is just one example of a kind of energy called electromagnetic radiation. Different kinds of electromagnetic radiation make up what we call the electromagnetic spectrum. The diagram below shows the spectrum from long "wavelength" radio waves to short "wavelength" gamma rays.

Radio telescopes

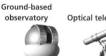

Spitzer

Ground-based observatory

Optical telescopes

International Ultraviolet Explorer (IUE)

Chandra

Swift

Radio waves	Infrared	Visible	UV	X-rays	Gamma rays

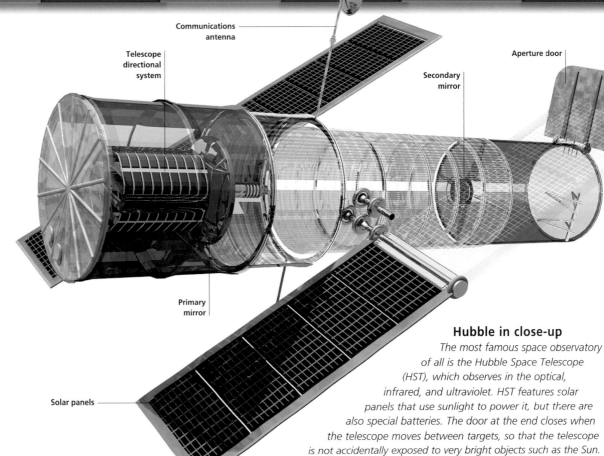

Communications antenna

Telescope directional system

Aperture door

Secondary mirror

Primary mirror

Solar panels

Hubble in close-up

The most famous space observatory of all is the Hubble Space Telescope (HST), which observes in the optical, infrared, and ultraviolet. HST features solar panels that use sunlight to power it, but there are also special batteries. The door at the end closes when the telescope moves between targets, so that the telescope is not accidentally exposed to very bright objects such as the Sun.

The light that your eyes can detect is only a tiny fraction of the entire range of radiation we call the electromagnetic spectrum.

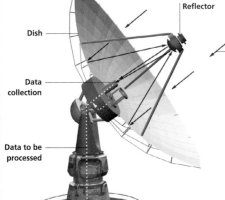

Reflector

Dish

Radio waves

Data collection

Data to be processed

Radio telescopes

To detect radio waves, astronomers use a special kind of antenna called a radio dish—much like a reflecting optical telescope. The rest is essentially the same sort of technology you might have at home to pick up radio signals via satellite for your television. The waves come in, bounce off the dish, are focused at the detector, then fed to a computer and processed.

Herschel's telescope

Sir William Herschel (1738–1822) was a German-born British astronomer, who had many claims to fame, in particular his discovery of the planet Uranus in 1781. Herschel built hundreds of telescopes in his time, for himself and for others, but the largest and most famous was the reflecting telescope shown here, completed in 1789. The diameter of its main mirror was 4 feet (1.2 m), the tube length was 40 feet (12 m), and for a time it was the most powerful astronomical instrument in the world. Using this telescope, Herschel found two new moons orbiting the planet Saturn.

Herschel's telescope was a marvel of eighteenth-century engineering.

Mauna Kea observatory

Optical observatories are often built on high mountains, where the air and sky are crystal clear. This dome, housing the Canada–France–Hawaii telescope, is perched 13,800 feet (4,200 m) above sea level on the peak of the volcano Mauna Kea, on the Big Island of Hawaii, USA.

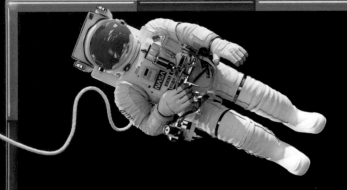

Visiting Space

Humans have been visiting space for almost as long as our probes have. The Soviets sent the first man into orbit less than four years after the first successful satellite, Sputnik 1. And within a decade of that, man walked on the Moon. In 1971 we started putting people into space for longer periods, aboard Earth-orbiting habitats called space stations. The first was the USSR's Salyut 1. The Americans followed in 1973 with Skylab. More recently there was the Russian Mir station, from 1986 to 2001, and now there is the International Space Station. Today, NASA is again showing interest in putting people back on the Moon, but it's still many years away.

On the Moon
This is astronaut Edwin E. Aldrin, Jr., standing on the Moon next to the American flag in July 1969. Aldrin and Neil Armstrong, who took this photo, were the first people to set foot on the Moon. Ten others followed them in five successful missions, before the Apollo program was scrapped in 1972.

First "walk" in space
Edward White, seen here, was the first American to "walk" in space, in June 1965. He left the safety of his spacecraft, called Gemini, but was still tied to it by a lifeline so that he could not float away.

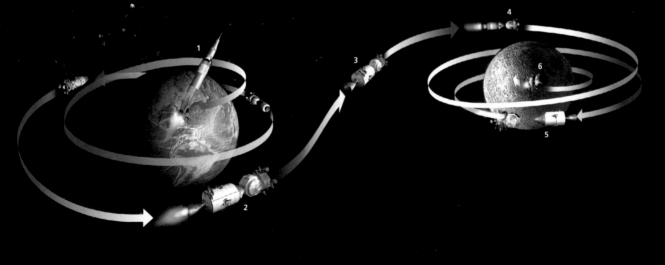

To the Moon . . .
Getting to the Moon and back involves many different maneuvers. After the launch (1), the command-and-service module (CSM) and the lunar module (LM), joined to each other, begin to make their way to the Moon (2 and 3). Once in lunar orbit (4), the LM and two astronauts break away from the CSM (5) and head for the surface (6), while the CSM waits in orbit with a third astronaut on board.

. . . and back
To return to Earth, the upper half or "ascent stage" of the LM blasts off from the Moon (1), leaving the landing feet behind. The LM docks with the CSM (2), to let the astronauts back in, then the LM is released (3) and the CSM leaves the Moon's orbit for Earth (4). Once in Earth's orbit, the command module (CM) separates from the CSM (5) and safely returns the astronauts to Earth (6 and 7).

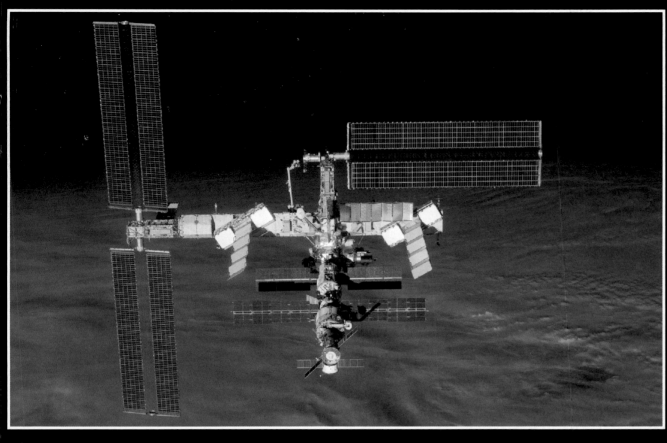

If you want to go into space, it may be affordable sooner than you think. There are already companies taking bookings!

Launching the Space Shuttle
The Space Shuttle is America's famous reusable space vehicle, which first flew in 1981. During take-off, the Shuttle is piggybacked on a fuel tank and two rockets called boosters. These all drop to Earth when the fuel is used. The boosters are recovered and reused, but the tank is thrown away. The three engines at the back of the shuttle provide the final push to get it into orbit.

Stage three

External tank drops away

International Space Station
The International Space Station is a milestone in international cooperation. This research station, orbiting 218 miles (350 km) above Earth, is jointly owned and funded by five space agencies, totaling sixteen countries. The station is not complete, but astronauts regularly go up there to help construct it. It probably won't be finished until 2010.

Stage two

Incredible "strength"
If you could go into orbit around Earth in the Space Shuttle, you too would be "weightless" like these astronauts. In space, you feel weightless because you and the spacecraft are "falling" around Earth together. It is easy to lose your sense of orientation and become "space sick."

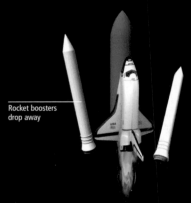

Rocket boosters drop away

Stage one

Spacewalk outside the ISS
This photograph shows astronaut Soichi Noguchi "walking" in space outside the Destiny laboratory, which is one of the compartments, called modules, that make up the International Space Station.

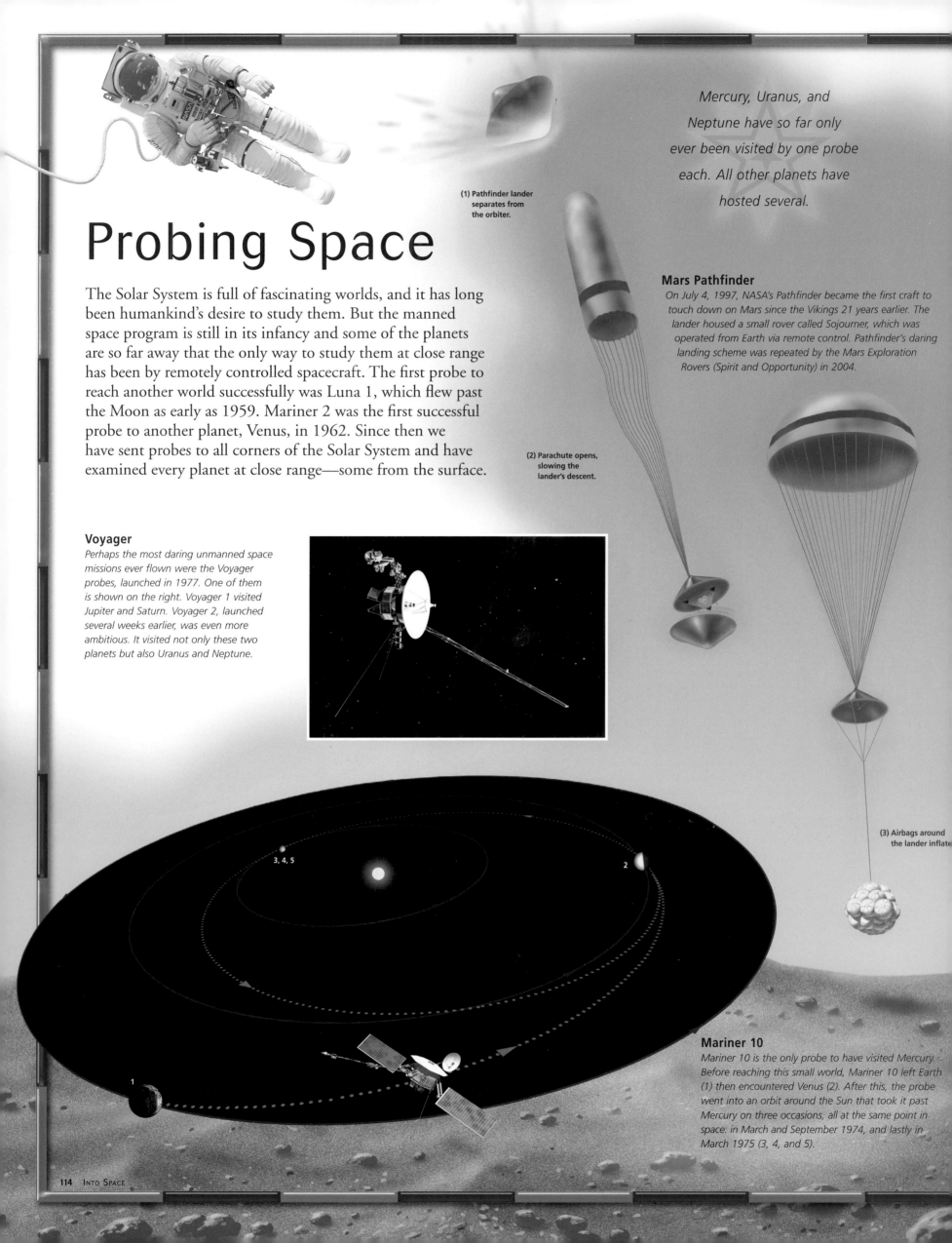

Probing Space

The Solar System is full of fascinating worlds, and it has long been humankind's desire to study them. But the manned space program is still in its infancy and some of the planets are so far away that the only way to study them at close range has been by remotely controlled spacecraft. The first probe to reach another world successfully was Luna 1, which flew past the Moon as early as 1959. Mariner 2 was the first successful probe to another planet, Venus, in 1962. Since then we have sent probes to all corners of the Solar System and have examined every planet at close range—some from the surface.

Mercury, Uranus, and Neptune have so far only ever been visited by one probe each. All other planets have hosted several.

(1) Pathfinder lander separates from the orbiter.

Mars Pathfinder
On July 4, 1997, NASA's Pathfinder became the first craft to touch down on Mars since the Vikings 21 years earlier. The lander housed a small rover called Sojourner, which was operated from Earth via remote control. Pathfinder's daring landing scheme was repeated by the Mars Exploration Rovers (Spirit and Opportunity) in 2004.

(2) Parachute opens, slowing the lander's descent.

Voyager
Perhaps the most daring unmanned space missions ever flown were the Voyager probes, launched in 1977. One of them is shown on the right. Voyager 1 visited Jupiter and Saturn. Voyager 2, launched several weeks earlier, was even more ambitious. It visited not only these two planets but also Uranus and Neptune.

(3) Airbags around the lander inflate

Mariner 10
Mariner 10 is the only probe to have visited Mercury. Before reaching this small world, Mariner 10 left Earth (1) then encountered Venus (2). After this, the probe went into an orbit around the Sun that took it past Mercury on three occasions, all at the same point in space: in March and September 1974, and lastly in March 1975 (3, 4, and 5).

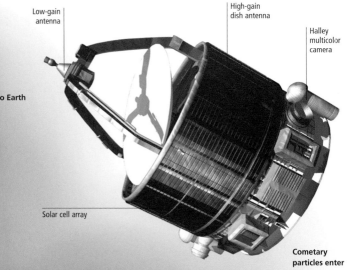

Giotto

When Halley's Comet was last seen in earthly skies, 1985–1986, it was met by a small squadron of spacecraft, of which Giotto (above) was the most famous. Giotto, launched by the European Space Agency (ESA), flew through Halley's tail and took the first close-ups of a comet's heart, its nucleus.

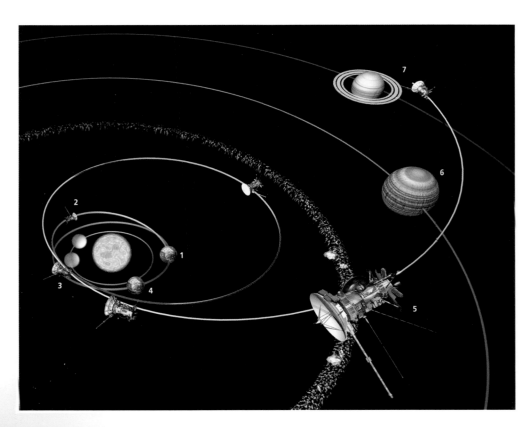

Cassini's path to Saturn

The most recent probe to Saturn was Cassini, which released the Huygens lander to study Saturn's moon Titan. After launch in 1997 (1), Cassini flew twice past Venus (2 and 3) and then past Earth (4), each time gathering speed. It crossed the Asteroid Belt (5) to reach Jupiter in December 2000 (6), and finally arrived at Saturn in July 2004 (7).

Future missions

Following is a list of major probes that have not yet completed their missions.

Rosetta: Launched March 2004, lander descends on the comet 67P/Churyumov-Gerasimenko in 2015

Mercury Messenger: Launched August 2004, flybys of Mercury in January 2008, October 2008, September 2009, Mercury orbit in March 2011

New Horizons: Launched January 2006, arrives Pluto July 2015

Dawn: Launched July 2007, flyby of asteroid Vesta October 2011, orbits asteroid and dwarf planet Ceres February 2015

Kepler: To launch October 2008, mission is to search for habitable planets

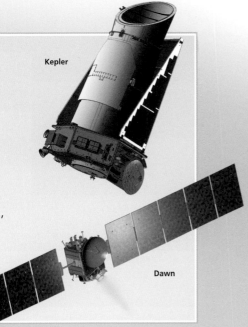

The two largest asteroids, Ceres and Vesta, have never been seen up close. That should change when Dawn (right) pays a visit.

Kepler

Dawn

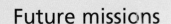

(4) Lander, cocooned in airbags, lands.

(5) The airbags deflate.

(6) The airbags retract and petals of the lander open.

(7) Sojourner rover leaves the lander and explores nearby.

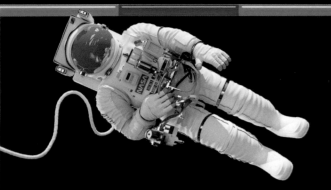

Life in the Universe?

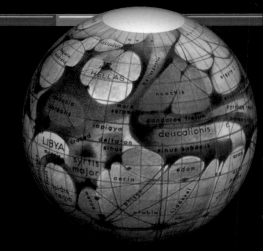

Martian map
This map of Mars was produced in the early 20th century by astronomer Eugène Michel Antoniadi. At the time it was believed by some people that Mars was covered in canals, dug by Martians to ferry water from the poles to the drier regions. Antoniadi doubted the reality of the canals and we now know that the canals were an illusion. Mars has, so far, proved lifeless.

Is there life beyond Earth? Frankly, we just don't know. And if it does exist, it could be a very long time before we find it. Astronomers are presently scanning likely stars for radio messages from distant beings, but so far no ETs have checked in. Perhaps we don't have to look. Since we developed radio and television, our transmissions have been heading into space. Maybe one day, aliens will notice our signals and drop us a message.

SETI Institute
SETI stands for the Search for Extraterrestrial Intelligence. The SETI Institute in California, USA, is dedicated to finding life in the Universe. Frank Drake and Jill Tartar are two of the Institute's most famous scientists. In 1961 Drake performed the first-ever search for extraterrestrial intelligence when he listened for radio messages from distant stars. But ET was not calling.

Titan
Titan (above) is the largest moon of Saturn and the only satellite in the Solar System with a thick atmosphere. It has been speculated that Titan could develop life in the future when the Sun grows larger and brighter. However, at the moment, Titan is very cold, its surface drenched in liquid methane and other bizarre substances. This photo was taken by the Huygens probe in January 2005.

Voyager's gold record

This golden record was placed aboard the two Voyager spacecraft, launched in 1977 to the giant planets. It contains a recording of various sounds that introduce the life and culture of planet Earth—just in case the craft are intercepted by an inquisitive alien species.

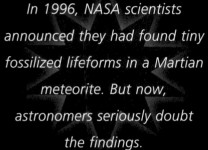

In 1996, NASA scientists announced they had found tiny fossilized lifeforms in a Martian meteorite. But now, astronomers seriously doubt the findings.

The search for Earth-like worlds

The European Space Agency (ESA) is developing an ambitious space mission that will find Earth-sized planets and then analyze their atmospheres for signs of gases that might indicate life. The mission will consist of three or four space telescopes, linked together by a central "hub" satellite. However, this technology is some way off: Darwin will not launch until 2015.

Alien ideas

What might aliens look like? Some think their shape will be governed by their environment, as life on Earth is. So, on very light planets with low gravity, aliens might be tall and gangly (left). Or perhaps, if life exists on a gas planet, with no surface, it will look like the flying aliens below. In truth, though, given how varied Earthly life is, it is very doubtful that life elsewhere will be like anything we can imagine.

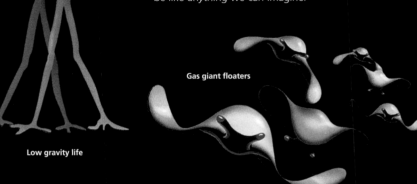

Gas giant floaters

Low gravity life

Arecibo

This is the largest radio telescope in the world (left), located in Arecibo, Puerto Rico. It is about 1,000 feet (305 m) wide. In 1974, this telescope was used to beam a message to a cluster of stars called M13. But because M13 is 25,000 light-years away, it will take the message 25,000 years to get there, then another 25,000 for us to get a reply—if there is one!

Europa

Europa (below), one of the four largest moons of Jupiter, is often mentioned by astronomers as a good place to look for life in the Solar System. Its surface is a thin shell of cracked, frozen water ice (left). But beneath it there is very probably a deep ocean of liquid water, which some think makes it habitable.

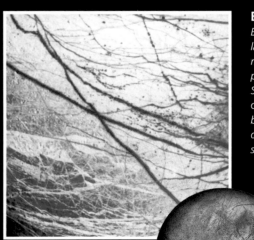

Space Exploration

1950s

1957
The Soviets' Sputnik 1 and 2 are the first artificial satellites of Earth

1960s

1962
The US Mariner 2 is the first probe to reach another planet, Venus

1976
NASA lands the first two successful crafts on Mars, Viking 1 and 2

1989
The Voyager 2 probe, launched in 1977, reaches Neptune

1970s

1980s

1990s

2000s

1966
Luna 9 makes the first soft landing on the Moon and sends back pictures

1986
The European Space Agency's (ESA) Giotto probe intercepts Comet Halley

2000
The probe NEAR-Shoemaker orbits and maps the asteroid Eros

2006
New Horizons probe launched with a mission to reach Pluto and beyond

OPTICAL TELESCOPES

NAME	LOCATION	MIRROR DIAMETER
Keck I and II	Hawaii, USA	394 inches (10 m)
Southern African Large Telescope	South Africa	394 inches (10 m)
Hobby-Eberly	Texas, USA	362 inches (9.2 m)
Large Binocular Telescope	Arizona, USA	331 inches (8.4 m)
Subaru	Hawaii, USA	326 inches (8.3 m)
Very Large Telescope	Chile	322.8 inches (8.2 m)
Gemini North (Gillett)	Hawaii, USA	319 inches (8.1 m)
Gemini South	Chile	319 inches (8.1 m)
Magellan I (Walter Baade)	Chile	256 inches (6.5 m)
Magellan II (Landon Clay)	Chile	256 inches (6.5 m)

FAMOUS OBSERVATORIES

NAME	LOCATION	ALTITUDE
Indian Astronomical Observatory	Himalayas, India	14,764 feet (4,500 m)
Meyer-Womble Observatory	Colorado, USA	14,148 feet (4,312 m)
Mauna Kea Observatory	Hawaii, USA	13,800 feet (4,205 m)
Paranal	Chile	8,650 feet (2,635 m)
Roque de los Muchachos	Canary Islands, Spain	8,200 feet (2,500 m)
La Silla Observatory	Chile	7,870 feet (2,400 m)
South African Astronomical Observatory	South Africa	5,770 feet (1,759 m)
Palomar Observatory	California, USA	5,620 feet (1,713 m)
Anglo-Australian Observatory	Australia	3,819 feet (1,164 m)

MANNED MISSIONS TO THE MOON

MISSION[#]	LUNAR LANDING	CREW
Apollo 11	July 20, 1969	Neil Armstrong, Edwin Aldrin, Michael Collins*
Apollo 12	November 19, 1969	Charles Conrad, Jr., Alan Bean, Richard Gordon*
Apollo 14	February 5, 1971	Alan Shepard, Jr., Edgar Mitchell, Stuart Roosa*
Apollo 15	July 30, 1971	David Scott, James Irwin, Alfred Worden*
Apollo 16	April 21, 1972	John Young, Charles Duke, Jr., Thomas Mattingly II*
Apollo 17	December 7, 1972	Eugene Cernan, Harrison Schmitt, Ronald Evans*

[#] The Apollo 13 mission was not able to land on the Moon * Command Module Pilots—crew who did not set foot on the Moon

PLANET MISSIONS

NAME	LAUNCH	TARGET
Mariner 2	1962	
Mariner 4	1964	
Venera 7	1970	
Mariner 9	1971	
Venera 8	1972	
Pioneer 10	1972	
Pioneer 11	1973	
Mariner 10	1973	
Venera 9 and 10	1975	
Viking 1 and 2	1975	
Voyager 1	1977	
Voyager 2	1977	
Venera 11 and 12	1978	
Venera 13 and 14	1981	
Venera 15 and 16	1983	
Magellan	1989	
Galileo	1989	
Pathfinder	1996	
Mars Global Surveyor	1996	
Cassini-Huygens	1997	
Mars Odyssey	2001	
Mars Exploration Rovers	2003	

OTHER MISSIONS

NAME	LAUNCH	TARGET
Luna 1 to 24	1959–1976	
Ranger 7 to 9	1964–1965	
Surveyor 1 to 7	1966–1968	
Vega 1 and 2	1984	Halley
Suisei	1985	Halley
Giotto	1985	Halley
Sakigake	1985	Halley
Galileo	1989	Gaspra, Ida, and Dactyl
Ulysses	1990	
Clementine	1994	
SOHO	1995	
NEAR-Shoemaker	1996	Eros
Cassini-Huygens	1997	Titan
Stardust	1999	Wild 2
Rosetta	2004	67P/Churyumov-Gerasimenko
Deep Impact	2005	Tempel 1

KEY

 Mercury Jupiter Uranus Moon Asteroid

Venus Saturn  Neptune Sun Comet

Mars

NOTABLE NUMBERS

3 Number of remaining active Space Shuttles, with the loss of Columbia and Challenger. They are Enterprise, Discovery, and Atlantis.

4.3 Number of days between the launch of Apollo 11 and its landing on the Moon, in 1969.

22 Number of people killed as a result of space travel, either in training or during actual missions.

27 Number of separate dishes that make up the radio telescope called the Very Large Array (VLA) in New Mexico. The dishes can be combined to work together.

91.2 Number of minutes it takes the International Space Station to complete one orbit of Earth.

20,000,000 Cost in US dollars of space tourist Dennis Tito's trip to the International Space Station in 2001.

7.92 Total number of days Dennis Tito spent in space during his trip.

100 Number of times farther from the Sun Voyager 2 is, compared to Earth.

16 Number of nations that contribute toward the construction of the International Space Station (ISS).

1957 Year the first space probe, Sputnik 1, went into space. Launched by the Soviets, it started the Space Race. In English it means "fellow traveler."

James Webb Space Telescope

The Hubble Space Telescope has enthralled us since its launch in 1990 with its stunning vistas of the cosmos. But it is growing old now and needs to be replaced with a telescope using the latest technology. Its successor, the James Webb Space Telescope (JWST), is due for launch in 2013. The telescope's mirror will be larger than Hubble's, at 256 inches (6.5 m) across. Among other things, astronomers hope that the JWST will be able to spot the very first galaxies that formed in the Universe.

Apollo 11 crew

If you were exposed to space you would not explode, as some movies suggest. But your blood and body fluids would freeze within a minute.

Apollo 13

The Americans had a near-miss in April 1970 with the third manned mission to the Moon, Apollo 13. Two days into the mission, an explosion aboard the spacecraft caused it to lose oxygen and power. The ship was traveling too quickly to simply be turned around, so it had to orbit once around the Moon, using the Moon's gravity to sling it back on an Earth-bound course. Fortunately the astronauts were all returned safely to Earth.

Mission insignia

SPACE EXPLORATION RECORDS

Longest single stay in space
Cosmonaut Valeri Polyakov holds the record for the longest stay in space. He spent 438 days in a row—more than fourteen months —aboard the Mir Space Station.

First woman in space
On June 16, 1963, at the age of 26, Russia's Valentina Tereshkova became the first woman in space. Tereshkova was launched aboard the Vostok 5 spacecraft. Almost three full days later she returned to Earth, having orbited the planet 48 times.

Laika

First animals in space
The first animal in space was a dog called Laika ("barker" in Russian), aboard Sputnik 2 in 1957. She was followed by a monkey called Gordo the next year.

Longest total time in space
The cosmonaut Sergei Avdeyev has spent a total of two years and one day in space, participating in many missions

Voyager 1

Farthest manmade object
As of August 2006, Voyager 1 has traveled about 9.3 billion miles (5.8 billion km) from Earth, farther than any other probe. That's 0.0016 light-years, or 100 times the Earth–Sun distance.

First space tourist
In 2001, American businessman Dennis Tito became the first paying passenger to go into space. He was aged 60 at the time.

Most space flights
The American astronauts Jerry L. Ross and Franklin Chang-Diaz have both been into space on seven separate missions.

First permanently manned space station
Launched by the Soviet Union in 1986, Mir was the first Space Station designed to be permanently occupied. The station lasted nearly fifteen years before finally being brought deliberately crashing to Earth (into South Pacific waters) in 2001.

Mir Space Station

1950s
In 1957, the Soviets launch Sputnik 1, the first artificial satellite of Earth. Sputnik 2, carrying the first animal into space, follows a month later. The US launches its first satellite, Explorer 1, in 1958—the same year that NASA (The National Aeronautics and Space Administration) is created.

Poster advertising the launch of Sputnik 1

1960–65
In 1961, the Soviets fly the first man into space, Yuri Gagarin, who orbits Earth once. John Glenn becomes the first American to orbit Earth in 1962. The Soviet cosmonaut Valentina Tereshkova becomes the first woman in space in 1963. And, in 1965, cosmonaut Alexei Leonov becomes the first man to "walk in space"— floating outside his spacecraft Voskhod 2, while tethered to the craft.

1968–69
In 1968, NASA's Apollo 8 becomes the first craft to carry humans beyond Earth's gravity, orbiting the Moon several times and returning home. In 1969, Apollo 11 lands the first men on the Moon, Neil Armstrong and Edwin Aldrin.

1970–75
In 1970, the crew of Apollo 13 narrowly escape disaster when their mission to the Moon fails. In 1971, Salyut 1 becomes the first space station. And on December 11, 1972, the final Apollo mission (17) carries the last humans to the Moon, Eugene Cernan and Harrison Schmitt.

1981
Maiden flight of the first American Space Shuttle, Columbia.

Columbia

1986
The Soviet Union launches its space station, Mir. The same year, the Space Shuttle Challenger explodes shortly after liftoff.

1998
Construction begins on the International Space Station (ISS). It will hold seven people when complete in 2010, and countries participating include the United States, Russia, Britain, Canada, and Japan.

2001
The aging Mir space station is crashed deliberately to Earth after nearly fifteen years in space. Meanwhile, the first occupants of the partially complete International Space Station—two Russians and an American—take up residence.

2003
The Americans lose another shuttle, Columbia. As a result completion of the ISS is delayed.

Glossary

A

absolute zero
The coldest possible temperature, equal to –459.67°F (-273.15°C).

active galaxy
A very bright and powerful galaxy. Astronomers suspect that most active galaxies contain supermassive black holes in their centers.

asteroid
A rocky, metallic, or carbon-rich body orbiting the Sun. The largest are hundreds of miles across, but most are much, much smaller.

Asteroid Belt
A region between the orbits of Mars and Jupiter where most asteroids can be found.

astronomical unit (AU)
The distance between Earth and the Sun, 93 million miles (150 million km). Astronomers use the AU as a unit of distance in the Solar System.

atmosphere
The thin envelope of gas that surrounds some planets and moons. The type of gas and its thickness varies from planet to planet.

aurora
Spectacular light show seen on Earth and some other planets. It happens when particles from the solar wind hit the atmosphere.

Saturn

B

Big Bang
A popular and successful theory for the creation of the Universe. The theory says that the Universe was created from an initial hot and superdense state that suddenly started to expand very rapidly.

Big Crunch
A possible end of the Universe, in which the Universe will collapse back to a single point, like the Big Bang in reverse. This is now considered unlikely.

billion
A thousand million, or a one followed by nine zeroes (1,000,000,000).

binary star
Two stars that orbit one another in the same way that Earth orbits the Sun. Binaries are very common.

binoculars
An optical device that is two small telescopes side by side, one for each eye. Binoculars do not have very high magnification, but they are great for observing clusters, nebulas, and star clouds.

black hole
A bizarre object whose gravity is so powerful that nothing, not even light—moving at 186,000 miles per second (300,000 km/s)—can escape from it.

blueshift
See Doppler shift

brightness
A measure of how bright an object appears to be, but not how much light it actually emits. An object that appears very bright may in reality be comparatively dim but close by. For a true measure of actual brightness, astronomers use luminosity.

brown dwarf
An object that forms like a star but that, having a very low mass, has no ongoing nuclear reactions in its core. Brown dwarfs are intermediate in size between real stars and giant planets.

C

celestial poles
The points on the sky around which all the stars seem to rotate. The north celestial pole is marked by a fairly bright star called Polaris. In the Southern Hemisphere, however, there is no bright star to mark the south celestial pole.

cepheid variable
A giant star that pulsates in and out, varying its brightness as it does so.

coma
The bright ball of gas and dust that surrounds the nucleus of a comet. The coma may be 60,000 miles (100,000 km) across, much bigger than the nucleus itself.

comet
A small object, only a few miles across, made from a mixture of ice and rock. As the comet approaches the Sun, the ice melts and forms a coma and a long, glowing tail.

command module
The spacecraft that carried astronauts to the Moon and back again during the Apollo missions in the late 1960s and early 1970s. At the Moon it deployed the lunar module, which descended to the Moon's surface with two astronauts inside while one remained in the command module.

constellation
A pattern of stars in the sky. There are 88 constellations in all, named after mythical beasts, gods, people, and other objects.

Copernican model
The Solar System with planets going around the Sun, according to Nicolaus Copernicus in the 16th century. His book eventually led to acceptance of this idea.

core
The central region of a planet, star, or galaxy.

corona
The thin outer atmosphere of the Sun. It can be seen only during an eclipse, when the bright light from the Sun's disk is blocked by the Moon.

cosmic background radiation
Radiation from the Big Bang that fills all of space and has a temperature of just a few degrees above absolute zero.

cosmos
A Greek word that is often used to mean everything that exists; another word for "Universe."

crater
A shallow depression in the surface of a planet or satellite, caused when an asteroid, comet, or meteoroid hits it at great speed.

crust
The outermost layer of a planet, comet, asteroid, or natural satellite.

D

dark nebula
A cloud of gas and dust in space that emits no light and is visible only when seen against a brighter background, such as an emission nebula.

day
See sidereal day or solar day

disk (of a galaxy)
The flat part of spiral galaxies.

Doppler shift
A change in the color of light emitted by an object in space, caused because the object is moving toward or away from Earth. Objects moving toward us appear slightly bluer than when stationary because the light has been blueshifted. The light is redshifted when the object is moving away.

double star
Two stars that seem close together on the sky because they form a binary system, or sometimes because of chance perspective.

dwarf planet
An object orbiting the Sun that is big enough to be round but not big enough to qualify as a true planet. Pluto, Ceres, and Eris are examples.

E

eclipse
A solar eclipse is when the Moon passes briefly over the Sun and blocks some or all of its light. A lunar eclipse occurs when the Moon moves into Earth's shadow, cast by the Sun.

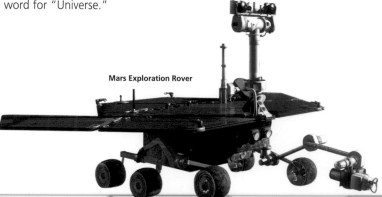
Mars Exploration Rover

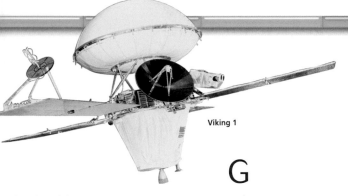

Viking 1

eclipsing binary
A binary star in which one star (as seen from Earth) passes in front of another as they orbit each other, partially blocking some of the light.

electromagnetic radiation
A form of radiation that includes radio waves, infrared light, optical light, ultraviolet light, X-rays, and gamma rays. Our eyes can only detect optical light from this spectrum.

ellipse
A closed curve resembling a squashed circle. Planets and moons move in elliptical orbits, some more nearly circular than others.

elliptical galaxy
A common form of galaxy structured somewhat like a giant football. Almost all of the stars in these galaxies are old, and there is little or no gas and dust to make new stars.

emission nebula
A cloud of gas and dust in space that emits light because it is energized by stars within it. The Orion Nebula is a famous example.

equator
The imaginary line drawn around the center of a planet, moon, or star that divides it into a Northern Hemisphere and Southern Hemisphere.

equinox
Two points in the year, on March 20 or 21 and September 22 or 23, when the Sun is directly overhead as seen from the equator. In the Northern Hemisphere, the March equinox marks the beginning of spring while the September one occurs at the start of fall. This is reversed in the Southern Hemisphere.

exoplanet
A planet orbiting a star other than the Sun. Also known as an extrasolar planet. More than 200 are now known.

extraterrestrial
A life form coming from beyond Earth. At present we do not know if any exist.

F

flyby
A type of space mission in which a probe does not enter orbit or land on the world it investigates, but instead records data as it flies past.

G

galaxy
A large structure composed of up to hundreds of billions of stars, gas, and dust. Galaxies can be irregular, spiral, or elliptical.

galaxy cluster
A large group of galaxies held together by their own gravity. Some contain thousands of members.

Galilean moons
The largest four satellites of Jupiter—Io, Europa, Ganymede, and Callisto—discovered by Galileo in 1610.

gamma rays
A form of electromagnetic radiation produced by energetic astronomical events, like colliding black holes or very powerful supernovas.

gamma-ray bursts
Incredibly powerful outbursts, believed to occur when ultra-massive stars explode at the ends of their lives and leave behind black holes.

gas giant
A massive planet made mostly from hydrogen and helium. Jupiter, Saturn, Uranus, and Neptune are usually all called gas giants, as are most exoplanets so far found.

globular cluster
A large star cluster, shaped like a ball, containing up to a million members. They are found on the outskirts of many galaxies, including our own.

granulation
The grainy pattern on the Sun's photosphere. Individual "granules" may be 600 miles (1,000 km) wide. They are created by hot gases rising to the surface of the Sun.

gravity
An attractive force between two objects. The closer the objects are to one another, or the more massive they are, the greater the force. Gravity is the dominant force governing motion in the Universe.

greenhouse effect
The heating of a planet's surface that occurs when solar energy is trapped by the planet's atmosphere.

Asteroid

H

helium
The second most common element, after hydrogen. It was created in the Big Bang, and it is also made inside stars during nuclear reactions.

Hertzsprung-Russell diagram
A graph astronomers use to show how the brightness of a star is related to its color.

hydrogen
The most common and lightest substance in the entire Universe. Stars and gas giant planets are made mostly of hydrogen gas, with some helium as well.

Venera lander

I

infrared radiation
A form of electromagnetic radiation emitted by warm objects. It is also known as heat radiation.

interstellar matter
The gas and dust between the stars. It is visible in huge structures called nebulas.

irregular galaxy
A galaxy that has no visibly consistent shape or form, unlike a spiral or elliptical galaxy.

K

Kuiper Belt
A donut-shaped region beyond Neptune, populated by worlds of rock and ice. A few of these Kuiper Belt Objects (KBOs), such as Pluto and Eris, are well over a thousand miles across.

L

lander
A probe designed to land on the surface of a planet in order to study its environment.

Moon impacting with Earth

lava
Molten rock from Earth's interior, usually seen erupting from volcanoes. When lava is hot it flows as a liquid.

light-year
The distance that light travels in a year—5.88 trillion miles (9.46 trillion km).

Local Group
The galaxy cluster that includes our own Milky Way as well as the Andromeda Galaxy. There are at least 47 members.

long-period comet
A comet that takes longer than about 200 years to orbit the Sun. Most come from the Oort Cloud, and their orbits are often steeply angled compared to those of the planets.

luminosity
A measurement of the actual physical brightness of an astronomical object, how much radiation it emits. Luminosity is measured in watts, a unit of power that is also used to describe lights in the home.

lunar module
The portion of an Apollo spacecraft that landed on the Moon. When the mission was over, part of the lunar module returned to the command module, which was in orbit around the Moon.

M

Magellanic clouds
Two small, irregular galaxies that orbit the Milky Way. You can see them in the sky from the Southern Hemisphere.

magma
Very hot, liquid rock found inside volcanoes and deep inside Earth. When it erupts to the surface, it is called lava.

magnitude
A measure of the brightness of an object on the sky. The fainter the object, the larger its magnitude.

main sequence
The period in the life of a star during which it converts hydrogen into helium in its core via a series of nuclear reactions.

Radio telescope

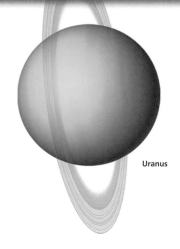
Uranus

mantle
On terrestrial worlds like Earth, the mantle is a thick shell of rock found just below the crust. Parts of it may be molten. In gas planets, the mantle goes deeper and is made from highly compressed fluids.

maria
Maria (singular "mare") are dark regions on the Moon, made from lava that flooded the surface and hardened long ago. It is Latin for "seas," because people used to think they were filled with liquid water.

meteor
A bright streak seen in the sky when a piece of debris from space (a meteoroid) hits Earth's atmosphere at great speed and burns up.

meteorite
A meteor large enough to survive its fiery descent through the atmosphere and reach the ground.

meteoroid
A small fragment broken off from a comet or asteroid, orbiting the Sun.

meteor stream
A trail of debris around the Sun, left by the passage of a comet. When Earth passes through these trails at certain times of the year, many meteors are produced, causing a shower of meteors.

Milky Way
The spiral galaxy in which the Sun and Solar System reside.

NASA astronaut

moon
A moon (lowercase "m") is a natural satellite of a planet or asteroid. The Moon (uppercase "M") is the name given to Earth's natural satellite.

multiple star
A star system composed of several stars that are all bound together and moving under the influence of their gravity.

N

near-Earth asteroid
An asteroid whose orbit crosses or comes close to the orbit of Earth.

nebula
A cloud of gas and dust that exists naturally in the space between the stars. It is Latin for "cloud."

neutron star
The highly compressed core of a once massive star, often spinning many times per second. Neutron stars are no larger than a city.

nova
An explosion—smaller in size than a supernova—that is caused in a binary star when a white dwarf, stealing matter from its companion star, becomes unstable because of its greatly increased mass.

nuclear reaction
A nuclear reaction, called fusion, is the process that occurs inside stars and hydrogen bombs. Atoms are smashed together at great speed to make new atoms, releasing a great deal of energy in the process.

nucleus
A nucleus (plural "nuclei") can relate to the center of an atom, the heart of a comet, or the center of a galaxy.

O

Oort Cloud
The Oort Cloud is a spherical cloud of comets surrounding the Solar System. It is made from trillions of frozen comet nuclei. It may be tens of thousands of astronomical units (AU) across.

open star cluster
A group of stars held together by gravity, spanning a few dozen light-years. The number of stars varies from dozens to hundreds.

orbit
The path followed by a star around a galaxy, a planet around a star, or a satellite around a planet. Orbits are usually elliptical, but some are very nearly circular.

orbiter
A probe designed to orbit a planet or moon in order to study it and perhaps map its surface in detail.

P

phase
The apparent shape of the Moon, which depends on how much of it is lit as seen from Earth. The phase is full when the Moon is fully lit, gibbous when mostly lit, crescent when only part is lit, and new when totally dark. Venus and Mercury also have phases, but you need a telescope to see them.

photosphere
The visible face of the Sun—not a surface in the true sense, because it is not solid. The photosphere has a pattern on it called granulation.

planet
Any spherical body that orbits a star, and whose orbit is clear of smaller objects. Ceres, for example, is not a true planet because its orbit is shared by many other asteroids. The Solar System has eight planets, and more than 200 are known to be orbiting other stars.

planetary nebula
A shroud of gas cast off by a star like the Sun when it becomes a red giant at the end of its life. The nebula shines because of the hot core of the star at the center, called a white dwarf.

probe
A machine sent by humans to investigate other places in space. They operate automatically under computer control but accept command from controllers on Earth.

prominence
A dense cloud of gas high up in the Sun's corona. So-called active prominences are very energetic, lasting only days. Less energetic ones, called quiescent prominences, may last several months.

Ptolemaic model
The Solar System as it was thought to be constructed, according to the ancient Greeks, and described in detail by Ptolemy. Ptolemy thought Earth was at the center, while everything else— the Sun, Moon, and planets—all went around it.

pulsar
A rapidly spinning neutron star. As the star spins, beams of radio waves flash past Earth, and the star seems to wink on and off like a lighthouse.

pulsating variable
A star whose brightness varies as its surface pulsates in and out.

Q

quasar
An active galaxy dominated by a bright nucleus, which is so far away that it resembles a star.

R

radiation
A term that may refer to light and other forms of electromagnetic radiation or to high-energy particles.

radio galaxy
An active galaxy that is a powerful source of radio waves.

radio telescope
An instrument, often shaped like a dish, used to receive and focus radio waves.

Reflecting telescope

red giant
A very large star that has run out of hydrogen in its core and has expanded and cooled. The Sun will one day become a red giant.

redshift
A change in color of light emitted by an object. This is often because of the Doppler shift, but is also caused by the expansion of the Universe.

reflecting telescope
A telescope that uses a mirror to collect and focus its light.

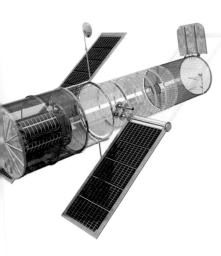

reflection nebula
A nebula that shines with a blue glow because it reflects the light of nearby stars.

refracting telescope
A telescope that uses a mirror to collect and focus its light.

rover
A wheeled probe that roams the surface of a planet or moon, under the control of scientists and engineers back on Earth.

S

satellite
Any small object that orbits another. The Moon is a natural satellite of Earth, while the International Space Station is an artificial satellite.

satellite galaxy
A small galaxy that orbits a larger one. The Milky Way has several, the most famous being the Magellanic Clouds.

short-period comet
A comet that orbits the Sun in less than about 200 years, such as Halley's Comet.

sidereal day
The time it takes Earth to rotate once relative to the stars—close to 23 hours 56 minutes.

solar day
The time it takes Earth to rotate once relative to the Sun, defined to be very close to 24 hours.

solar flare
A sudden, powerful blast of energy from the Sun, which releases streams of subatomic particles.

Solar System
The name given to the Sun and the system of planets, asteroids, and comets that surrounds it.

solar wind
A steady stream of subatomic particles that blows constantly away from the Sun at high speeds.

space shuttle
America's reusable spacecraft, used for putting satellites into orbit and carrying out repairs on them.

space station
A large satellite orbiting Earth, big enough for astronauts to spend extended periods of time living and working inside.

space telescope
Any telescope in space, such as the famous Hubble Space Telescope. Space telescopes can detect forms of electromagnetic radiation that are normally absorbed by the atmosphere.

spiral galaxy
A type of large galaxy that is flat like a disk but has a bulge in the center. The disk includes a spiral pattern traced out by young stars.

star
A globe of gas that shines of its own accord because of energy released by nuclear reactions in its core.

subatomic
Smaller than an atom.

sunspot
Regions on the Sun that are darker than normal because they have a lower temperature. Individual sunspots can easily be bigger than Earth.

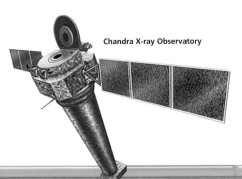
Chandra X-ray Observatory

Space Shuttle

supercluster
A cluster of galaxy clusters. They are among the largest structures in existence.

supermassive black hole
A very massive black hole, up to several billion times the mass of the Sun, found at the center of most, if not all, galaxies.

supernova
An exploding star. Massive stars explode at the end of their lives, when they can no longer generate nuclear reactions. Others, called white dwarfs, can explode when they attract gas from another star nearby and become unstable.

supernova remnant
The nebula created from the explosion of a star in a supernova.

T

telescope
An instrument with powerful magnification used by astronomers to view objects in the sky.

terrestrial planet
A small planet made mostly from rocky and metallic compounds, in contrast to the makeup of gas plants. Mercury, Venus, Earth, and Mars are the four terrestrial planets in the Solar System.

tides
The rise and fall of oceans on Earth caused by the gravity of the Moon and, to a smaller degree, the Sun.

trillion
A million million, or one followed by twelve zeros (1,000,000,000,000).

Trojan asteroids
Asteroids that share the orbit of Jupiter. Some are bunched up before Jupiter in its orbit, while others are bunched up behind it.

U

ultraviolet radiation (UV)
A form of electromagnetic radiation emitted by a range of objects in space. The Sun is a powerful UV source, but we are mostly shielded from harm by our atmosphere.

Universe
Everything that exists around us, including space and time, energy, and matter.

V

variable star
A star whose light output goes up and down with time.

visible light
Also called optical radiation, this is the region of the electromagnetic spectrum to which our eyes are sensitive. It is mostly harmless, but it can be dangerous if it is too powerful, as in a laser.

W

wavelength
The distance between two peaks (or dips) in a wave.

white dwarf
When hydrogen fuel inside a star runs low because it has reached old age, the star expands to become a red giant and later throws off its atmosphere. Only its core remains, which astronomers call a white dwarf.

Mercury

X

X-rays
A high-energy form of electromagnetic radiation emitted by energetic objects in space.

y

year
The time it takes for Earth to complete one orbit around the Sun—365.24 days.

Z

zodiac
While the Sun, Moon, and planets move around the sky, they move through a thin strip of sky called the zodiac. It crosses thirteen constellations—not just the usual "signs of the zodiac."

Index

Credits